- DIDN'T AGRESSIVELY FIGHT FOR INDEPENDENCE

- OLD AIRPLANES GOOD ENOUGH FOR DEF 27
    -- PROBLEM WHEN A NATION DIDN'T SEE NEW TECH.

- FOCUSED ON TACTICAL DOCTRINE NOT OP TO STRAT 36

- LAWS SOMETIMES HAVE ADVERSE EFFECTS ON EMERGING ENTITIES.

- LACK OF STANDARDIZED TRAINING 64

- AIRPOWER IS TOO COMPLEX TO RESIDE IN A REACTIVE STATE. TAKES TOO LONG
    TO PRODUCE PLANS AND GENERATE EXPERIENCE. IS IT ANY LONGER THAN
    THE ARMY ? 70

- SOCIALISM + S/D THE WEEK 71

- THE STRAT OF AF DIDN'T MATCH FRANCE GRAND STRAT OF LONG WAR 75

- AIR AF SUBSERV TO ARMY, THEN THEY MUST EXERCISE W/ EACH OTHER
    TO TEST C² OUT. THIS BIG PROBLEM IN TRANSITION FROM PEACE TO WAR 101

- PASSIVITY DUE TO WWI CARNAGE AFFECTED MOBILIZATION OF LOVE EN MASSE. 106

- FRENCH VIOLATED CW: ACTIVE DEFENSE STRAT. SHOULD HAVE
    BEEN STRUCTURED TO PREEMPTIVELY ATTACK. PASSIVE
    STRAT. DEFENSE VS ACTIVE STRAT DEF. 132

D1257645

The Forgotten Air Force

SMITHSONIAN HISTORY OF AVIATION AND SPACEFLIGHT SERIES

Dominick A. Pisano and Allan Needell, Series Editors

Since the Wright brothers' first flight, air and space technologies have been central in creating the modern world. Aviation and spaceflight have transformed our lives—our conceptions of time and distance, our daily routines, and the conduct of exploration, business, and war. The Smithsonian History of Aviation and Spaceflight Series publishes substantive works that further our understanding of these transformations in their social, cultural, political, and military contexts.

THE FORGOTTEN AIR FORCE

French Air Doctrine in the 1930s

Anthony Christopher Cain

SMITHSONIAN INSTITUTION PRESS
Washington and London

Copy editor: Anne Collier Rehill
Production editor: Duke Johns
Designer: Janice Wheeler

Library of Congress Cataloging-in-Publication Data
Cain, Anthony Christopher.
    The forgotten Air Force : French air doctrine in the 1930s /
    Anthony Christopher Cain.
      p. cm.
    Includes bibliographical references and index.
    ISBN 1-58834-010-4 (alk. paper)
      1. France. Armée de l'air—History.   2. Air warfare.   I. Title.
    UG635.F8 C34 2002
    358.4'03'094409043—dc21   2001049280

British Library Cataloguing-in-Publication Data available

Manufactured in the United States of America
09 08 07 06 05 04 03 02   5 4 3 2 1

∞ The paper used in this publication meets the minimum requirements of the
American National Standard for Information Sciences—Permanence of Paper for
Printed Library Materials ANSI Z39.48-1984.

All photos and figures are courtesy of the Albert F. Simpson United States Air Force
Historical Research Agency (photos: AFHRA K-113.108-1, vols. 49, 50, 53, 56, 57;
figures: AFHRA 145.91-135U, 145.91-146, 248-211.59, and 415.604). For permission
to reproduce illustrations appearing in this book, please correspond directly with the
Agency. The Smithsonian Institution Press does not retain reproduction rights for
these illustrations individually, or maintain a file of addresses for photo sources.

Dedicated to my wife, Mechieal Cain

Contents

Foreword

Military victories—some sage argued—have thousands of fathers, but military defeats are orphans. Actually, military defeats spawn hundreds of authors, and the Fall of France in 1940 must have more adoptive parents than any other recent defense catastrophe. Reflecting the adage that nations get the military systems they deserve, the French capitulation—bearing all the signs of national shame caught in the photograph of Adolf Hitler dancing a jig near the famous fairway coach of Compiègne—provided endless evidence, real and imagined, of the range of political, economic, psychological, and social flaws of France. Much of the focus eventually turned in more careful form upon the weaknesses of the armed forces, specifically the army and its exaggerated commitment to positional defense. Yet the inability of the French air force to win air superiority over the battlefields of France and Belgium allowed Luftwaffe ground support squadrons to attack the French mobile ground forces with impunity, thus contributing to the ability of the German mobile forces to penetrate the Ardennes and wage the campaign of maneuver that routed the Anglo-French armies. The air-ground defeat sent the Royal Air Force flying for home and the British army into the surf of Dunkirk. It is a story of sound and fury, but too often the failure of the French air force has not attracted the careful autopsy it deserves.

Through this ground-breaking and innovative analysis, Lieutenant Colonel (Dr.) Chris Cain brings balance to interwar European airpower history, a field traditionally dominated by Allied strategic bombing campaign studies and the climb and crash of the Luftwaffe's fortunes. Using air doctrine as the launching point from which to assess French military effectiveness during the 1930s, Dr. Cain's extensive archival research reveals how the Armée de l'air's comprehensive doctrine manuals sought to link tactical capabilities and operational structures with strategic objectives. The French government granted the Armée de l'air independence from the army in 1933, but interservice rivalries, an uncertain diplomatic environment, nearly a decade of parsimonious funding for research and development, and competing demands for air resources thwarted efforts to realize airpower's doctrinal vision.

Airpower history often focuses on offensive or defensive doctrinal components. This work develops the term *reactive doctrine*—a significantly broader understanding of airpower doctrinal studies—to explain how competing demands placed upon the French air arm intellectually and operationally constrained the Armée de l'air. To resolve these competing demands for various types of airpower within an era dominated by the "Maginot Line mentality," French airmen envisaged airpower within a context of *lutte aérienne:* "air battle." More accurately, however, this conception assumed a seamless theater war strategy in which airpower simultaneously performed offensive, defensive, and cooperative roles.

The parallels to contemporary strategic dilemmas are striking. Instead of developing a core set of capabilities, the Armée de l'air tried to react to every demand the government (especially the army and navy) placed upon it. In the process, air service leaders compromised their fundamental doctrinal tenets, which stressed the strategic decisiveness of a unified air war.

Dr. Cain offers another significant contribution, through his analysis of the relationship between doctrine and the institutional structures designed to transmit doctrinal precepts to air force members. Until now, interwar critiques have centered upon tactical performance, with few attempts to analyze the institutional arrangements that spawned tactical failure. The Armée de l'air failed to fuse its doctrinal vision of lutte aérienne with a training system to fulfill modern air force requirements. Consequently, the Armée de l'air did not wed its doctrinal precepts with a system of purposeful exercises and maneuvers. As argued in this book, although scenarios for major air maneuvers anticipated accurately the scope and thrust of Germany's 1940 attack, French air leaders failed to employ their doctrine's vision of integrated theater-wide air and ground war in their maneuvers.

One crucial measure of how effectively a nation organized for twentieth-century war centered on its mobilization and operational planning systems. For France, these proved especially critical during the interwar period. Dr. Cain shows how the Armée de l'air's mobilization system proved ineffectual for the task it was designed to accomplish. Chronic shortages of skilled personnel, equipment, and spare parts haunted French airmen throughout the 1930s, sowing the seeds for defeat as they persisted into and during the Battle of France. French intelligence and operational air planners identified Germany's, Italy's, and Spain's critical, exploitable weaknesses, but metropolitan military deficiencies, coupled with increasingly urgent demands from the army for greater control over air operations, confounded planning efforts. Ultimately, institutionalized structural flaws cost the French dearly in the six-week battle, contributing to the Third Republic's demise.

Defeat often provides military institutions with the insight and motivation required to reform doctrine and operational force employment. Triggered by its 1940 German defeat, the Armée de l'air's reform process began almost immediately. Drawing upon an almost unknown set of original reports archived in the the Service historique de l'Armée de l'air, Dr. Cain analyzes lessons French airmen learned from their 1930s failures and 1940 combat experience. He demonstrates that French airpower leaders carefully examined the lessons of war, evaluated their doctrine and operational capabilities, and used their conclusions to advocate an intellectual foundation upon which to build a more effective aviation component. Occurring within the context of harsh German oversight and Vichy collaboration, that this covert assessment materialized at all speaks highly of the dedication, professionalism, and patriotism of the airmen who performed the study.

No explanation can absolve the French air force of its part in the Fall of France. Chris Cain makes no attempt to do so. Rather, he expands our grasp of the ways in which Armée de l'air leaders thought about airpower, attempted to prepare their forces for combat, and, ultimately, learned harsh lessons from their humiliating defeat. Students of twentieth-century French military history have needed such a study for a long time—this one insightfully fills that void. Chris Cain probes beyond accepted interpretations, while creatively exposing and interpreting the complexity intrinsic to French airpower's interwar evolution.

Allan R. Millett

Mason Professor of Military History, Ohio State University
Coauthor (with Williamson Murray), *A War To Be Won: Fighting the Second World War* (Cambridge: Harvard University Press, 2000)

Preface

The airmen and politicians who led the Armée de l'air as it served the Third Republic worked diligently to create a military institution that they believed met
French defense needs. Their efforts reveal the difficulties that arose when airpower theory clashed with established notions of how to employ air forces. Reactive doctrine crept into every aspect of the service, because the airmen failed
to argue effectively for a distinct vision of warfare predicated on the air
weapon's dominance.

Air force leaders transmitted doctrine and values to operational and tactical
commands by several institutional channels. At the lowest levels, airmen
learned basic technical skills. Pilot training, aircraft and engine maintenance,
radio operator training, and gunnery schools provided specialized instruction
that met the basic job requirements for manning combat units. These schools
also gave members their first exposure to air doctrine, concealed in the form
of technical training. After individuals completed basic technical training and
reported to their assigned tactical units, exercises and maneuvers became the
primary means of transmitting and refining air doctrine. Performance and behavior in day-to-day learning, and, more importantly, in annual exercises indicated the degree to which air force members accepted or rejected official doctrine. The amount and frequency of change in the structures and methods of the
French educational system also provide insight into institutional values and tactical effectiveness.

The defeat of 1940 rocked the nation's military institutions. The air force, in
particular, shouldered a large portion of the blame for the military's poor per-

formance. Its leaders sought to derive lessons from the battles of the war, so that the disaster of 1940 would not reoccur. They launched an investigation into the conduct of the air war, and officers from combat and support specialties responded to requests for reports on their experiences. In the harsh, painful process of self-examination and critique, air force personnel identified important areas for doctrinal and institutional change.

Acknowledgments

A writing project such as this may seem to be the product of a single mind. Yet no one who attempts such a task emerges with this impression intact. The list of those to whom I owe emotional and intellectual debts is long. At the Air Command and Staff College, Colonel John Warden (ret.) and Lieutenant Colonel (Dr.) Larry Weaver (ret.) established an atmosphere that encouraged and rewarded intellectual development. Colonel Weaver's tireless efforts to set up the advanced-degree program allowed me to begin this project; his timely and insightful feedback on each chapter helped me to complete it. Colonel (Dr.) Jim Forsyth and Dr. Rich Muller allowed me to focus on completing the manuscript. Colonel Tommy Dickson (ret.) encouraged my research efforts and provided essential technical resources that made my time in Paris more productive. Dr. Bill Dean and Major Vicki Rast (Ph.D.) provided intellectual and emotional support well beyond the call of duty.

A grant from the Institute of National Security Studies made possible my trip to the Service historique de l'Armée de l'air at the Château de Vincennes, just outside Paris. Général (C. R.) Hugues Silvestre de Sacy offered his kind assistance and that of his staff, while I gathered the primary material that formed the core of this study. His permission to scan thousands of documents made my research efforts much more practical. Patrick Facon, François Pernot, and Marie Catherine Villatoux listened patiently to my ideas and did not condemn me for butchering their native tongue. Professor Facon graciously commented on organization and provided critical advice on sources. Laurent Henninger of the Centre d'études d'histoire de la défense also offered encouragement. Ron

Myers, Dennis Case, and Milton Steele at the Albert F. Simpson Historical Research Agency provided outstanding technical support, with procuring the photographs of interwar French aircraft. Without the expert help of these historians and archivists, this manuscript would remain ill-formed.

At the Ohio State University, Professors John Guilmartin, Mark Grimsley, John Rothney, John Burnham, and Geoffrey Parker served as excellent professional role models. My primary dissertation adviser, Allan Millett, struck the ideal balance between enthusiasm for the project and direction. Dr. James Corum at the USAF School of Advanced Airpower Studies provided valuable comments that improved the manuscript. At the Smithsonian Institution Press, Mark Gatlin and Nicole Sloan helped to give this project life. Annie Rehill carefully edited the manuscript and helped refine the raw material into a polished final product. With so many top-notch scholars and advisers guiding my efforts, one might anticipate a flawless product; however, I cannot lay any blame for the shortcomings of this work at their feet. They offered their best advice; any blemishes resulting from my failure to capitalize on their wisdom are mine.

As much as the aforementioned individuals contributed to the completion of this project, my family suffered its birth pangs. My children, Jessica, Micah, and Ryan, have more often than not seen their father with his nose in a book or glued to a computer screen. Yet when I remembered that they are infinitely more important than any piece of historical literature, they welcomed me with unconditional love and affection. My wife, Mechieal, remains the rock upon which our family depends. She shouldered the responsibilities of both mother and father while I traveled to Paris, and she listened patiently to my endless musings about the writing process. Mechieal honors me with her love and companionship; any success I attain stems from her unfailing devotion, loyalty, and support—I gratefully and lovingly dedicate this effort to her.

1   Introduction

No military action may occur, on the land or on the sea, without aerial participation; freedom of
action is assured only when one possesses mastery of the air.[1]

During the interwar period, and especially after 1933, French airpower leaders pursued doctrines and developed institutional structures that led to a
unique expression of airpower. The French case was singular because, unlike
American, British, and German airmen, the leaders of the Armée de l'air tried
to create a force capable of applying airpower to nearly every security challenge
that emerged in the years following the Great War. Since the early days of military aviation, airpower theorists had proposed that the key to understanding and
capitalizing on the revolutionary nature of the air weapon lay in acknowledg-
ing the offensive nature of aerial combat. The French, however, developed a
doctrine and accompanying force structure designed to provide reactive
airpower.

The term *reactive airpower,* as it applied to the French case, describes a complex conception of aerial warfare. Although French airmen did not use it in this
sense, they would have felt very comfortable with the term and its implications.
To them, the ability to react meant more than simply battling with an aggressive enemy for initiative and aerial advantage. The strategic challenges of the
1930s forced French aviators to develop doctrine and forces applicable to a
broad range of strategic, operational, and tactical tasks. Consequently, France
came to possess an air arm that stressed offense, defense, reconnaissance, air

interdiction, strategic bombing, close air support, airborne assault, and colonial operations. Nations that specialized in one or two of these missions developed doctrine, training methods, aircraft, and support structures that yielded a more efficient and effective military force when war erupted in 1939–40.

The French, who opted for an aviation component capable of reacting to every strategic, operational, and tactical task, were rarely efficient. What is surprising about the French approach is that the air arm proved remarkably effective as an instrument of strategic deterrence for most of the 1930s. In 1940, however, the effects of attempting too many roles and missions caught up with the French air force: as the blitzkrieg crashed down on France, the air force could not effectively help to counter the onslaught, owing in part to the many things required of it.

The attention devoted to virtually every conceivable aspect of air warfare made the French approach to the interwar aviation revolution unique. American and British airmen concentrated on theories of strategic bombardment as the institutional model for doctrine, force structure, and organization. German air leaders toyed with strategic bombing until 1938 or so, but politico-strategic requirements and industrial capabilities forced a turn to air superiority, interdiction, and close air support as the primary doctrinal missions. The Red Air Force nearly disappeared as an organization that generated doctrine after the purges in 1937–38. The loss of Marshal Tukhachevsky and other innovators limited thinking in the Soviet air arm to doctrines of air superiority and close air support.[2] As for Japan, the vast distances of the Pacific and Asian theaters combined with interservice rivalry to relegate aviation to integrated yet supporting roles for the Imperial fleet and the army.[3]

The fundamental aim of this study is to assess the operational effectiveness of the French air force as it prepared for war against Nazi Germany.[4] To obtain an objective appraisal of a particular institution's effectiveness, one must assess political, strategic, operational, and tactical characteristics. In this way, a true composite may be developed of how military institutions carry out their assigned tasks.

Studies of how French aviation performed in May and June 1940 focus largely on strategic designs or tactical performance. Such efforts yield insight, in the case of strategic studies, into how French politicians and diplomats thought about airpower in the context of European politics. As for analyses of tactical performance, one may gain an appreciation for how combat experiences shaped individual lives, but such knowledge often fails to communicate the underlying operational and institutional causes for combat outcomes. The common result of tactical narratives is the propagation of the patriotic "knights of the air" school of French airpower historiography. Personalities and events loom so large, in this tradition, that one rarely discerns the underlying structural developments that shaped the institutional character. In any event, few studies shed light on how the French air establishment prepared intellectually and organizationally for operational warfare.

Those who try to explain how the French military attempted to solve the strategic problems of the interwar period enter an emotionally charged arena. Many assign blame for the defeat or condemn members of the military for failing to adopt more effective, "modern" methods of warfare in time to defeat the Germans. Robert J. Young writes that historians and pundits alike attribute the defeat in 1940 to conspiracy, treason, incompetence, stupidity, paralysis, and degeneration.[5] Rather than tilting at these explanatory windmills, this study follows Professor Young's example as well as those of Robert A. Doughty and Eugenia C. Kiesling, both of whom ask questions of the French military from the perspective of the 1930s rather than from a position of perfect knowledge of the outcomes of the 1940s.[6]

In the 1930s, French leaders recognized that using airpower to deter Germany and to bolster the network of alliances with countries in Eastern Europe meshed well with the inherently offensive nature of the air arm while offering attractive economy of force options.[7] Moreover, plans to support allies with airpower in the event Germany launched a war in the East allowed politicians to claim purely defensive intentions in Western Europe, thereby preserving the moral high ground in diplomatic negotiations with the Germans. Relying on airpower in the East also permitted the army to remain faithful to its doctrine of firepower and fixed defenses. French leaders at the time understood that the army's choice of a defensive doctrine made sense; it was a rational decision based upon calculations of historical experience, existing force structure, national demographics, and political will. Finally, strategic predictions in the early 1930s caused French air force leaders to expect a war in 1936 or, at the latest, 1938.[8] These expectations shaped decisions to modernize the Armée de l'air with the best aviation technology available at the time—technology that proved to be a generation too old in 1939–40.

A reasonable perspective assumes that the men who answered the call to lead France and her air force in the 1930s were neither decadent, nor traitorous, nor stupid. Most of France's political and military leaders during the interwar period survived the trial by fire in the First World War. These men were intensely patriotic, highly intelligent, and intimately familiar with the sacrifices that war demanded. Knowing the horrible price that was possible, they tried their best to prepare the nation for war using the information and resources at hand. To be sure, they made some bad decisions. But these did not always stem from impure motives, just as good decisions do not always guarantee victory in battle.

Since the end of the Riom trial in 1942, air force historiography followed three schools of thought: the first assigned blame for the defeat of 1940, the second focused on political-military relations of the Third Republic, and the third revised earlier perspectives in the search for lasting conclusions about airpower and military institutions. Early assessments of how the Armée de l'air performed followed the judgments established at the Vichy-ordered trial. Marshal Philippe Pétain directed the High Court of Justice to single out political leaders like Léon Blum, Pierre Cot, and Guy La Chambre for failing to prepare the nation for war.

On the military side, the air force bore the brunt of the blame for the military defeat. According to this approach, the judgment of the High Court of Justice was essentially correct. Third Republic politicians, especially those of the Popular Front, squandered time and money in futile attempts to appease Germany while fatally weakening the nation's military and social institutions. The air force, which became an instrument of the Left under Pierre Cot's tutelage, added insult to injury by refusing to fight in the critical battles of May and June. Following this tradition to its conclusion, one finds that the army was not responsible for the defeat of 1940, because French land forces could not compete on par with German air-land superiority.

A special issue of the *Revue historique de l'armée,* published in 1969, illustrates the persistence of the combined effects of shame and myth on the historiography of the air force throughout the 1950s and 1960s. The editors devoted the 167-page issue to the history of French military aviation. Fifteen authors, including serving airmen and staff members at the Musée de l'air, contributed articles that trace efforts to build the air service. The disdain shown by the authors for the interwar period—when the air force gained independence from the army and navy—is interesting. Seven articles focus on early efforts to conquer the skies. The creativity, heroism, and valor of France's early aviation community represent the main themes that emerge from this sampling of articles. National honor peaked during World War I, according to the authors of this interpretation of French airpower history.

The balance of the issue contains studies of post–World War II developments and how they reflect the legacy of the early years. There is no attempt to describe how interwar air leaders organized the service for peace and war, how air doctrine evolved, how the air force contributed to the strategy-making process of the 1930s or to the battles of 1940.

The second school of air force historiography focused on political-military relations. Robert W. Krauskopf's dissertation, written in 1965, remains one of the best studies in this tradition.[9] Krauskopf acknowledged how the Riom proceedings influenced the tone of scholarly attention directed toward the air service. He looked beyond the effects of the trial, however, to explain how France's military aviation deteriorated during the 1930s while that of Germany, her principal rival, grew. But those who follow this approach focus primarily upon the interaction between ministers and generals, thereby giving short shrift to the equally important operational and tactical mechanisms with which the airmen expected to fight the next war.[10]

Since the mid-1970s, historians have been revising earlier assessments of the interwar French air force. The revisionists preserved elements of the heroic traditions of the First World War and the early 1920s, but they also began to explore the processes that led to the development of the independent air force. Authors such as Patrick Facon, Patrice Buffotot, François Pernot, Pascal Vennesson, and Claude d'Abzac-Epezy mined the archives at the Service historique de l'Armée de l'air, at Vincennes, to create a more complete narrative of the interwar French air force.

The revisionists acknowledge a reasonable degree of air force culpability for the defeat of 1940, but they reject the extremes of the earlier Riom-dominated tradition. Theirs is a richer version of air force history that looks for causation in institutional structures, social composition, and operational factors while building upon the conclusions of the political-military explanations of the 1960s. Moreover, the revisionist historians find links between the air force of the interwar years and the one that survived the German occupation to play a role in the resistance and subsequent liberation.

The Armée de l'air obviously failed to perform its assigned operational missions in 1940. But military organizations, as a rule, do not willingly plan to suffer defeat; the French air service was no exception.[11] The magnitude and rapidity of the defeat in 1940 concealed French airmen's efforts to prepare for war in the 1930s. As Eugenia Kiesling correctly points out, neither the American disaster at Pearl Harbor nor Russia's near collapse at the hands of Germany in 1941 evokes the derision that the French experience does.[12] The way that the Battle of France ended and the subsequent consequences for the nation set the defeat of 1940 apart from other catastrophes of the Second World War. Third Republic leaders surrendered the field with operational and tactical options unexplored. Compounding the shame and humiliation of the defeat was the deceptive material strength that the air force possessed when the government ordered its forces to cease resistance in June.

Archival sources show that French aviators articulated a robust concept of how aviation could contribute to a war against Germany. Between 1933 and 1940, service leaders laid the philosophical and material foundations for combat performance in 1940. The processes by which airmen developed doctrine, trained and equipped aviation units, and prepared for mobilization and war provide the framework for this study.

The first clues to understanding how the leaders of the Armée de l'air reacted to the challenges of the 1930s reside in the various aviation doctrines published between 1933 and 1940, and in the processes by which the airmen developed and refined them. Throughout the troubled 1930s, members of France's military aviation community remained acutely aware of their nation's expectations, as well as of the air arm's strengths and weaknesses. But military solutions to the problems presented by German political and military aggression were not always obvious, nor were they always palatable to the French public. One must attempt to understand how strategic and political pressures affected the attitudes, options, and actions of the Armée de l'air.

Histories of interwar airpower doctrine often focus on how strategic bombing concepts evolved to produce the campaigns that devastated Germany and Japan. The results of the bombing campaigns against the Axis powers in the Second World War appeared to vindicate arguments of early airpower theorists by showing how aviation could decisively alter the nature of warfare. The limited evidence that those in the 1930s confronted, however, offered only uncertain answers to questions about how best to employ airpower in modern war. The promise of airpower, in other words, was often greater than the combination of political will and aviation technology could deliver. This was especially true in interwar France. Significantly, the historiography of aeronautical doctrine devotes scant attention to explaining how French ideas about the use of airpower evolved.[13]

The strategic airpower theories of Giulio Douhet influenced French airmen in the 1920s and 1930s as they struggled to resolve the challenges presented by rapidly changing aeronautical technologies and a shifting strategic environment. The Armée de l'air's aviators were not dogmatic, however, in their acceptance or rejection of Douhet's ideas. Like the British, Americans, and Germans, French aviators selected only those concepts from Douhet's writings that applied to their political, social, and military situation. As innovative as some of Douhet's ideas were, the French recognized the Italian's theories for what they were: a departure point. Each nation, each air force, had to tailor basic airpower theory from multiple sources to form usable doctrines.

The Gordian knot that French aviators puzzled over was how to satisfy the diplomat's demands for a strategic force capable of projecting power toward Central and Eastern Europe as well as the army's demands for aerial intelligence and air superiority on the battlefield.[14] The result of their efforts to juggle these often competing and contradictory demands for scarce aerial resources was a reactive airpower doctrine, backed by institutional structures and operational plans, that represented the consensus among air service members on how best to employ air forces for national defense. That their efforts met with so little success in the Battle of France masked the energy and creativity the airmen expended to create an institution that they believed met their nation's defense needs.

Doctrine serves no purpose without training institutions and facilities to insure that it filters down to combat units. One key to arriving at an assessment of operational effectiveness is to evaluate the ability of an organization to convince its members that the institution is on the right ideological and doctrinal path. Air force leaders transmitted these themes to operational and tactical commands by several institutional channels. At the lowest levels, airmen learned basic technical skills. Pilot training, aircraft and engine maintenance, radio-operator training, and gunnery schools provided specialized training that met the basic job requirements for manning combat units. These schools also gave members their first exposure to air doctrine concealed in the form of technical training.

Maneuvers, exercises, and wargames became the primary means of transmitting and refining air doctrine after individuals completed basic technical training and reported to their assigned tactical units. Performance and behavior in day-to-day training and, more importantly, in exercises and wargames indicated the degree to which air force members accepted or rejected official doctrine. The degree and frequency of change in the structures and methods of the French training and education system represent one indicator of member satisfaction with institutional values and provide insight into operational and tactical effectiveness.

In the interwar period, mobilization represented the final strategic task between peacetime and war. Air service leaders created a system designed to transform the nation's war potential into operationally effective forces. This system's performance during the interwar years foreshadowed the operational and tactical deficiencies that plagued the Armée de l'air when war came in 1939 and 1940. To a large degree, the air service's failure to convert human and material potential into effective tools for war determined the ultimate level of operational effectiveness that French airmen could achieve against their Axis adversaries.

Strategic and operational planning also convey a sense of an institution's operational effectiveness. For the Armée de l'air, war-planning efforts in the 1930s reflected the reactive doctrine that evolved during seven years of service independence. French air campaign planners proposed strategies to attack the German war economy across a strategic and operational spectrum that resembled campaigns pursued later by American and British bombing advocates. In the French case, however, the requirement to support the army's defensive operations limited the Armée de l'air's initiative and ability to achieve strategic and operational objectives by pursuing an independent air campaign.

The final phase of doctrinal development occurs when military institutions make adjustments during and after combat. In the French case, the defeat of 1940 rocked the nation's military institutions. The air force, in particular, shouldered a large portion of the blame for the military's poor performance. Yet in defeat, the leaders of the institution sought to derive lessons from the battles of the war so that the disaster of 1940 would never reoccur. After the defeat, air force leaders, under the rubric Commission G, launched an investigation into the conduct of the air war. Officers from combat and combat-support specialties responded to requests for reports on their wartime experiences. In the harsh, painful process of self-examination and critique, air force personnel identified important areas for doctrinal and institutional change. The history of this process remains largely absent from English-language accounts of the interwar French air force.[15]

The overriding conclusion that emerges from this study is that military institutions are incredibly resilient. The French air force shared the burden of national defense with their countrymen in a time of strategic uncertainty and unprecedented technological change. Airmen often found their actions constrained by economic and political bonds that forced them to act in ways that at times contradicted sound military judgment and doctrinal precepts. Yet aviators rose to defend their nation, suffered the humiliation of defeat, and endured the chaos of enemy occupation to emerge with the basic structures of their institution intact. Far from being a story of decadence, treason, or stupidity, such a tale fits surprisingly well within the *chevaliers de l'air* traditions of the early days of French military aviation.

2   Sources of Reactive Air Doctrine

The progress of aviation, marked by a considerable increase in the power, the speed, and the radius of action of its machines, offers enhanced possibilities for cooperation with the Army.[1]

Doctrine and organizational change often stem from recent combat experience. Two primary events offered the fledgling French air arm opportunities to learn lessons from the combat application of airpower. The first was the Great War. No influence was more pervasive on how French air doctrine developed than the historical legacy of the First World War. Between 1914 and 1918, Allied and German aviators pushed the limits of aviation technology in efforts to help restore mobility to the deadlocked struggle on the Western Front. In the process, all of the major airpower missions, with the possible exception of airborne assault, emerged in nascent form.[2] By 1918, French military specialists concluded that airpower contributed to the commander's ability to "see the enemy . . . to assist artillery and to control its fires—to fight in close liaison with the infantry; to protect the soldiers from detection and raids by the enemy . . . and to throw his bombardment squadrons directly into the battle as a new arm of intervention."[3] *Supporting Air Doctrine*

The second combat experience that contributed to French airpower occurred in colonial operations, especially in the 1925 Moroccan Rif War. Taken together, the two wars offered French airmen a snapshot of aviation's potential across the breadth of the conflict spectrum.

French Airpower and the Legacy of World War I

France emerged from World War I as the world leader in military aviation.[4] Her factories equipped her own air force as well as those of her allies. Her training facilities kept a steady stream of pilots, gunners, observers, and mechanics flowing toward the fighting fronts. Her position as the world's aviation leader seemed secure, at least within the European aviation community, at the end of the war—especially when screened by the terms of the Versailles treaty that prevented Germany from developing and maintaining a military aviation capability.[5] Even the dramatic demobilization that came with the peace that followed Versailles failed to shake the nation's confidence in the air service.

Although the French government recognized the need to preserve a degree of institutional identity for the air arm after the war, it did so within the confines of the land army. The Aéronautique militaire was the army's aviation branch for most of the 1920s. Because aviation remained a combat arm of the land service, the first published aviation doctrine derived from that institutional identity. The *Instruction sur l'emploi tactique des Grandes Unités,* the army's basic doctrine manual, remained virtually unchanged between 1921 and 1936 regarding the army view of airpower employment. "The progress of airpower," remarked the authors of the 1936 manual, "offers to the army increased possibilities for cooperation." Although such progress may have spawned optimism among airmen and air theorists, the same technical advances were available to enemy powers. Consequently, French army commanders expected aviation to provide "an organization and reinforcements corresponding to the various elements of aerial defense . . . in order to allow the land forces to shield themselves from enemy airpower and to repulse its attacks."[6] This perspective reflected little change in the attitude of army leaders from the days of World War I, when the primary mission for aviation had been to observe the enemy lines and to warn of possible attacks.

The cornerstone of reactive air doctrine was the requirement, born in the world war experience and imposed by the army during the 1920s, for the air force to devote significant energy and resources to supporting land warfare objectives. As national strategy and army doctrine settled around an emphasis on the fixed front and in-depth defenses, airpower leaders had to devote significant resources to defending the airspace along the front lines. Thus the precedent for reactive air doctrine stemmed from the tension between army requirements for airpower to provide security for the corps battle areas and from airmen's visions of aviation's offensive striking power.

In the early interwar years, theories of strategic bombardment had not replaced the World War I paradigms that defined the roles and missions of the air service in terms relating to the outcome of land combat. Aviation units remained subordinate to ground units, even to the extent of assigning to ground commanders the responsibility for selecting airfield locations.[7] By the end of the war, the French military establishment had identified five missions for the air service: observation, pursuit, bombardment, aerostation (captive balloons), and antiaircraft defense.

In the positional warfare of the Western Front, observation aviation contributed to the ground commander's objectives more significantly than any other form of airpower. One contemporary text noted the importance of maintaining "perfect liaison with the [ground] commander . . . in order to know what to look for . . . failing this, the hours of observation will be perfectly useless."[8] This report devoted fifty-three pages of instruction to air observation and only eight to pursuit, five to bombardment, nine to aerostation, and eight to antiaircraft defense.

In the 1930s, as French ideas about land warfare solidified around the continuous front and the methodical battle, army leaders came to rely even more heavily on having abundant observation aviation resources. This demand for aerial observation support became an important source of reactive air doctrine in the years leading up to World War II.[9]

While observation supported the ground commander's ability to control the pace and scope of the battle, pursuit aviation evolved early in the war to win the battle for air superiority. Ground commanders assigned pursuit missions primarily to secure freedom of action for friendly observation aircraft. French thinkers gradually applied this airpower role within a defensive context, because of the operational constraints of positional warfare and the limited range and striking power of World War I–era airplanes. As one text described the role of pursuit aviation, "the essential missions of pursuit consist in: a) protection of friendly aviation; and b) attack of enemy aviation."[10] If battlefield conditions required pursuit units to perform outside these essentially defensive constraints, commanders assigned pilots to accomplish reconnaissance missions or to attack enemy troop formations.

Bombardment operations represented the only doctrinal use of aviation for offensive purposes during the war. The limited range and payload of early bombardment-type planes did not prevent French planners from recognizing the potential advantages that derived from reaching toward the sources of enemy combat power. The instructors at the École militaire et d'application du génie distilled the aviation lessons from the world war into an air-service course. The result of their efforts was a doctrinal statement that concluded that the most efficient method of employing bombardment aviation was in "prolonging the action of artillery and supplementing its action whenever artillery is powerless either due to the great distance from, or the fugitive nature of the target."[11]

Despite airpower's potential to affect lucrative targets behind the front, the army maintained that the advantages of bombardment in direct combat were best realized when "the special means and efficacy of the Air Service are placed at the service of the ground troops."[12] In other words, the World War I experience led French land warfare–oriented military strategists to establish a paradigm that limited bombardment aviation to a role as long-range artillery. While army leaders recognized the theoretical potential of long-range bombardment, the French general staffs valued the more tangible direct influence of bombardment aviation that obtained when the ground commander exercised control of aerial bombardment missions.

The physical characteristics of the World War I battlefield tied aerostation, or captive balloon observation aviation, more closely to the missions of tactical-level ground units than any other air-service mission except for antiaircraft defense. Army commanders assigned aerostation units missions that were similar to those performed by observation aviation. The primary task of balloon units was to observe the battle area in the immediate proximity of ground forces. Observers kept watch for enemy assaults, adjusted friendly artillery fire, and directed the efforts of antiaircraft artillery units. From the army's perspective, aerostation was difficult, if not impossible, to employ effectively in a war of movement, or where foliage and terrain shielded enemy movements. The air force regarded aerostation units as easy prey for prowling enemy pursuit planes. To protect the courageous but highly vulnerable balloonists, air planners had to strengthen antiaircraft defense units and increase the number and frequency of pursuit patrols. Thus the army's reliance on aerostation for close observation of enemy maneuver along the front limited the range and freedom of pursuit units.[13]

The last mission French doctrine identified for aviation during and immediately after World War I was antiaircraft defense. Defensive counter air (DCA) missions fell into two categories: a) surveillance and reconnaissance; b) protection. In the surveillance role, DCA units collected information on enemy aerial movements and forwarded it to higher-level headquarters. Higher command echelons used the information to alert antiaircraft batteries, direct fire missions, or launch pursuit aircraft to intercept enemy flights. Protection missions consisted of direct measures to counter enemy aviation or balloon operations.[14]

As aviation technology advanced during the 1920s, French military professionals continued to speculate about the best way to integrate airpower into the all-important land battle. One author asked if "deep aerial attack will be suffered by all, and through massive bombardment of what one may call 'vital centers' of the enemy nation, will airpower be capable of ending a war in its early days and of halting the progress of the army's heavy war machines?"[15] Even

OBS, ART, AA DEF

with the technical progress of the 1920s, the author concluded that such an outcome was impossible.

Air forces, like navies, were expensive institutions to create and to maintain, and one of the characteristics of airpower that was recognized by land and air specialists alike was that there would never be enough aviation assets to go around. Moreover, the large number of targets in the "vital centers" of an enemy nation precluded a rapid end to a war solely through aerial attacks. Finally, according to the author, the key lesson from the Great War was that "the war depends upon the armies on the march."[16]

Early interwar studies of how airpower developed during the Great War spanned a continuum that included, on one hand, unabashed optimism about aviation's revolutionary impact on the conduct of war and, on the other hand, hyperconservative caution. One author remarked that the experiences of World War I proved that even a small force of two hundred planes "could in three missions destroy, or at least seriously disorganize three divisions." The effects of this aerial coup would directly benefit the army by "creating [at least] three important breaches that the cavalry may easily use to great benefit."[17]

Some airpower advocates interpreted the historical evidence from the Great War as promise of greater contributions from aerial attacks, despite the pervasive memories of the stalemated front that dominated French perceptions of future wars. In 1925, Major (later General) Keller acknowledged the supporting role assigned to aviation in the "unified battle." Yet he refused to limit his vision, having recognized aviation's potential to reach beyond the land-bound armies. According to Keller, aviation should "take flight and go far from the battle to throw the weight of its bombs to shift the balance of the attack against the sources of enemy supplies in order to triumph over economic and moral factors which are indispensable to success."[18]

The problem airmen encountered when searching for war-winning formulas based on political, economic, and moral effects lay in the difficulty in measuring the efficiency of such efforts against desired results. Although Keller and other like-minded aviators may have hoped to expand the role and prestige of the air arm by extrapolating air theory from the limited experience of the war, others countered that aviation had done little material damage to German industry or morale. This position found its way into the service regulations and there assumed the air of dogma. As one author wrote, "the moral effects and tactical results of aerial bombardment . . . are hardly proportional to the deadly effect of bombs . . . therefore, the material efficiency of bombardment is, in every case, the first result to seek."[19]

After examining the results of World War I bombing missions, conservative strategists concluded that support for operations along the front represented the best use of bombardment aviation. According to the army-cooperation viewpoint, men and material were the appropriate targets, not industries and morale.

After 1928, the focus of articles about the World War I experience changed, in the aviation-branch journals, from trying to distill knowledge and principles about air warfare to chronicling how aviation performed in various battles and operations. This new trend in professional writing about the war reinforced the army's view that the proper role for aviation remained the support of land operations—primarily through aerial observation and the missions that supported air superiority over the battlefront. To support this thesis, authors concentrated on campaigns that had occurred early in the war. The months of August and September 1914 had witnessed significant aviation action along several areas of the frontier, as aerial observers provided timely intelligence information about German movements. Studies of the early months of the war also emphasized aviation's limited striking power, owing to the lack of technological sophistication in military aircraft and armament used by the combatants. Viewed in the context of evolving French defensive doctrines, the critical contributions of airpower that had allowed army commanders to shift forces and to help prevent a disastrous breakthrough promised to help save the day once again, if Germany were to make another attempt to conquer the *métropole*.[20]

French strategic airpower advocates refused, however, to concede the field to their army-cooperation brethren. One author asked plaintively if it was "permitted to consider the [independent] Air Division as an organism capable of playing a strategic role under the direction of the High Command?"[21] But the combined-arms paradigm that forced the Aéronautique militaire into a primary role as a supporting arm compelled even this argumentative author to structure his ideas about air warfare in terms of the "battle of arms" in which observation, pursuit, and bombardment assumed roles similar to cavalry, infantry, and artillery. The air division, despite its potential to achieve strategic effects, remained tied to the land battle and was "best articulated with a packet of pursuit to the East, a packet of bombardment in the center, and a packet of pursuit on the left."[22]

As the 1930s dawned, the French government began to consider the role that air forces should play in national strategy. This caused changes in service organization and doctrines, as aviation assumed greater importance. The Aéronautique militaire, the aviation branch of the army, became the Forces aériennes to indicate the unique contributions that airpower brought to the military strategic mix. Later, in 1933, aviation completed the transformation from combat branch to independent service when the Forces aériennes became l'Armée de l'air.[23] As the debates about independence and the proper role for the new institution occurred, airmen turned once again to the Great War to find historical models for how best to employ aviation in an independent role. In this case, the campaigns of 1918 furnished the best evidence for authors to argue for the autonomous, offensive use of airpower.

One of the best examples of a study that showed the efforts to achieve strategic effects—those aimed at the war-making potential of the enemy rather than at the forces engaged on the operational or tactical fronts—was one of an air campaign proposed in July 1917. The premise for the proposal stemmed from the unfortunate geographical situation that prevailed in northeastern France. As the author of the air campaign expressed, "[t]he most powerful factor of German resistance is his current possession of the iron in the Lorraine and Luxembourg regions, from which he draws 76 percent of his war material consumption, his naval and railway construction."[24] Much of the coal, iron ore, and related industries were (and remain) near the German border. When the fronts stabilized in 1914, this industrial potential fell into German hands.

The central idea behind this strategic campaign involved an attempt to isolate from German exploitation the critical mineral resources in the region by interdicting the rail traffic that carried coal and iron ore to foundries in the Saar, the Ruhr, and other parts of Germany. French air strategists determined that marshaling yards at Thionville, Luxembourg, Woipy, Athus, Pétange, Conflans, and Longuyon, all within 40 kilometers (24.8 miles) of one other and within 100 kilometers (62 miles) of French airfields, represented the critical choke points that serviced this industry.

The key to success, according to the air planners, was to throw the entire weight of the night heavy bombardment forces into the effort against the marshaling yards. By doing so, "one could seek not only their disruption, but their annihilation through massive heavy bombardment."[25] By selecting a few critical targets and applying the principle of massed aerial attack over a sustained period, airmen hoped to deal German war industry a crippling blow.

Unfortunately, the raids failed to produce the anticipated results. This was due, in part, to a combination of poor navigation techniques, bad weather, bombing errors, enemy countermeasures, and repair efforts. The greatest flaw in the execution of the campaign, however, was the gross underestimation of the tonnage required to achieve the desired effects. Each mission carried only an average of eight bombs, and aircrews rarely delivered all their ordnance on the assigned targets.

The failure of the French high command to approve the all-out effort envisioned by the airmen compounded the problems. From January to October 1918, the air service launched only ten missions against the rail yards at Thionville, the most important of the seven target sets. Additionally, a two-month gap between each raid against Thionville allowed German repair crews ample time to restore to full operation any damaged facilities.[26]

In 1930, aviators seized upon the potential represented by this strategic bombing campaign to justify increased reliance on airpower. Despite the lack of tangible results against the iron-ore transportation system in 1918, airmen concluded that "the attack of economic objectives could prevail in the period of cover [*couverture*] and concentration, during stabilization when the land operations lose their importance, and toward the end of an armed conflict, to definitively overcome the morale of the enemy population and government."[27]

Under the tutelage of their land service comrades, French airmen adopted a philosophy, for most of the 1920s, that the proper role for air forces was to support the objectives and actions of army commanders. As the 1930s brought glimpses of strategic uncertainty, however, they realized that even if France adopted a limited vision of aviation employment that tied the air arm to battlefield operations, other nations would most likely exploit all the possibilities of airpower. The debate of the 1930s centered on how to reconcile the army's need for aviation with the increasingly real capabilities that air forces could provide in terms of speed and striking power.[28]

BRT • AMERICA WERE ISLAND NATIONS.

Airpower Contributions in the Rif War

Throughout the 1920s, the air service remained a combatant arm of the army. Army leaders saw little potential for revolutionary developments in aviation, especially with the limited technology of the day. Yet French airmen were among the few aviators to gain valuable combat experience in the 1920s, heralding a new age for aerial warfare. In 1925, the insurrection that had smoldered for more than ten years in the Moroccan protectorate burst into full-fledged war, as rebel forces under the leadership of Abd-el Krim mounted an offensive that threatened to push lightly manned French garrisons out of the country.

While Resident General Marshal Hubert Lyautey shifted his mobile columns to counter Krim's incursions, his aviation commander, General Paul Armengaud, deftly responded with air evacuation of wounded soldiers, aerial bombardment, close air support, reconnaissance and observation, and aerial supply. By blocking the path to Fez, the capital, French troops, supported by air forces, thwarted Krim's efforts to rally larger numbers to his cause. Lyautey, who had advocated a broader role for airpower in colonial operations as early as 1912, credited Armengaud's 37th Aviation Regiment with saving the French cause.[29]

When viewed from a British perspective that emphasized the primacy of independent air operations, the performance of the French air service in the Moroccan Rif War of 1925 appeared lackluster. According to one British analyst, "the offensive power of the air forces was entirely unappreciated or completely ignored."[30] The cooperative role officially assigned to the French colonial air arm served as ammunition for those who thought that airpower was best applied under the aegis of army commanders. From the French perspective, however, the Rif War represented significant progress and innovation from the World War I paradigm of aviation employment. Airmen gained credibility and increased autonomy while they showed that, when properly applied under the command of a knowledgeable airman, aviation could become the primary weapon used to accomplish strategic objectives.

French colonial aviators brought the assumptions of continental doctrine to the colonial administration task. The metropolitan influence was evident in one Tunisian aviator's description of the air service role in 1921: Aviation was "1) to cooperate in the surveillance of the Saharan confines . . . 2) to constitute a force at the disposition of the Commander, in case of insurrectionist troubles in the interior of the Regency; 3) to prepare personnel for their wartime role, either in exterior theaters, or in metropolitan theaters."[31]

Despite this conservative description of aviation's potential to contribute to colonial security, the North African environment quickly forced French airmen to reassess their relationship to colonial land forces and to other colonial institutions. For example, the pursuit mission was superfluous because the North African tribes that fought against the French armed forces had no airplanes. Additionally, the aerostation mission proved cumbersome and ineffective because of rugged terrain and the highly mobile nature of colonial warfare.

Aviation leaders emphasized how the air arm supported army pacification operations. The air service participated in the French protectorate administration in Morocco from the outset, by providing territorial reconnaissance and surveillance of insurgent and tribal movements. Aviators carefully advertised aviation's unique institutional characteristics, but in a way that did not threaten the primacy of, or criticize the contributions of, the larger institution of the army. In the process of refining the institutional characteristics that eventually set the air service apart from other Moroccan institutions, aviators drew upon the values, goals, and institutions of the protectorate government rather than upon those of the army. These values, goals, and institutions evolved under the influence of a particular colonial philosophy promoted by Marshal Lyautey and under conditions of conflict between Moroccan and French societies.[32]

The Agadir Crisis of 1911 had culminated more than half a century of French maneuvering for access to Moroccan territory. Internal instability and extensive debt to French banks provided the justification for intervention in the sultanate. French leaders judged Moroccan society as always on the edge of anarchy, because of the chaos caused by the sultan's economic policies, the nomadic nature of the tribes, and the native willingness to resort to violence to avenge even the smallest insult.[33]

The settlement of the Agadir Crisis divided North African territory between France, Spain, and Germany, with France gaining a free hand in Morocco. The French government assumed the responsibilities of protector and signed the Treaty of Fez in 1912, formalizing the relationship. Paris chose Marshal Hubert Lyautey to administer the country as resident general.[34]

Lyautey was an outspoken, self-styled expert on colonial administration. He had served under General Galliéni in Madagascar and Indochina and had become familiar with Galliéni's ideas on colonial administration, but he developed his own theories of colonization. He served as resident general of Morocco from 1912 until 1925, when opposition at home to his policies and, in Morocco, the Rif War prompted the government in Paris to relieve him in favor of a more politically malleable successor.[35]

Lyautey sought to maintain a thinly veiled illusion of a partnership between the French rulers and their Moroccan subjects. He regarded the sultan and his representatives as legitimate, though junior partners in ruling the territory. In the resident general's view, Morocco's main enemy was instability and, although he preferred to use peaceful methods to introduce French civilization, he was prepared to respond with violent military measures. These included aerial bombardment of civilian areas, to ensure that French pacification efforts succeeded. French officials tolerated dissent from the Moroccan natives only within strictly defined boundaries.

Aviation provided economy-of-force advantages that were important not only in the colonial environment in which ground forces in isolated outposts guarded vast stretches of territory, but also in the postwar métropole, which did not look favorably on costly military expenditures. Lyautey petitioned the war ministry in June 1914 for more powerful aircraft engines for his observation airplanes and, more importantly, for an airman, "un Officier spécialiste de la direction de l'Aéronautique," to manage the aviation effort.[36]

In contrast to the limited effects envisioned for airpower in a continental war, aviation's rapid-response capability and long reach delivered material destruction and great psychological dislocation in colonial warfare. In areas where tribal insurrection flared up, according to one aviator with extensive experience in Morocco, Commandant Barthélemy, "the arrival of airplanes going to bombard and strafe the enemy . . . never fails to return calm rapidly to the rebellious regions."[37]

The regular movement of tribes and their herds between mountain and valley grazing areas represented a significant source of instability that complicated

French attempts to subdue the countryside. Controlling the movements of the nomadic tribes became a central issue in the French endeavor to claim fertile pastures for systematic farming. Airpower supported efforts to control seasonal migrations by monitoring the traditional routes taken by the tribes and their herds. Commandant Cheutin, commander of Morocco's 37th Aviation Regiment from 1918 to 1925, reported that "aviation greatly assisted the interdiction of nomads from the mountains down to the plains, by maintaining surveillance and directing ground units to intercept the nomads. Without aviation, *the army could not perform its assigned mission.*"[38] Cheutin's description of this mission revealed his identification with the goals and values of the protectorate rather than a mission orientation toward army tasks.

Rabat became the nerve center that shaped the character for the emerging colonial air service institution. Commandant Cheutin lobbied successfully to locate the regimental headquarters at Rabat, "close to the Marshal, the Directorate of Information, and the main Protectorate services." The proximity to Lyautey's headquarters and center of colonial government allowed the aviation commander to advise the resident general on how best to employ the air force to accomplish colonial objectives. Cheutin wrote: "The Moroccan Aviation Commander is, of course, the technical adviser to the Commander-in-Chief."[39]

This informal structure, however, led to the arrangement of a formal chain of command in which the aviation commander became an equal participant in protectorate strategy councils. The air commander exercised autonomy by intervening in the chain of command between individual ground commanders and the aviation squadron commanders. Cheutin expressed his pride that "Group commanders have full authority over their squadrons." He went on to comment that "from the point of view of instruction, discipline and use . . . they maintain a close link with the commander of the Intelligence Service and insure that the squadron bases and emergency landing fields are always in good condition."[40]

The independence from land-service interference that resulted from the protectorate command arrangements filtered down to the aviation group and squadron levels in the form of responsibilities that included more than just flying missions assigned by army staffs. Moroccan air service leaders held squadron commanders responsible "not only for the administration and instruction of personnel, the maintenance of equipment, but also to take part . . . in important combat operations."[41]

This command structure represented a significant departure from that of the world war, in which the ground commanders had exercised rigid control over all aspects of the aviation mission. Now air service leaders selected sites for airfields to accomplish the objectives of protectorate strategy, rather than to support specific ground operations. When required, squadrons deployed to areas that were closer to the action in order to support outposts engaged in combating insurgents.

The ability of the air service to evacuate wounded and sick personnel also enhanced the prestige of the emerging institution among leaders of the army and the protectorate government. Colonial aviators pioneered aeromedical evacuation, and by 1925, the Moroccan air service included airplanes dedicated to the aeromedical evacuation mission. Because of the demands of this task, air service and medical personnel cooperated to suggest the development of specially designed airplanes (the Breguet 14T *bis*). These allowed for increased safety and better care of wounded and sick personnel during transport. Aviators allied themselves with representatives in the medical field to formulate rules for the new role. These regulations covered setting up of airfields near well-equipped hospitals, criteria for selecting personnel for aerial transport based on medical treatment needs, safe altitudes (owing to the effects of flying in unpressurized airplanes), and specialized training requirements for flight crews assigned to transport the wounded and sick.[42]

The European doctrine that subordinated aviation to ground commanders proved impractical and inefficient in the fluid environment of colonial warfare. The continental system that evolved during World War I had been effective in combat between symmetrical military opponents where the war aims had been relatively unlimited. But in the limited war that prevailed in the colonies, against enemies employing asymmetrical forces and strategies, options for using force required more sophistication and careful study.

Lyautey and his administration assigned missions to the 37th Aviation Regiment that reflected the new institutional character of aviation and the difference between the European and colonial tactical environments. In 1924, the regimental commander declared that "aviation acting *alone* fills the following missions: reconnaissance, bombardment, liaison and transport, artillery adjustment, medical transport, and *various missions of interest to the civil and military organizations of the Protectorate*."[43]

Bombardment aviation experienced a significant change, in terms of expectations, from the World War I paradigm. Rather than the physical destruction of property and personnel, aviators now connected the results of bombardment missions to Lyautey's desire to convert the natives to the French cause. This represented a dramatic break with earlier ideas that emphasized the material rather than morale effects of bombardment operations. During pacification operations, Cheutin followed Lyautey's doctrine and discouraged indiscriminate killing and destruction. He explained that "the end sought after is evidently not to kill many of the dissidents, but to bring about their rapid surrender, since on the day they accepted [French rule] . . . they became allies of fidelity and devotion beyond reproach."[44]

By 1924, members of the 37th Aviation Regiment aligned air service values in Morocco with Lyautey's economic and social stability goals. The range, speed, and quick-response airpower provided allowed French forces to "assure the security of the country with minimum troops."[45] In contrast to the description of the limited role of aviation in colonial operations presented earlier, by 1924 the air service leader proclaimed that "Moroccan aviation [played] an important role in: a) the preparation of operations; b) participation in combat; c) the exploitation of success."[46] Rather than speaking to the resident general through the ground commander, the aviation regiment commander advised the commander in chief on all aspects of aviation employment at the highest levels of protectorate government.

The Rif War served as the catalyst for accelerating the development of the separate institutional identity of the Morrocan air force. Aviators did not energetically push their case until the protectorate faced the Riffian attack toward Fez in 1925. During and after the Rif War operations, air service personnel confidently advertised airpower effectiveness as a rationale for army and protectorate leaders to recognize aviation as a separate institution. Aviators applied the tactics and operational concepts that had evolved since 1920 to defend the larger institutions of the army and the protectorate. As the Riffian threat heightened tensions, members of the aviation community developed greater confidence in the doctrinal changes that applied to the Moroccan environment.

The coalition of northern tribes led by Abd el-Krim had battled Spanish forces for control of northern Morocco since 1921. Krim sought to "create a republic with a resolute government, firm sovereignty and a strong national organization which was to be a modern state like France and Spain, but of course an Islamic one."[47] By 1924, Spanish military incompetence coupled with Riffian fighting skill and knowledge of the terrain had resulted in a decisive defeat of the Spanish army.[48]

Lyautey recognized the threat posed by the Riffian tribes and positioned his mobile groups to deal with attacks into the French zone. His "stick and carrot" strategy of using small units to pacify local tribes and to begin economic development remained unaltered despite the insurgents' growing confidence after the defeat of the Spanish. Because of Lyautey's reliance on a thin line of lightly fortified outposts, French forces remained extremely vulnerable to attacks all along the northern zone claimed by Krim's Rif Republic.

The Riffian tribes attacked the northern sectors of French Morocco in April 1925. Krim's hard-fighting rebels quickly surrounded or defeated Lyautey's troops in their isolated outposts. Despite the early Riffian successes, Lyatuey remained confident in his pacification strategy. He had little choice, in fact, because he lacked the forces to remove the rebel threat by permanently occupying all of northern Morocco. More importantly, he did not want to subject the Moroccan economy to the ravages of an all-out war. He wrote that "the power and danger of Abd el-Krim as well as his stated ambitions are incontestable; there are, nevertheless, fissures, divisions, and weak points on which action backed up by and advised by political measures, that I have already begun, could easily intervene."[49] Given the resident general's preference for political and economic strategies, and the distance between the French outposts and their reinforcements, aviation became his primary weapon to stabilize the front and set the stage for the counteroffensive.

Aviators assessed the situation somewhat differently than did the resident general. The change in the situation from day-to-day pacification operations signaled a new role for aviation that essentially revolved around the need to preserve from an external threat the security of protectorate territory. One aviator described the situation at the beginning of the rebel advance: "Along a front of more than 100km the danger is everywhere, there are no reserves . . . the command is severed from its outposts and cover. The true reserve, the only reserve capable of maneuvering in this pitiful condition, is aviation."[50] This assessment of the situation reflected the grim nature of French military prospects at the beginning of the Rif War. It also indicated, however, the realization by air service personnel that their institution deserved respect based on airpower's ability to contribute to the protectorate defense.

As the rebel offensive unfolded, Lyautey adjusted his strategy by choosing which key outposts he would defend. He ordered troops in selected outposts to hold their positions, and he organized the remainder of his forces for an eventual counterattack. The fourteen air service squadrons assigned to the northern front assumed responsibility for preventing further territorial loss. Lyautey charged the 37th Aviation Regiment with the following missions:

- discover and track the enemy line of advance;
- develop bombardment objectives;
- attack targets with bombs and machine guns;
- resupply and protect surrounded outposts;
- assure the safety of mobile columns;
- participate in combat.[51]

Although listed fourth on the priority list, the importance of resupplying and protecting surrounded outposts became crucial in terms of the air service's independent institutional identity.

Krim's rebels isolated the French troops from their regular supply columns, forcing them to husband scarce provisions of food and water. The pressure of determined rebel attacks also caused the troops to use ammunition at increased rates. Aviators understood their comrades' plight and devised emergency measures to keep the French lines from collapsing entirely. The airmen communicated with outpost commanders by radio, visual signal, or, if possible, by landing (often in the face of intense small arms fire from rebel forces) to deliver supplies and pick up the commander's dispatches.

The experience of the outpost at Aoulaï illustrated the value of aviation to these installations during the critical period of the war. For four days (3–6 May) the post commander signaled to pilots, "We are encircled, we are under attack." The aviation commander stepped up bombardment missions to the area by attacking rebel artillery emplacements that were firing on the compound's interior. On 8 May, the surrounded post signaled that the "Situation is grave—losses exceed more than one-third of effective personnel—Help us—We are under attack." Aviators increased the degree and frequency of the bombardment missions, so that by the afternoon of the eighth, the sector commander sent the following message: "Excellent work by aviation in checking the intense attack on Aoulaï, enemy artillery has been quiet since 8:30 a.m. Harassment of the enemy by aviation should continue until nightfall to prevent enemy movement and artillery adjustment before morning."[52]

Although aviation could assist soldiers in the fortified positions with keeping enemy forces at bay, time was not on the side of the French soldiers when it came to food, water, and ammunition. The demands for succor in the face of enemy artillery and infantry attack became even more urgent when soldiers confronted thirst and starvation. Aerial bombardment had not broken the siege at Aoulaï, and the commander signaled on 12 May that "We have water for less than four days—Help us." Airplanes, flying at extremely low altitudes, dropped supplies into the compound that allowed the surrounded soldiers to maintain their defenses. A relief column arrived on 15 May to lift the siege and drive the rebel forces away. In all likelihood, survivors of the siege of Aoulaï did not echo the signal that the mobile group commander in charge of the relief column sent to airplanes flying overhead: "We no longer need you."[53]

In retrospect, Lyautey's strategy of applying political and economic pressure against Abd el-Krim's Rif Republic worked. Lyautey's opponents in France, however, used the crisis to have him removed, thus opening the door for harsher colonial policies toward Morocco's native peoples. Aviators judged their performance in the emergency and concluded: "The campaign proves clearly how and how much aviation can help Morocco, to begin the work of the other arms and in the conquest of the land . . . The coming months will show that it is capable of giving results of another type: aiding in the peaceful conquest by the sugar and whip method, aviation perhaps being the better whip."[54]

By the spring of 1926, Abd el-Krim surrendered in the face of a French combined air-ground campaign. The French government had replaced Lyautey the preceding fall, but the institutional relationships that he had allowed to develop and flourish between the air service, the army, and the protectorate government remained. The immediate concern for colonial forces after Abd el-Krim capitulated was to pacify the remaining dissident tribes. Airmen and soldiers viewed this as a return to the pacification and social programs that they had engaged in since 1920. Because of the air service's support for economic development and territorial security, the colonial government and the army granted it de facto recognition as an independent institution.

To protect and enhance hard-won institutional prestige and autonomy, aviation leaders emphasized what airpower could do, not what it might be able to do. Colonel Paul Armengaud, who replaced Cheutin as 37th Aviation Regiment commander only months before the Rif War flared, reported to Lyautey that "aviation, as powerful as it can be, cannot achieve victory by itself. It can prepare for it, but the land should be effectively occupied."[55]

This concise statement reflected the real limits of aviation in the colonies. At the same time, Armengaud's words indicated his awareness that the institution provided a unique ability to support both security and economic development in the North African colony. Lyautey commended the 37th Aviation Regiment and confirmed the status of the air service as an independent institution within the protectorate when he said that the "squadrons have greatly aided the programs of the operations groups and inspired the ground troops with a double measure of confidence, gratitude and admiration."[56]

Armengaud returned to France after the Rif War and added his voice to the growing debate over the organization and role of the air service in national defense. In 1928 he published a study of aviation's contribution to the Rif campaign that distilled for the public several lessons regarding airpower. Armengaud described the operational conditions that prevailed in Morocco, then transferred the lessons from the colonial context to a hypothetical European war. Those who argued that *la petite guerre* of the colonies held few lessons for *la grande guerre* on the continent missed a valuable opportunity to advance the body of military aviation knowledge, according to Armengaud. The key to profiting from the Rif War lay, he said, in assessing "in what measure those lessons would be valuable for a European war."[57]

The 37th Aviation Regiment units operated most effectively when concentrated, Armengaud observed. In future European wars, he argued, enemy aviation would attempt to apply this principle to cover the army's mobilization and advance and to strike a mortal blow against French aviation. Moreover, the numbers of airplanes that nations would employ would continue to grow. Armengaud wrote: "The war in Morocco marked an evolution in the number of planes assigned to the units charged with assault missions."[58] The correct response to this troubling development would require a doctrinal change *(une nouvelle conception)*. Aviation would best serve the war effort by concentrating rapidly and proceeding to the frontier ahead of the army.

This was indeed a revolutionary proposal, when considered in light of the World War I doctrine that relegated aviation units to a role subordinate to land commanders. What was more revolutionary, however, was the realization that the range and speed that were inherent characteristics of airpower would ensure that "the entry into the line of all aviation upon mobilization [would] be *quasi-immediate*."[59] Armengaud opened the door for independent aerial action that could shape the course of the war effort.

To allow aviation units to range ahead of the armies required a new organization and command structure. In the first place, land commanders would find themselves preoccupied with organizing large numbers of men and vast amounts of material before shifting to the task of moving their units into the battle line. To insist that aviation wait for the army commander could cost the nation valuable territory and resources. The answer, Armengaud argued, lay in the model that prevailed in Morocco, where the aviation commander reported independently to the commander in chief. But, he cautioned, to best employ air forces the nation must grant airmen command authority. In the next European war, "the senior aviation commander should be the effective chief, not only of the general reserves, but of all of the available airpower."[60]

But how should airpower contribute to the war effort if the front stabilized into a continuous battle line, as it had done during the Great War? Armengaud found this question difficult to answer using the example of the Rif War. In the first place, few strategic targets supported the Riffian attack. Second, the critical need during the war was for close air support for the surrounded units and aerial interdiction of rebel supply lines. Finally, aviation technology had not progressed enough to support deep penetration of enemy rear areas. Armengaud built a case that argued for an independent role for aviation, but his combat experience supported a close cooperative function. He related that airpower had functioned in Morocco "like a synthesis of the cavalryman, of the gunner and of the infantry machine-gunner. We will never forget our interview with Captain Duboin, the heroic and famous defender of Aoulaï, on the day after his relief. He told us, and he has re-echoed it several times: 'I thought that I understood airpower, I know today how much I misunderstood about it. What I have seen is a revelation for me. Airpower is the synthesis of the three arms.'"[61]

Although he suggested that airpower could have decisive strategic effects by intervening in rear areas to instigate "terror, isolation, and the abandonment of towns," the need on the front was for a maximum effort to support army assaults.[62] The answer was to employ airpower as a flexible, independent arm that tailored combat power to the needs of the theater.

Armengaud advocated strengthening the trend toward independent air operations based on his analysis of the successful experience in the Rif War. But he did not favor abandoning the army altogether. Army leaders would continue to need the benefits that aviation provided, perhaps even more than in the Great War. While some in the aviation community pushed for independence and strategic bombing capability, others, like Armengaud, favored a more methodical approach that guaranteed their army brethren the air support they needed. Nevertheless, both traditions—the subordinate role played by airpower during the First World War and the cautious search for increased autonomy that derived from the Rif War—contributed to the reactive doctrine that emerged in the 1930s and that the Armée de l'air would ultimately carry into battle in 1940.

Other Influences on Air Doctrine

Institutional battles in the late 1920s and early 1930s also contributed to how reactive air doctrine developed. The French government and the military struggled to define the most effective organizational scheme for the nation's military aviation. In 1928 the government established an air ministry to manage operations, training, and procurement matters. The decree that created the ministry failed, however, to grant full autonomy to the new institution. Land and naval commanders retained control of aviation units slated to cooperate with their combatant commands. Moreover, the law prevented the air minister from altering the structure or the deployment of aviation units without prior approval from the minister of war. The air service remained attached to the army by this umbilical for nearly five years.

The late 1920s and early 1930s witnessed a surge of technical developments in aviation. France's air industry was no exception to this phenomenon. Unfortunately, this period also saw the onset of the global economic crisis; the United States and other countries suffered first, but France too eventually felt the pinch. Fears for the economy, coupled with an active disarmament movement, served as a brake on modernization initiatives for the air force until the mid-1930s. Rather than adopting a focused procurement policy that linked assigned missions with technological capabilities, the air ministry opted to support aviation industries by pursuing a prototype procurement strategy *(politique des prototypes)*.[63]

According to this approach, current aviation technology functioned well enough for present defense purposes. Additionally, the technology changed so rapidly that politicians wished to avoid placing large orders for aircraft that were destined to become obsolete in the near future. Theoretically, the prototype policy allowed aviation contractors enough government business to remain solvent, while at the same time it promoted research to keep French aeronautical technology current with the latest engineering developments. Unfortunately, the result was that the air service spent the first half of the 1930s operating with aircraft that looked like and performed on par with those that had flown in the First World War.[64]

By 1933 the government decided to end the organizational and bureaucratic twilight zone that had plagued the service since 1928. New presidential decrees awarded a higher degree of autonomy to the air service. At the same time a youthful professor of international law, Pierre Cot, took over as air minister. Cot expressed strong support for collective security under the aegis of the League of Nations; he also spoke out in favor of European disarmament. At the same time, however, he deeply distrusted Germany and the rising tide of fascism. Cot believed that airpower could provide the requisite collective security in the guise of an international reprisal force, as European nations dismantled their dangerous land forces.

The new air minister set out to reform the air ministry and to shape the character of the Armée de l'air. He intended to reorganize the service to make it more effective as a war-fighting element of the defense establishment, while simultaneously reforming procurement practices and modernizing equipment. Given the political culture of the Third Republic in the 1930s, it is no surprise that Cot's sweeping agenda achieved mixed results.

Cot faced a situation in which French strategy in Europe depended heavily on alliances with weaker countries in the East (Poland, Czechoslovakia, and Rumania, in particular) to keep the threat of a resurgent Germany in check. The army, for all practical purposes, abandoned hopes of launching offensives into Germany to relieve the pressure on French allies in Eastern Europe, thus leaving the air force to represent the French determination to honor the treaties with the Eastern partners.[65] Unfortunately, when Cot took office the air service was ill prepared, either materially or doctrinally, to succor French allies by launching aerial strikes against Germany.

To complicate matters further, Cot recognized that a war that began in the East could quickly turn on France in the West, thereby placing demands on the air service to provide air support for the army.[66] He could not afford, therefore, to build a fleet of bombers designed to strike deep into Germany and the East at the expense of ground support, fighter, and reconnaissance aircraft. Even worse, by 1933 the effects of the Great Depression began to exert their full weight on the French economy after a deceptive grace period.[67] Weighing all these factors, Cot opted to jettison the politique des prototypes in favor of a plan to purchase a multiplace, multipurpose aircraft—the bombardment-combat-reconnaissance, or BCR. With such a vehicle, the independent air arm could meet the demands of economy, metropolitan defense, and collective security. But the BCR, an airplane designed to do everything, did nothing well.

Cot's tenure as air minister lasted until 1934, when his chief of staff, General Victor Denain, replaced him after the near-coup in February that followed the notorious Stavinsky affair.[68] Denain commanded respect with politicians and aviators alike. He was a veteran of the First World War who had led the air effort against rebels in the Levant during the 1920s. As air minister he pursued Cot's modernization plans, thus providing much needed continuity and stability at the highest level of the service.

Plan I, the production plan that Cot and Denain assembled, forecast the acquisition of 1,010 new airframes over a period of three years. From the outset, Plan I met with difficulties. The aforementioned effects of the Depression tightened the fists of the traditionally parsimonious French legislators. Aircraft production plants experienced the atrophy that comes from long periods of little or no work. And Denain's initiative to pressure industry leaders to relocate important aircraft industries away from the Paris region, where they presented easy targets for enemy bombardment, to deeper in the nation's interior compounded production problems. Finally, German rearmament sparked French fears of a war in 1936 and prompted Denain to push for accelerating the plan's production schedule. He cut the original optimistic timetable of three years to an impossible-to-achieve eighteen months.[69]

After 1936 the French strategic position took on an increasing aura of emergency. Germany grew stronger, particularly with respect to airpower, and the alliance systems in the East that had once promised to draw the German menace away from metropolitan France began to evaporate. Denain's tactic of overestimating the German threat when addressing legislators in order to impart a sense of urgency for rearmament programs had the undesirable effect of shaking public confidence in the readiness of French aviation. Moreover, the experiences with Plan I exposed the French aircraft industry's dismal inadequacy to the task of gearing the nation for war against a major airpower.

The Popular Front that assumed the reins of government in 1936 returned Pierre Cot to the air ministry. Cot resumed his duties determined to complete the initiatives he and Denain had launched during his first term at the air ministry offices on the Boulevard Victor.[70]

At Cot's urging, and with Prime Minister Léon Blum's support, the government passed a new law nationalizing the armaments industries. Cot used this to
pressure reluctant manufacturers to modernize assembly processes and to relocate to more secure areas in the south and west. Not surprisingly, he failed to
turn the industry around. Firms such as Breguet, Liore, and others resented the
government's intrusion and lobbied aggressively to stop Cot's meddling.[71] With
the unwillingness or inability of French industries to meet demands for faster
and better production results, the government began to look overseas, particularly to the United States, for new airplanes.[72]

While the Popular Front government struggled to cope with industrial concerns at home, international events diverted its attention and threatened to destroy
the cohesion of the fragile Leftist coalition. The Spanish Civil War forced Blum
to choose between Great Britain (France's most important ally against the German threat) and support for a Leftist government in Madrid. Cot pushed the government vigorously to support Spain's Republican government. He promised to
deliver airplanes and logistical support to bolster the Spanish government's
cause, but Blum bowed to pressure from the British abroad and the Right at home
by declaring that France would remain neutral regarding the Spanish problem.

By choosing national interest over ideology, Blum proved that he was no
slave to Socialist dogma. However, French Communists viewed Blum's decision as a betrayal of the Popular Front ideal. Blum and Cot established a limited clandestine supply line of planes and supplies to the beleaguered Spanish
Republicans, but the French material was too little in quantity and of inferior
quality compared to the German and Italian equipment supplied to Franco's
forces.[73] Ironically, the French air contribution significantly constrained the Na-
tionalists in the early days of the war. When Lieutenant Colonel Jose Yagüe
launched his dramatic drive on Madrid from Sevilla early in August 1936, he
felt constrained to move only at night because of his concern for "Red" (mean-
ing French) airpower.[74]

While events in Spain and Eastern Europe rocked French foreign policy, Cot
launched a series of initiatives aimed at reforming the air force. He thought that
the rank structure was too top-heavy, that the senior officers were too entrenched
in the philosophies of the last war, and that promotion boards favored staff officers over their brethren who concentrated on operational and tactical expertise.[75]
Consequently, Cot forced many senior generals to retire while awarding commissions to nearly four hundred noncommissioned officers. He streamlined and
reorganized the air staffs and combat commands to make them more efficient.

Regardless of the necessity for such sweeping reforms, the abrupt way that
Cot implemented them sparked resentment within the service. For the remain-

der of his tenure in office, Cot fought on one hand the army and navy's efforts to erode the autonomy of the air service, and on the other his unpopularity with his own hostile officer corps.[76]

Guy La Chambre replaced Cot as air minister in 1938 and served in that capacity until the declaration of war.[77] La Chambre recognized that Cot's reform initiatives had cast a pall over the entire service, and he acted to restore the troops' confidence in the ministry. He chose General Joseph Vuillemin as his chief of staff. Vuillemin possessed impeccable operational credentials for the job. He was a bona fide war hero and world-famous explorer who had led a daring aerial expedition across the Sahara in the 1920s. During the interwar period, Vuillemin had served as bombardment group commander and inspector of bombardment forces for the air service.

The team of La Chambre and Vuillemin promised to focus the service on critically important issues—purchasing and flying new airplanes—rather than wasting airmen's time on political and doctrinal nonsense. La Chambre soothed the army's ruffled feathers by granting General Gamelin, an old friend and chief of staff for national defense, a measure of control over air forces deployed in the different operational theaters.[78] Vuillemin acknowledged that the army's war plans placed a heavy burden on the air force for reconnaissance and pursuit aviation support. After 1938, visions of independent aerial operations gave way to a policy of cooperation and support for land forces. In any event, both aviation leaders were more concerned with rearming the air service with modern, competitive airframes.

With the completion of Plan I in 1937, airmen realized that the planes designed in the late 1920s and purchased in the mid-1930s would suffer horrible losses when confronting front-line equipment flown by Hitler's Luftwaffe. La Chambre pushed the Chamber of Deputies to authorize credits for a new modernization plan (Plan V). This time the emphasis would be on purchasing specialized fighter, bombardment, and reconnaissance aircraft instead of opting for an all-purpose machine like the ill-fated BCR.

Fighter types made up the lion's share of the new program, owing to the emphasis on metropolitan defense. French manufacturers still lagged behind the state-of-the-art design innovations and mass-assembly production techniques used by the other great airpowers.[79] Industry representatives promised to deliver a more modern air fleet no earlier than late 1941 or early 1942 at best—far too late to allow the Armée de l'air to cope with the anticipated German onslaught. La Chambre desperately sought to obtain large numbers of American-built Curtiss pursuit planes, but by the late 1930s American public opinion severely limited the volume of airframes available and the pace of their delivery.[80] Despite vigorous negotiations from French politicians, the Armée de l'air could only field four groups of American-built Curtiss H-75 pursuit planes for the Battle of France.[81]

Adding to the mounting sense of urgency for the French air force, in September 1939 the agreement between the air leaders and Gamelin took effect. The immediate consequence was a complete reshuffling of the command structure of the air service, in February 1940. La Chambre and Vuillemin broke up Cot's autonomous aerial regions and divided the air units piecemeal fashion among the various army command theaters. Air commanders found themselves subordinate to army commanders, often with no established lines of communication between air bases and army theater headquarters.

To make matters worse, national mobilization brought on by the declaration of war hopelessly complicated the critically important coordination required to integrate the air and land efforts. As war descended upon the French air forces, the lack of command coordination resulted in predictably poor use of air resources. William Bullitt, United States ambassador to France, described a conversation between General François d'Astier de La Vigerie and the air minister: "Almost every evening I had to lift up my telephone and take the initiative to inform the commander of the army and of the group of armies that I had, for the following day, a certain number of formations without missions, adding, 'Have you any to give them?' Their reply was invariably the same: 'We thank you very much but we do not have use for them.'" General d'Astier added that a mixed group of fighters and bombers attached to an army corps did nothing during ten to fifteen days.[82]

Efforts to coordinate the allied war effort were no better off than the air-land dilemma. Pierre Cot wrote that "what is most lacking between France and its allies is the absence of technical and military accords, prior to war, between our Air Forces."[83] While Cot criticized the lack of coordination between the two allied nations, British leaders expressed concern over the material state of the French air force. The French responded that although they understood the importance of aerial rearmament, they were doing all that was possible. In the last eighteen months before the declaration of war, the French repeatedly requested larger British airpower commitments for the continent. The British responded by agreeing to deploy light and medium bombardment units to northern France, but balked at the notion of weakening the Home Defense fighter force to help stop a German attack against their continental ally.

In any event, even had the British deployed larger numbers of aircraft to help the French cause, there was virtually no coordination between the two air staffs.[84] The British bombers shared the fate of their French counterparts, as commanders sent them into battle in penny-packets where the German fighters and antiaircraft guns ground them up.[85]

Since 1918 the French air service had become accustomed to dealing with competing demands for its resources. When granted independence in 1933, the members of the Armée de l'air had no institutional model within the metropolitan military structure upon which to base an independent role for airpower. Pierre Cot set out to provide that model, by ordering the air staff to write and publish a series of comprehensive doctrine manuals that spelled out the institutional position on every possible aviation mission. In doing so, Cot and the men who developed the air service's basic doctrine inadvertently reinforced the growing predilection toward reactive airpower.

3   Writing and Publishing Reactive Air Doctrine

The considerable technical progress and the evolution of aviation doctrine among the world's powers has required us to envisage a new role for airpower in the event of a conflict.[1]

In the 1930s there was great controversy, as there is today, over how to develop air doctrine.[2] In the Armée de l'air, competing demands at the strategic, operational, and tactical levels exerted pressures on how airpower doctrine evolved in the critical years before World War II. Additionally, instability within the governments of the Third Republic filtered into the process, thus complicating the task. Despite the pressures brought on by the influences on the quest for a viable aviation doctrine, the leaders of the Armée de l'air published statements that described how they intended to use airpower to defend the nation against an aggressive enemy.

In 1933, after much debate, the French government reorganized the national defense structure and, while retaining the air ministry of 1928, created the Armée de l'air as an independent service.[3] On one hand, granting airmen autonomy from the army and navy appeared to be a logical and progressive move. Airpower had contributed in numerous ways to the successes of the Great War, and, with the apparent technological changes on the horizon in the early 1930s, aviation seemed on a path that emphasized the need to capitalize on the unique capabilities afforded by military aviaton.

On the other hand, if France remained committed to ideals of collective security and disarmament, the creation of a large independent air force capable of

33

striking targets deep in neighboring countries represented a contradiction in national strategy. Moreover, the emerging land warfare doctrine that relied upon fortified frontiers and massive firepower, the methodical battle, required a robust aviation component to provide observation, air superiority, close air support, and battlefield interdiction.

Consequently, the law that created an independent air service within the French military establishment decreed, "the Air Force should be capable of participating in aerial operations, in combined operations with the Army and the Navy, and in territorial air defense."[4] From the outset, the Armée de l'air supported demands from its sister services while trying to develop formulas that expressed the best application of airpower. The broad outline of the duties that members of the new service would perform reflected the tradition of cooperation and support for land and naval operations that had existed since World War I. Thus the air service appeared destined to drift among the various options for using aviation to pursue national interests.

Airmen tried to remain faithful to visions of an independent role for the Armée de l'air, while simultaneously supporting legally mandated roles that centered on cooperating with the army and the navy. Existing doctrine failed to provide a framework within which the members of the new service could operate. Pierre Cot, the minister for air, aimed to establish adequate doctrine that airmen could use as a guide in the plethora of strategic, operational, and tactical situations in which they would find themselves in the 1930s.

Types of Military Doctrine

One of the first tasks military professionals encounter when developing doctrine is to distinguish among the various types that they intend to create. The job is relatively simple if the existing tenets conform to the broad needs of the service; in this case, the task becomes one of revising or updating the existing doctrinal formulas. When creating guidelines for entirely new technological or strategic purposes, however, the chore becomes much more difficult. New doctrines often threaten established values, beliefs, and practices—thus causing conflict within the institution and with other military organizations. When this happens, the authors of the new doctrine must carefully define the type that their service needs. At least three sorts of doctrine serve as institutional guideposts for military professionals.[5]

Fundamental doctrine identifies the basic institutional values of a particular military service. It describes the characteristics that allow application of combat power in distinct media and is more abstract, thus more theoretical than other types. In the interwar period and, some would agree, even today, the theoretical basis for airpower thought remained sketchy at best.[6] For the French air force, the writings of Giulio Douhet may have represented the most concise source of fundamental doctrine.[7] Douhet's conception advocated the creation of air forces organized to strike enemy air bases and cities in order to gain command of the skies and to establish conditions that led to the destruction of the enemy civilian population's will to fight. This formula clashed somewhat with the liberal disarmament ideals that characterized much of the Socialist agenda to which Cot and his colleagues adhered. The Italian's visions of offensive striking power remained an attractive departure point, however, from which French airmen could justify service independence and autonomy.[8]

Organizational doctrine describes on one hand how services interact, and on the other how they organize internally to conduct combat and other operations. With the advent of modern, technologically sophisticated armies, navies, and air forces came the need for a common understanding of how to unify the separate efforts in order to achieve common strategic and operational objectives. The interservice conflicts that arose during the interwar development of air doctrine stemmed, in part, from airpower's ability to range beyond the reach of land and naval forces. Airmen conceived of war at the strategic level, as in the case of British and American strategic bombing doctrines, or at the operational level.

These new visions of military effectiveness questioned the utility of established methods of warfare. Thus the most difficult obstacle French airmen confronted when developing organizational doctrine lay in identifying areas of common ground, assigning service priorities, and selecting command arrangements that allowed the services to integrate their capabilities without compromising fundamental service doctrines. Throughout the 1930s, the leaders of the Armée de l'air struggled with representatives from the land and sea services over the most effective organizational air doctrine for national defense. The failure to resolve conflicts with the other services contributed significantly to the reactive doctrine that characterized the French air service's approach to aerial warfare; this forced the airmen to conform to organizational formulas that threatened or compromised the tenets of their fundamental doctrine.

Finally, tactical doctrine defines how military forces intend to employ specific weapon systems in battles and engagements. In many instances, this is the simplest form of doctrine to construct. Yet by focusing on the specifics of tactics and maneuver, military professionals may become complacent, too technically minded, and may lose step with the strategic and operational context that drives the war effort.[9] The conflicts that arose between the Armée de l'air and the other services over fundamental and organizational guidelines caused French airmen to focus on producing tactical doctrine to the exclusion of nearly every other doctrinal task. The leaders of the Armée de l'air found that it remained one of the few areas that they could explore in relative freedom from sister service interference. The product was an air service that came to rely heavily on technical and tactical expertise, thus leaving airmen poised to react to strategic and operational circumstances rather than prepared to seize and exploit the initiative.

Relationships between formal and informal tenets can also characterize military doctrines. The degree to which formal, written guidelines coincide with operational and tactical procedures describes the sophistication and maturity that exists between formal and informal institutional values, practices, and norms. At the beginning of the development process, there may be a close correlation between formal and informal doctrines. This applied, to a great extent, to airpower philosophy during and immediately after World War I. Combat experience, technological limitations, and the absence of sound theory resulted in a widely accepted informal doctrine that most airmen and soldiers embraced. In other words, formal and informal doctrine corresponded to the tactical guidelines that had worked under fire. Informal doctrine emphasized the supporting roles that airpower could perform in a static operational and tactical land theater context. After the war, however, air theorists began to reflect upon the experiences of the conflict; the difference between formal and informal doctrines became greater as the body of airpower theory diverged from the World War I realities.

Several events may prompt changes that reduce the discrepancies. The first circumstance that can motivate military professionals to bring formal and informal doctrines closer together occurs when the body of military theory expands. Often, but not always, this may result from direct experience in combat.[10] For aviation, the Great War represented the catalyst for military applications of airpower. Second, technological change may widen the gaps between formal and informal doctrines; thus an advance in technology may provide incentives for changes in thought. This was the case in the late 1920s and early 1930s within nearly every major airpower.[11] New airframe designs, better engines, increased payloads, and longer range for aircraft heralded a technological shift that expanded the possibilities for military aviation beyond the boundaries established during the Great War.

Changes in strategic circumstances may also dramatically affect informal and formal doctrines. In the interwar period, the failure of collective security and disarmament, the worldwide economic depression, and the resurgence of a belligerent Germany kept French diplomats and military strategists off balance. As the strategic landscape changed, French airmen repeatedly examined the relevance and adequacy of their doctrines. The result caused air service members to lose confidence in their ability to close the gaps between formal and informal doctrines.

Finally, the doctrine-development process comes full circle as military professionals try their ideas in combat. There is no more painful experience in war for a military organization than the discovery that deeply held values and beliefs about how best to employ a particular specialty are woefully lacking. Some degree of irrelevance is inevitable, but if the institutions fail to foster imagination, innovation, and initiative, the outcome may prove disastrous and irreversible.

The Armée de l'air and Fundamental Air Doctrine

In 1933 Pierre Cot and the leaders of the Armée de l'air set out to resolve two related processes. The first was to promote a flexible and complete doctrine that addressed fundamental, organizational, and tactical needs within the new service. The second was to ensure that the principles remained relevant by narrowing the gaps between formal and informal doctrines. The first process addressed concerns held by airmen and members of the other services; the second dealt with concerns within the air service. The foundations of air doctrine would allow airmen "to realize the most judicious employment of the materials in service, to conceive and to prepare the new doctrine based on the materials that modern technology will permit putting into service in the years to come."[12] The vision that Cot attempted to communicate to the airmen was one of establishing the continuing utility of the independent service within the national defense establishment.

One of the most important questions Cot and his staff faced was what type of air service to create. One thing was certain: the existing paradigm that tied French airpower to a model of land warfare characterized by stationary fronts would prove decidedly inadequate for the wars of the future. Cot anticipated a German surprise attack aimed at delivering a quick knockout blow to French military and industrial power. German military, economic, and material conditions, he argued, favored a short war rather than a long conflict. "The short war assumes the offensive—the continuous offensive. And the offensive assumes a considerable superiority of means."[13]

Cot argued that for France's best interests, airpower remained the most flexible and effective instrument available to draw the Germans into a long war, if war should occur. The Armée de l'air required a complete revision of French airpower doctrine and structures to prepare the new service intellectually and structurally to counter the German threat. Cot wrote: "Until 1933 we had military aviation, but not an Air Force. Our airpower was entirely at the disposition of the Army and the Navy, its material and its doctrine being oriented only toward cooperation missions."[14] This emphasis away from airpower as a supporting element for the other services defined the broad outlines of the fundamental doctrine that Cot urged upon the Armée de l'air.

In a 1933 report to the president, Cot emphasized the flexibility he hoped to instill in the new air arm. "Instead of air forces that are strictly specialized with respect to particular missions, it is necessary to have an air force capable of taking part, to defend the nation, either in purely aerial operations, or in terrestrial or naval operations."[15] Cot assumed an active role as his air ministry launched the doctrine-development process. In his view, "the personal role of the Minister was to choose and to define doctrine, just as to choose and to determine the operational plans, as a function of the Minister's doctrine, was the role of the Chief of Staff."[16]

Cot aimed to create a service that could react to any mission the nation required of it. The new air minister was not naïve, however. He realized that events in Germany did not bode well for the French Republic. The Germans would attempt to overcome the restrictions that the Versailles treaty imposed upon their military. Therefore, according to Cot, airmen could ill afford "to believe that a new war [would] resemble that which we have known. To fail to realize that the new possibilities of aerial technology offer new tactical possibilities, and consequently expose our country to new dangers, in a word, lacks imagination."[17] Examined in the context of new operational potentialities and looming strategic dangers, the aerial weapon presented a sword that could cut both ways.

The Armée de l'air represented a new, technologically sophisticated force that promised decisive results in war. But regardless of airpower's ability to achieve conclusive effects, it would certainly prove essential to any future European conflict. Imagination and innovation would become the defining institutional characteristics that Cot sought to foster in his doctrinal and structural revisions for the new service. In order to achieve Cot's objectives, the service would have to abandon conventional thinking that emphasized airpower's material and technological limits. One author speculated, "modern airpower can possess today the tactical and strategic power to assume a preponderant role in a future conflict. Surprise, maneuver, concentration of means, direct and constant intervention against the enemy's sources of supply—with all the promise that they offer—are they not entirely possible for the Air Force?"[18]

The imagination and vision that Cot sought to instill among the airmen rested upon a free exchange of airpower ideas. His initial directive to the officers who would write and employ the air doctrine reflected this philosophy. "These ideas," he wrote, "do not express a rigid, inflexible aerial doctrine. They should serve as a theme for reflection. They do not reject critiques. Much to the contrary, they are intended to provoke."[19] In the early days of service independence, the Armée de l'air appeared poised intellectually to formulate and to embrace new ideas about fighting the nation's wars.[20]

Early on, the leaders of the new service confronted the increasing instability that characterized the European strategic environment in the 1930s. Cot's assessment of German plans for a rapid, decisive war meant that the addition of airpower increased the civilian population's concerns about enemy aerial attacks. These promised to bring war to the doorsteps of every citizen.[21] According to one staff officer, "the feeling of security procured by our population through the existence of a solid army profiting from an organization of fortified frontiers is found to be shaken: each family feels threatened, every town feels targeted. From a conception of war more or less localized to the area of the armies, is substituted one of a total war exercising its ravages on the entire nation."[22] The possibility that conflict could rapidly spread to encompass the nation, its infrastructure, and its social fabric helped to frame the requirements for new ideas about how to wage war in the air.

French airmen used the term *lutte aérienne* (aerial battle) to describe the central concept of how to counter an enemy with the potential to hold every town at risk. This term allowed the aviators to consolidate all aspects of airpower into one expression, because it was flexible enough to encompass offensive, defensive, and cooperation missions. "Thus the Armée de l'air should orient itself to adapt to methods that correspond to new aspects of lutte aérienne. These new methods emphasize the predominance of collective combat over the individual combat that characterized the last war to a great degree."[23] The expression also revealed the revolutionary potential of the air weapon to win wars. The key to waging successful lutte aérienne lay in massing air forces to accomplish common objectives.

The complexity of lutte aérienne required a new understanding of warfare. General Vuillemin, a future air force chief of staff, observed: "The historical experience of air war does not constitute a collection of 'offensive or defensive' battles separated by time, by orders, or by delays. It presents the character of a single 'fight' which prolongs itself during the entire duration of the war, and it pertains to the battle of attrition with alternatives of success and failure. In this battle, offensive and defensive operations are found constantly juxtaposed, sometimes even combined."[24] Vuillemin argued that to couch perceptions of lutte aérienne in terms of land or naval warfare concealed the complexity and the decisive potential that airpower brought to the modern war effort.

The legal requirement for the air force to support army and navy operations forced the airmen to forge a conceptual link between their emerging doctrines and those of the traditional services.[25] Despite the airmen's visions of decisive air campaigns, the characteristics of lutte aérienne that made it politically acceptable within the Third Republic centered on the flexibility that allowed the Armée de l'air to accommodate and support contemporary conceptions of land

and naval warfare. For cooperation with the army, in particular, airmen created a doctrine that emphasized providing security for the army during mobilization and defensive operations. Pierre Cot observed, "in the current technological conditions, the belligerents will endeavor, in the first place, to paralyze their adversaries by bombing their military centers, by hindering troop and material transports, by blocking industrial mobilization, and by throwing civil populations into disarray."[26] Thus the leaders of the Armée de l'air shouldered the twin burdens of protecting the fragile civilian population and the army, as it concentrated its combat effectives and moved them into contact with the advancing enemy.

The prospect of rear areas thrown into disarray suggested that a clash of air forces, rather than of armies, would characterize the initial battles of a future war. In such a clash, the air force assumed responsibility for offensive and defensive missions as integral parts of lutte aérienne. The key to winning in aerial warfare lay in carrying the fight to the enemy. Air forces could target entire enemy societies in order to "destroy the enemy air force by bombing its bases, hangars, and air fields, and fuel depots; disrupt mobilization and concentration of the enemy armies by bombing principal communication nodes, barracks, and mobilization centers; and target national morale by bombing large towns."[27]

In the early days of air force independence, the army demanded a fixed number of airplanes for air superiority and reconnaissance support. Based upon army estimates, the air force agreed to dedicate two hundred reconnaissance and pursuit planes to service army needs. But the possibility of an aerial war occurring without a corresponding ground battle resulted in a demand by the air service that "the Commander of the land forces will put, each time that he is able, a portion of this allotment at the disposal of the Air Department for use in the lutte aérienne."[28] If the predominant effort dictated that air forces carry the weight of the war effort, land units would, in principle, support the Armée de l'air as it waged the aerial battle.

The conceptual structure of lutte aérienne that accommodated defensive applications for airpower represented a significant departure from prevailing interwar theories that focused on the offensive character of aerial warfare. The French airmen attempted to include defensive applications for aviation in their expressions of fundamental doctrine, in order to conform to the basic outlines of French national military strategy. The gravity of the German threat, however, meant that no single service could assume the responsibility for national defense. Therefore, as one airman concluded, "modern airpower could, and should, intervene to the benefit of land and naval operations in a larger way than that of cooperation."[29]

The logical solution to resolving the question of integrating defensive and offensive missions into a unified lutte aérienne was to turn offensive aerial strategies to defensive purposes. "In the aerial domain, as in the terrestrial domain, only the offensive can yield decisive results. This is why only bombardment aviation is capable of attacking the enemy's vital areas; to carry the war in all circumstances over his territory remains incontestably one of the essential factors of the power of the air arm."[30] Therefore a single component of the air service could satisfy requirements of national defense by simultaneously waging an offensive and a defensive lutte aérienne that targeted the entire enemy society. While the airmen grasped the complexity contained in the structure of lutte aérienne, their army brethren acknowledged only defensive aspects aerial warfare.

Thus the fundamental precepts of French air doctrine contained a controversy: was it offensive missions designed to carry the war to the enemy that defined the character of the new service, or was it defensive missions that relegated the air force to a role as a protective shield for the army? The debates that continued throughout the 1930s, both within the service and with members of the other services, failed to resolve this central issue of fundamental doctrine. Consequently, the members of the Armée de l'air remained in a netherworld of ill-defined priorities about their service's role in a future war.

French fundamental airpower doctrine in the 1930s developed, to a large degree, because of technological as much as theoretical developments. For the French air force, technology presented a dilemma upon which efforts to produce doctrine threatened to founder. On one hand, limited experience with existing aircraft designs suggested that airpower had little to offer in independent aerial warfare. Additionally, the pressures of disarmament policies, economic stress, and national reluctance to appear provocative served as a brake on technological and doctrinal development.

On the other hand, as French leaders became convinced that another European war was inevitable, aviation technology promised to offer a relatively inexpensive solution to the national defense conundrum. In other words, the technology-doctrine nexus contributed to the uncertain and halting evolution of French reactive airpower thought in the 1930s.

Pierre Cot and General Victor Denain, his chief of staff and later his successor as air minister, attempted to solve the technology-doctrine dilemma by directing the air force to procure multiplace, multirole airplanes designed to perform multiple missions: "[T]he multi-place airplane gives us the possibility to satisfy these two needs [offense and defense], but not necessarily simultaneously. By a modern application of the old principle of economy of force, this machine allows us in effect to fulfill, according to the circumstances, the missions of bombardment or cooperation and to solve in a satisfactory manner the much-talked-about problem of reconnaissance aviation."[31] Cot arrived at this assessment by weighing several perceptions about the strategic environment, the capabilities of French aviation industries, the needs of the army and navy, and the needs of the air force.

The view of an enemy dedicated to waging quick, offensive, total war produced the fundamental doctrinal precepts of lutte aérienne. Cot found French aviation industries mired, however, in inefficient, outdated production methods. If the air force was to rearm quickly, either the industrial capability would have to change, or the service would have to compromise its desires for large orders of modern aircraft types. He wrote: "It is necessary first to consider not only the position taken by France in international negotiations on limiting aerial armaments, but also the budgetary repercussions which are involved with a radical modernization of our air units . . . The renovation should then be conducted with a new spirit of economy, substituting quality for quantity."[32]

Additionally, the army and the navy closely monitored the service to ensure that Cot and the airmen did not jeopardize air support capabilities for land and sea missions. Finally, the airmen developed competing views on the proper technological path to pursue. Aviators adopted positions that emphasized airpower as both an independent and supporting force, subordinate to the army in the national defense scheme. Cot used his authority as air minister to resolve these competing demands for airpower technology.[33]

In 1933 the air minister elected to procure the multirole bombardment combat reconnaissance (BCR) plane as a compromise solution that addressed the external competing demands upon the air force while preserving the service's ability to perform in independent lutte aérienne. Nevertheless, the BCR drove the Armée de l'air into a doctrinal and technological box canyon. The BCR established severe technological constraints on airframe and engine development philosophies for all French aircraft for most of the decade that preceded the Second World War. The multirole airplane was too slow and had insufficient payload capacity to perform effectively as a bomber, was too heavy and thus too slow to do well as a fighter, was too lightly armed to work as a close support platform, and was too vulnerable for a reconnaissance platform. In other words, the airplane designed to perform many roles performed none well.

From a doctrinal perspective, the BCR established technological limits on nearly every aspect of aviation guidelines. The multiplace, multipurpose BCR drove the French to rely on organizational and tactical doctrines predicated upon formations for protection, rather than on high-performance fighter escorts. The key protective advantage gained in formation flight applied primarily to the bombardment mission. According to French doctrine, "one crew or one formation can only hope to accomplish their mission if they assure themselves freedom of maneuver with minimum acceptable security."[34] Thus the formation discipline emphasized in the doctrine took precedence over other operational and tactical schemes. While this formula was adequate for long-range bombardment strikes, it left a hole in the operational and tactical philosophy for pursuit, close support, and reconnaissance missions.

The Armée de l'air and Organizational Doctrine

In many ways, the reactive air doctrine with which the Armée de l'air fought in 1940 was a product of the service's failure to create an effective organizational doctrine. This shortcoming obtained, in part, from a weak institutional bargaining position vis-à-vis the army and navy. This does not fully explain, however, why the airmen were not more forceful in their defense of independent roles for airpower. Some airmen, like Generals Paul Armengaud and Joseph Vuillemin, argued that defensive and cooperative missions and the accompanying subordinate role for airpower represented the most sensible ways to employ aviation. The chorus of competing voices from the army and the navy in the formative years of the French independent air service only made the task of creating organizational doctrine more difficult.

The first hurdle was the issue of who commanded French air units. When viewed in light of the lutte aérienne, this seemed simple—airmen should maintain operational control over the complex defensive-offensive aerial battle. Things were never that easy, however. The law that had created the independent air service erected an obstacle that complicated command relations between airmen and their land and sea counterparts. The language built into Article 1 of the law required the air force to participate in cooperative missions with the army and the navy.[35] This provided the justification for land and sea officers to keep their younger sister service in a subordinate role.

Air leaders assigned dedicated aviation units to the army commands, in an attempt to use an organizational device to circumvent the legal mandate. This idea had its roots in the early days of service independence, when Pierre Cot tried to make a clean break with the army. Cot reasoned that a properly organized, equipped, and trained air force would serve the needs of army commanders more effectively by waging lutte aérienne in independent air operations. Therefore, in order to appease the army's demands for air resources, Cot placed short-range, light aviation *(aviation légère de défense)* at the disposal of regional army commanders, as a component of the air reserves. These reserve units supported the army by performing local air superiority, reconnaissance, and artillery spotting missions. The air minister wrote: "By thus constituting, organizing, and training these squadrons we could eventually make parts of our Air Force available for other missions."[36]

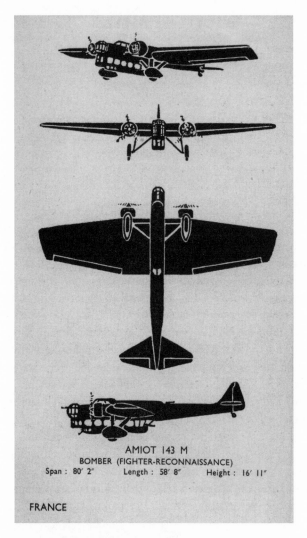

AMIOT 143 M
BOMBER (FIGHTER-RECONNAISSANCE)
Span : 80′ 2″   Length : 58′ 8″   Height : 16′ 11″

FRANCE

Figure 1. Amiot 143 M (bomber-fighter-reconnaissance),
  1934
Engine: Gnôme-Rhône K-14 (2), 880 hp
Payload: 1000 kg bombs (2,204.6 lbs)
  Front gunner, 2
  Rear gunner, 1
Weight: Loaded 7,128 kg (15,714.39 lbs)
Speed: 4,000 m (13,120 ft.) 315 km/hr (195.3 mph)
  6,000 m (19,680 ft.) 298 km/hr (184.8 mph)
Ceiling: 9,500 m (31,160 ft.)
Range: 600 km (372 miles)

Issued January, 1939 with A.L. No. 1

FARMAN 222
BOMBER
Span : 118′ 0″   Length : 69′ 0″   Height 17′ 0″
FRANCE

Figure 2. Farman 222 (bomber), 1938
Engine: Gnôme-Rhône K-14 Krsd (4), 700 hp
Weight: 15,200 kg (33,509 lbs)
Speed: 4,000 m (13,120 ft.) 325 km/hr (201.5 mph)
Ceiling: 7,800 m (25,584 ft.)
Range: 2,000 km (1,240 miles)

POTEZ 540

BOMBER (FIGHTER-RECONNAISSANCE)

Span : 72′ 6″ Length : 53′ 2″ Height : 12′ 9″

FRANCE

Figure 3. Potez 540 (bomber-fighter-reconnaissance), 1935
Engine: Hispano-Suiza 12xbr (1), 550 hp
Payload: 1,000 kg bombs (2,204.6 lbs)
    Gunner, nose 1
    Gunner, rear, 1
Weight: 5,560 kg (12,257.58 lbs)
Speed: 4,000 m (13,120 ft.) 320 km/hr (198.4 mph)
Range: 1,250 km (775 miles)

POTEZ 630
Multi-seater Fighter Leader and Fighter
Span 52'-5¾"   Length 36'-7½"   Height 9'-10"
(56703)   B

Figure 4. Potez 630 (bomber-fighter-reconnaissance), 1938
Engine: Hispano-Suiza 14Hb (2), 670 hp
Payload: 20 mm canon, 2
  Machine gun, nose, 1
  Machine gun, rear, 1
Weight: 4,174 kg (9,202 lbs), bomber
  3,734 kg (8231.98 lbs), fighter
  3,695 kg (8146 lbs), reconnaissance
Speed: 450 km/hr (279 mph), bomber
  320 km/hr (198.4 mph), fighter
  430 km/hr (266.6 mph), reconnaissance
Ceiling: 9,000 m (29,520 ft.), bomber
  10,000 m (32,800 ft.), fighter
  10,000 m (32,800 ft.), reconnaissance
Range: 1,300 km (806 miles), bomber
  1,000 km (620 miles), fighter
  1,000 km (620 miles), reconnaissance

From Cot's perspective, this solution eliminated missions that threatened to whittle away at service autonomy. The formula contained the added benefit of transferring the material legacy of the *politique des prototypes,* a fleet of obsolete airplanes, out of the front line inventory into the reserve units destined to accomplish cooperation missions.[37]

The generals and admirals recognized a swindle when they saw one. Army leaders, in particular, used the precedent of having detached air units placed under the authority of land commanders to ensure that land cooperation units received priority in air doctrine and plans. By the time the air ministry published the *Règlement de manoeuvre de l'aviation* in 1937, the leaders of the air service recognized that the army had hoisted them on their own petard. The reserves assigned to cooperate with army regional commands became Regional Air Groups of the Army, and the air commanders for those groups found themselves subordinate to army commanders (Grandes Unités terrestres).[38] Army commanders tasked the reserve aviators under their authority for all missions.

Senior aviators performed roles analogous to those of airmen in World War I. Their tasks included executing missions passed down from army headquarters, advising army generals on the best use of airpower, training air service personnel, and maintaining the equipment assigned to the aviation units. The *Règlement* specified that the aviation commander "advises the commanding general of the Army of the difficulties which could arise from a technical point of view; he proposes, or takes on his own initiative, all useful measures to repair them."[39]

 Rather than eliminating an unwanted mission as Cot intended, the establishment of the Regional Air Groups of the Army entrenched the cooperation mission deeper into organizational air doctrine, thus guaranteeing that reacting to tactical situations in the proximity of the army corps remained a high priority for the Armée de l'air. But the greatest, and most detrimental, result that stemmed from Cot's attempt to foist an unwanted mission upon the army was to reinforce a subordinate role for airmen in the eyes of army leaders.

The cooperation mission for the aviation légère de défense units gradually migrated from the reserves to the front lines. In the process, the air units that might have performed long-range reconnaissance or bombardment missions found themselves placed under the authority of army commanders. The airmen reconciled themselves to this arrangement by remaining focused on the lutte aérienne, particularly on the defensive aspects of their fundamental doctrine. In peacetime, or in the early days of a conflict, the air force commander in chief coordinated aerial actions with his army counterpart. In principle, the army commanders tasked the aviation units at their disposal as they saw fit, while the air force fought "against the aerial expeditions of the enemy to halt their strikes as close to the lines as possible and to attack them along their routes with maximum effort."[40]

In reality, at the instigation of hostilities the air force reverted to an on-call arrangement that subordinated the formerly independent service to regional land commanders. As the air staff described this arrangement, "the elements thus sent as reinforcements will pass to the orders of the Commander of the air forces of the affected land echelon."[41] The air staff failed to anticipate, however, the effects on air service capabilities that resulted from the army view that the "Commander of the air forces" remained a mere technical adviser to the army commander, rather than an equal partner in the process of formulating operational plans.

This uncertain and unwelcome state of affairs affected heavy aviation, or bombardment forces, as well as pursuit units. If an enemy attack threatened to overwhelm army units in a particular region, the air force agreed to divert all available heavy aviation assets to stabilize the situation. This requirement resulted in an ill-defined set of priorities for the bombardment units. Generally, the first priority for the bombers remained the destruction of the enemy air force, but because of the necessity to protect the army, the heavy bombardment aviation units had to remain ready to abandon their missions "to support terrestrial operations by attacking troops and communications of the enemy with all or part of their forces."[42]

To heighten the uncertainty in this situation, the air units would find a confusing command arrangement as their primary mission changed. "This action will occur either under the direct orders of the Air Force Commander-in-Chief, or by temporarily placing a certain number of units at the immediate disposal of the land commander."[43] No other organization within the French military establishment operated with such a confusing organizational doctrine.

The connection between the Armée de l'air and the navy was even more difficult than the convoluted relationship that existed between the air and land services. To the airmen's credit, they made a genuine attempt to comply with the intent of the 1933 law that directed their service to develop a cooperative partnership with the sea service. The 1937 *Règlement de manoeuvre de l'aviation* specified, "if maritime cooperation formations of the Air Force should be trained in destruction missions of interest to maritime operations, it is important that all formations or all aircrews be allowed to participate in the search, collection, and diffusion of maritime intelligence."[44] This organizational task occupied more coordination and compromise than either the navy or the air force could achieve.

The air force resisted establishing dedicated naval cooperation forces, such as the aviation légère de défense that operated in army support missions. The airmen finally stated emphatically: "There are no aviation formations normally granted to the Grandes Unités navales in the Air Force."[45] For its part, the navy jealously guarded its authority over missions that pertained to coastal defense and power projection from the sea. The sea service planned to place air units under the direct command of maritime prefects.

Air force leaders chafed under the navy's refusal to grant even limited authority for air missions that occurred near maritime operating zones. Missions could arise, in the opinion of the navy ministry, that required air units to "coordinate with naval operations—such as the attack of enemy bases or coastal areas."[46] However, because such missions remained within the general purview of naval operations, the air units "should be placed under the orders of the naval commander."[47]

With cold logic, the navy ministry concluded that the proper role for senior aviators in maritime power projection was to "assure command of the formations, to act as technical adviser to the Maritime Forces commander, and to assure the liaison with the Commander-in-Chief of the Air Force. In other circumstances, the presence of an air commander placed next to a maritime commander does not seem necessary."[48] The navy formula relegated senior aviators to roles as mere technical advisers and messengers, with no influence on either campaign strategy or operational execution. This prescription mirrored the treatment airmen received at the hands of the army.

When the issue of coastal defense arose, the navy's resistance to alter its existing command structures stiffened. The navy organized and controlled the aerial defense of sensitive ports and coastal areas, through an arrangement whereby the army provided antiaircraft artillery to the navy, but the navy exercised command over the defensive units. The navy ministry perceived the addition of pursuit aircraft to the coastal defense mission in much the same way that it did the antiaircraft artillery provided by the army. The navy ministry concluded: "It will be the same for pursuit assigned to the authorities charged with defending sensitive points; the higher authority (in practice, the maritime prefect) can, at any time, act to coordinate or to concentrate the action of the air forces participating in the pursuit."[49] In other words, the navy could not conceive any rationale for an enhanced role for senior Armée de l'air commanders, either in offensive or in defensive maritime operations.

The effect of the sea service's refusal to alter existing command and control arrangements, coupled with the army's persistent clamoring for more air resources to shield and support its mobilization and defensive efforts, helped to ensure a flawed and reactive organizational doctrine for the air force. With their efforts mired in disagreements over the division of command authority, the airmen turned to developing organizational issues within their own service. Here, unsurprisingly, they met with little more success than they had in other doctrine-development efforts. The air service attempts to articulate how the Armée de l'air could offer a unique contribution to the nation's strategic problems seemed destined to fail, because the airmen did not resolve conflicts regarding an independent lutte aérienne and the army and navy demands for air service resources.

The vehicle that the air force used to codify its doctrine was the four-part *Règlement de manoeuvre de l'aviation,* published, as we have seen, in 1937. The air staff released the first three parts in a single volume and issued part 4 separately. The titles—"maneuver regulation"—reveal much about the difficulty the Armée de l'air encountered in producing fundamental and organizational doctrines. The *Règlement de manoeuvre* reflected the interservice compromises that characterized the debates regarding roles and missions that the air service would perform. The *Règlement* also reflected compromises within the air service itself, regarding the nature of lutte aérienne and the character of modern warfare. The result of the internal and external compromises that the air service made to create an acceptable doctrine was a doctrinal emphasis on tactical concerns rather than on strategic or operational possibilities for airpower employment.

The way that the air staff chose to organize the four parts of the service's basic doctrine reflected an emphasis on tactical matters. The architects of the new doctrine intended part 4 to answer "all questions relating to the use of aviation . . . in a single regulation."[50] The first three parts of the *Règlement,* by contrast, described "the attributes of air force command regarding aviation instruction, the means of command and control, and aviation instruction by aircraft type," respectively.[51] In other words, the organizational scheme of the doctrine manuals emphasized how to employ airpower before the airmen had been guided to think about why to employ it.

This bottom-up approach reduced the potential for encountering within the air service troubling conflicts regarding the independent lutte aérienne. At the same time, the in-depth treatment of command relationships found in the first two parts provided a detailed outline of the authority that remained to air commanders when they performed cooperation missions with other services. Furthermore, by establishing policy regarding instruction and command and control before elaborating on situations that emphasized using airpower's attributes, the service could assure that the institutions and infrastructure required to sustain the air force's combat power had a philosophical outline from which to guide further service development. The basic directions that emerged from the *Règlement* were to "prepare for war," to instill "the will to overcome," and "to teach the means of acquiring victory."[52]

The authors of the *Règlement de manoeuvre* divided lutte aérienne into two main categories that corresponded to the organizational roles the air service performed. In the first, bombardment and pursuit units allowed aviation to act as an arm of destruction for both offensive and defensive purposes. Reconnaissance and intelligence constituted the second basic organizational category in which aviation offered unique capabilities. Additionally, the doctrine anticipated auxiliary missions that aviation could perform more rapidly and effectively than other services. These fell into the general classifications of transport and camouflage (smokescreens, and so on).[53] The organizational divisions allowed for a degree of consistency between the fundamental roles envisioned for lutte aérienne and the tactical execution of missions defined throughout the *Règlement*.

The formation was the basic organizational unit within the scope of nominally independent air operations. This applied to pursuit, bombardment, and reconnaissance missions, regardless of the type aircraft employed. The formation remained a fixture of French air force organizational doctrine, because of the Armée de l'air's reliance on the multirole airplane for most of the 1930s. Formations of multirole aircraft allowed the Armée de l'air to adapt rapidly to the tactical requirements of the moment. "The ability to operate in the third dimension confers upon airpower the possibility to choose the area of the most favorable winds, the economical means to acquire speed. It requires the adversary to stage his defenses, then to divide them. Finally, the different altitudes used for the routes presents several particular advantages."[54] The formation allowed the Armée de l'air to concentrate its efforts in both offensive and defensive roles. It also capitalized on airpower's inherent flexibility.

Air force leaders argued that the key to success in modern lutte aérienne lay in achieving surprise using massed aerial formations.[55] Furthermore, French organizational doctrine emphasized the desirability of achieving a combination of results in destruction missions. The effects described in the *Règlement* contained a range of mission tasks:

Aerial maneuver should seek to obtain a rendering of the maximum available effects by combining attacks in order:
- to produce, as much as possible, the effect of surprise;
- to disrupt the alert and lookout posts;
- to divide and disrupt the enemy forces;
- to act by proportional concentrations against important targets;
- to obtain the best pattern of weapons on the targets;
- to present in all aspects the optimum defense and to halt the free play of the enemy defenses.[56]

Therefore the organizational doctrine published by the French air force focused on producing effects at the tactical and operational levels of war.

The Armée de l'air's organizational doctrine did not purport to replace the contributions of the army and the navy; rather, it aimed to describe how airpower could add to the efforts of the other services as they defended the nation. Yet without a clearly articulated description of how their operations supported air strategy, the French airmen failed to convince the other services that airpower could make an independent contribution to the war effort. Two doctrinal flaws led to a focus on the details of tactical employment: the failure to build upon the existing body of theory to create a coherent and comprehensive fundamental air doctrine, and the failure to resolve organizational conflicts with the army, the navy, and within the air service.

The Armée de l'air and Tactical Doctrine

Tactical principles in the Armée de l'air derived from the broad outlines established in fundamental and organizational doctrines. Because both of these contained unresolved conflicts regarding the standards for employing airpower, tactical doctrine tended to remain flawed as well. It generated less controversy, however, because it was more specific and more directive in nature than were the other two doctrinal forms. Moreover, because the Armée de l'air's tactical guidelines did not infringe upon traditional land and sea missions, army and navy leaders expressed less concern regarding the form and substance of the air force's opinions about how to conduct tactical engagements.

The commander's role became the focus of tactical doctrine, just as lutte aérienne became the focus of fundamental doctrine and the formation became the focus of organizational doctrine. Tactical commanders played the pivotal part in accomplishing aerial missions by exercising strict control over all tactical aspects. "For all combat missions, the chief's place is at the head of the unit he commands."[57] This emphasis on personal leadership meant that the Armée de l'air risked losing its best commanders in aerial combat.[58]

To prepare formation commanders to cope with the risk that leading operations entailed, and to create a system that recognized and rewarded aviators with leadership potential, the air service devised a graduated system of aircrew qualification standards. Flying personnel received basic qualification training in the various flight schools. Tactical unit commanders assigned the newly qualified flyers to basic qualification crews *(non confirmé)* for entry-level tactical training. Unit commanders declared individuals fully mission-ready *(bien confirmé)* after observing proficiency in tactical specialties. Finally, a crew formed of mission-ready specialists received the bien confirmé designation, while certain crews earned the special classification of elite crew *(équipage d'élite)*.[59]

The French air force divided tactical units into flight sections of two or three airplanes. In order to mass defensive and offensive firepower, sections formed together into squadrons *(escadrilles)*. Each escadrille contained two or three sections. Finally, two or three escadrilles could join to form a group. Just as each section commander controlled tactical engagements from the lead airplane in his section, group commanders flew in the lead position of each group formation.

The *Règlement* prescribed that in the lead position, the commander was in "the best place to make decisions which to order, according to the situation: changes in the course of the formation's flight, speed, altitude, target, modify the separation between squadrons, and even on occasion abort the mission."[60] This conception of how to orchestrate command for aerial missions appeared similar in scope and purpose to missions conducted by cavalry units in the army.[61]

The goal in formation flight was to overwhelm enemy defenses, in the case where French airpower assumed an offensive role, or to mass superior firepower to thwart an enemy aerial attack in the case of defensive operations. The commander's role was critical to ensuring that the formations preserved tactical unity and self-defensive capabilities. "It could be necessary to arrange the specially armed and very maneuverable elements, to keep the assailants out of range; to suffer shock without weakening; and, [in order] to permit a heavily loaded formation to preserve its cohesion, to pursue its route and, if the battle draws near, to present to the assailants a powerful barrier of massive and combined firepower."[62]

In times of peace, the air service expected group commanders to supervise the training, maintenance, and administration of their assigned personnel and equipment.[63] At the tactical level, the French remained certain that qualified commanders could lead their crews to overcome the enemy, whether in the offensive, defensive, or supporting roles.

French tactical doctrine assigned destruction missions to bombardment and pursuit aviation. Because these two tasks could assume both offensive and defensive qualities, they meshed with the concepts of lutte aérienne and the organizational structures that required the Armée de l'air to support land and naval campaigns. Air service groups could include crews trained and equipped to perform both missions, or the same crews could receive individual taskings for either mission.

Tactical manuals divided bombardment operations into day and night bombardment categories. This conformed to World War I practices. The specialized training and equipment required to fly and to navigate safely at night made the distinction necessary. Night bombardment, although tactically advantageous because of the security and the inherent potential to achieve surprise, never assumed a large role in the Armée de l'air. The French air service failed to provide enough trained aircrews to create a significant force of night bombing groups. In any event, the only distinction made between day and night targets in tactical doctrines centered on the visibility of the target.[64]

French tactical doctrine included unusual recommendations for coping with enemy defenses, which would concentrate near the types of targets—railway lines, electrical power facilities, roads, airfields, ships, port facilities, and enemy industrial areas—proposed by the French tacticians.[65] Bomber tactical prescriptions instructed crews to vary their attacks according to the disposition of enemy defenses in the immediate target area. The authors of the manuals asserted that low altitude strikes tended to achieve better accuracy than those attempted at higher levels. Crews could choose to envelop the target using a concentric circling maneuver, to attack along the longitudinal axis of a target, or to attack across the axis of a target.

Moreover, tactical doctrine specified that the mission commander could direct the airplanes in his formation to adopt different strike tactics against the same target—at the same time—to confuse enemy defenders.[66] Tactical doctrine appeared based upon an article of faith that a successful bombardment mission occurred when the bombers reached the target and dropped their weapons in the general area; discussions of accuracy and targeting science did not figure in tactical doctrine publications.

The Armée de l'air planners devoted much time and energy to identifying and prioritizing enemy targets for bomber lists. In the early 1930s, bombardment targets reflected French fears that German aerial attacks would focus on civilian population centers. French plans included attacks against *objectifs militaires et de représailles* to erode German popular support for aggressive government policies while simultaneously bolstering confidence among French civilians. Air force planners anticipated that "repetitive incursions of bombers, even if not accompanied by effective destruction, will rapidly obtain results" among the German work force.[67]

Railway lines presented particular problems. Small errors in bomb placement could result in little damage to the tracks and roadbeds. If planners selected the wrong ordnance, repair crews could put the line back in service quickly. Air service leaders charged the Centre d'expériences aériennes militaires at Reims to recommend the most effective tactics for railway attack missions. Flight-test personnel concentrated on low altitude *(vol rasant)* and shallow dive bombing *(attaques en léger piqué)* experiments, using a variety of aircraft speeds. A second set of experimental variables involved attacks across the axis and in parallel with the axis of the rail line.

The experiments revealed that the air service required special training procedures and tactics to achieve optimum results against rail networks. The bombardiers could not depend on conventional bomb sighting equipment, the pilots could not fly standard bomb run profiles, the munitions personnel could not load standard fuses. Many of the bombs dropped in the experiments missed the tracks, because they ricocheted after striking the ground. Others exploded prematurely or failed to detonate at all.[68] Despite these difficulties, the German railway network remained an important tactical bombardment objective.

Electrical-power generation and transmission facilities supported critical military and industrial targets. French bombardment planners began collecting information on the German electrical industry as early as 1926.[69] According to the air staff, it was possible "to determine for each large industrial region in the Reich . . . a certain number of public or private thermal plants, transformers, and hydro generators which, if attacked simultaneously, will permit the *isolation* and disorganization of the total system of production in these regions."[70] Once again, French planners prepared detailed target dossiers that included photographs and navigation charts for the most important of these.

French tactical doctrine also included a role for bombardment aviation in the air-superiority battle. The self-defending bomber formation could contribute to this mission in two ways. First, the aircraft could wage a campaign of attrition against German pursuit and bomber forces as they encountered the enemy en route to targets in German territory. This legacy of the BCR era remained a permanent fixture of French tactical doctrine. Destroying the enemy air force on the ground represented the second method French airmen planned to use to gain air superiority.

Despite the detail and the level of analysis contained in the bombardment dossiers developed by the air staff before the war, the Armée de l'air never displayed more than a passing tactical interest in such targets. The most important concern, doctrinally, turned gradually from airpower's potential to affect enemy morale and material abilities toward measures designed to support friendly army units along the frontier. The French bombardment arm stopped short of forging a connection between the theory of lutte aérienne and the vulnerabilities contained within the various target sets represented in the bombardment dossiers. Army demands for air support prevented serious consideration of systematically attacking any target that did not relate directly to the outcome of the terrestrial battle. This condition also applied to pursuit aviation units.

The tactical doctrine for pursuit remained dependent upon the skills and intuitions of the fighter pilots who manned this arm. The pilots practiced maneuvers and patrol procedures that differed little from the basic flight methods used in the Great War. Destroying enemy air forces and maintaining air superiority defined the outlines of pursuit tactical doctrine. The only variation in mission content concerned who delegated mission taskings. Pursuit units could operate under the orders of air force, army, or Défense aérienne du territoire (DAT) commanders. The DAT organization controlled air defense and alerting networks during peacetime. As the armed forces mobilized, DAT forces merged their responsibilities and capabilities with those of the army and air force. Regardless of which organization required pursuit support, tactical mission structures conformed to similar formulas.

Three types of missions applied when these units supported land operations: security *(couverture)*, protection, and free pursuit.[71] Security operations tied pursuit patrols directly to land maneuver units. Mission tasks centered on defeating enemy pursuit and bomber attacks against friendly troop concentrations. Pursuit also operated in the couverture role to prevent enemy reconnaissance aircraft from observing French troop movements. Patrol discipline formed a critical doctrinal principle for the couverture mission, because pursuit received mission assignments from specific army units. Before attempting to engage an enemy patrol, leaders observed their formations to determine if they threatened the assigned unit. If the French patrol commander could bring other defensive units to bear (artillery or free pursuit units) by notifying command echelons, he would avoid aerial combat. But if the commander perceived that the enemy formation represented a threat to the unit he protected, he committed his patrol to intercept the enemy airplanes.[72]

Protection missions differed from couverture in that they tied assigned pursuit patrols to protect friendly airplanes and observation balloons, rather than army formations. Units assigned to this mission operated with more freedom than did those protecting land combatants. Pursuit units in a protective role were free to attack any enemy aircraft that entered their assigned zones. The critical rule stated that pursuit patrols should not become so distracted, when chasing an enemy patrol that crossed their zone, that they allowed an undetected enemy to attack an aircraft or balloon under their protection. To prevent this occurrence, pursuit patrols usually worked together, in pairs or in groups.[73]

Free pursuit missions allowed the patrol to search for the enemy within the theater, to the limits of its operational range. This option allowed maximum tactical flexibility and initiative while, theoretically, instilling the greatest fear and uncertainty in enemy air forces. Patrols involved in free pursuit could also augment bombardment formations that targeted enemy airfields, by surprising enemy pursuit patrols as they attempted to intercept the French bombers.[74]

DAT pursuit missions resembled the tactical categories defined in the land support role. Pursuit units could provide direct security, oriented security, contact/concentration, and night pursuit under DAT control. Direct security ensured the protection for a specific target area or feature. This resembled the couverture role performed by pursuit units assigned to an army zone of operations. Oriented security differed by grouping several important targets into a patrol zone. Contact/concentration involved observing enemy formations and reporting their movements to the DAT lookout network. Finally, night pursuit operations combined the DAT searchlight and lookout network with pursuit patrols to detect and intercept enemy formations.[75]

Pursuit aviation remained the most tactically independent of all French aviation categories. Army commanders agreed that the primary mission centered on gaining air superiority. The same did not apply to the observation units that provided aerial reconnaissance to army and Armée de l'air headquarters, as the land campaign unfolded.

If pursuit aviation represented the most independent tactical expression of airpower in the Armée de l'air of the 1930s, reconnaissance was the component that remained most closely tied to army needs. The air service used the term *aviation de renseignement* to encompass three categories of missions: reconnaissance, observation, and liaison. Reconnaissance and observation involved two closely related information-gathering missions, the former the search for information regarding enemy movements and activities; the latter maintaining contact with enemy forces and reporting changes in their disposition. The final category of reconnaissance aviation, liaison missions, required aviators to observe and adjust artillery fire efforts along the front.[76]

Aerial reconnaissance and surveillance of the battlefield had emerged in the early battles of World War I and remained a fixture of airpower employment throughout that conflict. Army commanders refused to allow this capability to erode in the Armée de l'air of the interwar years, and the army successfully lobbied to force the air service to make aerial reconnaissance an important secondary tactical mission for pursuit and bombardment formations. The *Règlement de manoeuvre* specified that all aircrews "will search in an assigned zone for information necessary for air operations and for combined operations with the Army and the Navy."[77] Although the authors of the *Règlement* made a token attempt to relate reconnaissance missions to the needs of the Armée de l'air, virtually the entire discussion about them—ninety-five pages—centered on how to execute such missions while supporting land or sea operations.

The essential features of successful reconnaissance missions involved processing and transmitting to the appropriate command echelon data obtained through aerial surveillance. The data came in several forms, the least technically complicated of which was a verbal or written report submitted by the aircrew upon completing a mission. Debriefing personnel conducted a postflight interview using standard questionnaires; after completing this, the tactical unit forwarded written reports to higher command echelons. The three-part written report included mission information about the airplane, the crew, and flight conditions, a chronological account of the information obtained in the course of the flight, and a detailed tactical description of enemy units observed.[78] Tactical units usually collected all reports for a single day before forwarding them to the next level in the chain of command.

Photographic data afforded confirmation of suspected enemy activity. Aviators took great risks to gather high-quality aerial photos of enemy movements. Like the verbal or written reports, however, photographic data often arrived at the higher echelons after significant delays, because of the developing processes at the tactical units. Photographs also introduced a level of uncertainty and complexity to the information-processing task. Trained interpreters had to identify positively the location and the types of information on the images. Photos could mislead even trained interpreters, if the aircrew failed to properly relate the route of flight used to obtain them. Enemy countermeasures, camouflage and deception, could complicate the task, resulting in erroneous conclusions.

Data could also arrive at ground units through radio or message transmission, though this method did not become universally available to the French air service during the 1930s. Some reconnaissance units resorted to dropping messages from their airplanes as they flew over their assigned headquarters during the Battle of France, because their aircraft did not have radios or their radios were incompatible with army communication equipment.[79]

The doctrine-development process in the Armée de l'air followed a complex path, filled with difficult issues that brought air service leaders into conflict with their counterparts in the army and the navy. The airmen articulated a fundamental doctrine that embraced the defensive vision that prevailed in the army. The lutte aérienne structure also accommodated offensive employment possibilities for aviation, promising to allow strategists to seize the initiative in a campaign in which the French maintained a strategic defensive posture. The offensive component of lutte aérienne threatened to ignore army and navy requirements for aviation assets; therefore land and sea service leaders waged a successful campaign to place air commanders in subordinate roles whenever the services engaged in joint operations. The resulting flawed organizational doctrine destroyed the authority of air commanders and left them to act as technical advisers rather than equal participants in developing operational strategy.

The airmen fared no better when they tried to develop tactical doctrines. The flawed fundamental and organizational formulas caused Armée de l'air leaders to couch all air service tactical efforts in terms of cooperative missions. Thus the pressures to conform to the needs of the sister services left the air force incapable of planning or executing independent missions. The Armée de l'air reacted at the strategic, operational, and tactical levels of war because doctrine demanded it. The same guidelines formed the conceptual foundation for the training system that prepared airmen for war.

4   A Training System for a Reactive Doctrine

We consider an Air Force. It is not only the warplanes, armed and crewed, prepared for combat, but a service fleet destined for the formation of pilots, for their training, [it is] the technical services for the transport of troops, for liaisons of all sorts of indispensable tasks for the life of this force.[1]

The training system that the leaders of the Armée de l'air established during the 1930s reinforced the reactive character of the service's doctrines. Airmen created institutions and programs designed to prepare the service to fight the type of war anticipated in the fundamental, organizational, and tactical doctrines. The basic philosophy represented the consensus among air service members regarding how best to use airpower to serve France's strategic, operational, and tactical needs. Air force leaders developed a training system designed to forge an aerial weapon capable of fulfilling the promise of their doctrines.

After serving as air minister in the Popular Front government, Pierre Cot stressed the importance of the training system. He wrote: "In every case, the superiority of our armaments, of our crews, of our trained reserves, and our staffs has compensated, very quickly, for German superiority."[2] Thus in Cot's eyes, and in the eyes of his colleagues in the air ministry and the air staff, the training system would serve as the great equalizer in the race to forge a modern aerial weapon. Unfortunately, the air service's tendency to react to events found its way from the doctrine into the training system and made the instruction programs one of the greatest obstacles to achieving operational and tactical effectiveness.

The core of the Armée de l'air's training programs lay in a variety of procedural, organizational, and physical traits that imparted structure to the system. At the procedural level, frameworks evolved to transform doctrine from abstract concepts into concrete instructions. These frameworks, in turn, guided activities designed to prepare the air force for war. Procedural characteristics ranged across a spectrum of personnel, recruiting, resource management, and operational issues. Organizational characteristics defined ways that the Armée de l'air managed procedural matters. Finally, the institution assumed form and substance by matching the established organizations and procedures against resources, personnel, and material to accomplish assigned tasks and missions.

These three aspects of the air service's training system— conceptual, organizational, and physical—influenced and ultimately reinforced the Armée de l'air's reactive nature during the interwar years. This prevailed not solely because of internal decisions—to suggest that any institution in interwar France was complete master of its fate would be ludicrous—but because of the ways in which air force leaders chose to function within the constraints of their political, social, and cultural context.[3]

The Armée de l'air's technical school system became one of the most important vehicles used to transmit and reinforce institutional norms, values, and doctrines to the men who manned the service's units. A well-developed school system was essential to building the air service in the years after it gained independence from the army and navy, because of the high degree of technical knowledge required to operate aerial combat systems safely and effectively.[4] The leaders of the Armée de l'air relied upon a rational, managerial approach to impart structure and credible combat capability to the various components of the published air doctrines. But the competition for airpower resources that caused the fundamental, organizational, and tactical doctrines to assume reactive characteristics filtered into the training system's institutional structures. The result was a training system, like the doctrines it served, that shifted with the winds of interservice rivalry, political instability, and strategic and operational uncertainty.

Several elements reinforced the tendency toward the reactive posture in the training programs operated by the French air service. The first was the structure of the system. The educational matrix that evolved in the 1930s did not derive from a master vision of modern war, but from a constant balancing of national defense and economic concerns. Although the authors of the fundamental doctrine described the complexity of modern aerial warfare in terms of a single *lutte aérienne,* more often than not the training system emphasized preparations for the defensive and cooperative components of that battle, thus leading to neglect of independent operational concepts that formed an essential element of fundamental doctrine.

The second element that exacerbated the reactive nature of the training system related to the air service's need to balance its intellectual and technical requirements against the available personnel. The air force needed dedicated, intelligent recruits to fill the cockpits and maintenance hangars of its tactical units. Entry into the service required satisfactory scores on a wide-ranging battery of tests. Applicants for officer and noncommissioned officer positions received examinations in French composition, language and literature, history, geography, arithmetic, algebra, trigonometry, geometry, physics, chemistry, and foreign languages.[5] For most of the decade, air service leaders struggled to manage personnel requirements and, simultaneously, to maintain a high level of quality in the training programs. This effort pushed them toward a reactive posture.[6] Finally, as French grand strategy drifted from one crisis to another, the air force training system followed, struggling to produce combat crews and trained support personnel to fulfill the strategic and operational missions the government demanded.[7]

The picture that emerges from an analysis of the documentary evidence of the training system is one of chaos and uncertainty. The mounting pressure of international political tension after 1936, coupled with the shockwaves of domestic political turmoil in 1934, 1936, and 1938, sowed chaos in the training system. The air force altered the system as national leaders altered their perceptions and strategies of how to cope with the German threat. Debates over the proper role for aviation in the context of national defense sowed uncertainty in the institutional structures that the service relied upon to indoctrinate new members.

The surprising outcome of the story is not that the Armée de l'air performed poorly in combat, but that it performed as well as it did. The combat record of the French air service against the Luftwaffe in 1940 remains a testament to the courage and tenacity of French airmen, rather than a product of the quality and effectiveness of their training and educational institutions.

The Training System

Instruction began as an integral element of the published service doctrines. The various *Règlements de manoeuvre de l'aviation* editions published in the 1930s represented the most accessible basic statement that described how the air service intended to prepare its new members to perform their missions. Doctrine established a central role for the air ministry and staff in designing, administering, and evaluating the various schools that came to form the system. According to organizational doctrine, the role of the air ministry was to assure "the coordination of programs concerning common instruction for Air Force personnel . . . camps for instruction and fields for application and fire instruction; reserve credits; and the essential fuels required for the formations [of the service] to function."[8] Thus the air ministry became the central clearinghouse for all instructional system matters. Air staff personnel at the ministry established training policy, regulated funding, managed personnel assignments, and evaluated the performance of the various training schools in the system.

With the complexity of the training systems required by the Armée de l'air came a correspondingly complex personnel management system that tracked the progress of recruits, reserves, and units. The inspector general of the air force controlled "the execution of the orders and directives of the Minister regarding every activity dedicated to preparing the Armée de l'Air for war."[9] The inspector general's authority was not absolute, however. He shared responsibility for administering the various combat training programs with his counterpart in territorial air defense (Défense aérienne du territoire, or DAT).

This administrative burden sharing was necessary because of the doctrinal and physical separation of the *aviation légère de défense* that formed the DAT units from the mainstream air commands. Together, the two inspectors general exercised authority over "all propositions concerning Air Force instruction, in the schools as well as in the tactical units."[10] Colonial aviation required a further division of administrative responsibility for training and education programs, owing to the remoteness of the colonies and the differences in equipment and operational missions. The division of missions, coupled with the air force's desire to retain unity of command over its personnel and equipment, created confusion throughout the 1930s. This prompted repeated meetings between the air force inspector general and his DAT counterpart.[11]

Outside the centralized air staff bureaucracy, subordinate commanders exercised responsibility for training and instruction—in principle. Confusion over this charge stemmed in part from changing emphases in the Armée de l'air's tactical roles at various points during the decade. These changes, in turn, derived from the changes in the political fortunes of the various air ministers between 1933 and 1940. Pierre Cot reorganized the command structure and the supporting staff roles for the air service to emphasize the potential that airpower could bring to bear on Germany through independent air operations. He created five regional air commands that corresponded roughly to the army's military regions.

In addition to their wartime roles, the combatant commanders exercised education and training responsibility over the forces assigned to their regions, over the logistics specialties tasked to support the front line units, and over the reserve units that trained and reported to their regions for mobilization. This all-encompassing accountability meant that the regional air commanders saw to the details of training camps, gunnery ranges, wargame and exercise planning, and coordination with the army and navy commanders who looked to the air service for cooperation and support.

At the most elementary level, airmen acquired formative instruction designed "to make each student gain the necessary knowledge of his function on the crew."[12] Once a prospective aircrew member successfully completed the formative phase, he moved on to applied instruction. This form of continuation training emphasized "combat operations; principles, functions, and procedures for employing new materials; increased proficiency; and instructor training."[13] Formative training occurred at various bases scattered throughout metropolitan France, while applied instruction usually remained the responsibility of the tactical units. Regardless of the type or location of the education, however, the air staff established the content and the duration of the syllabi.

The centralized management of the training system that began with the ministerial-level policy guidance broke down as the components of the system, the various schools and training bases, evolved in the 1930s. Ultimately, the leaders of the air service found themselves in the unenviable position of managing many small technical schools scattered throughout the French countryside. Those that conducted flight training further distributed air resources, by establishing the headquarters and administrative support sections at the designated training base and then creating small fields in outlying areas, where detachments of instructors and students accomplished the flying portion of the curriculum.

One air staff chart depicted the organization of the flight school system in three of the five air regions.[14] The top of the chart shows thirty *écoles élémentaires,* or basic flight schools. Students then moved on to one of eight *écoles auxiliares* for more advanced flight procedures training. From there they went to one of two *écoles principales;* this represented the final stage of flight training before students received assignments to one of three main combat specialties. The commander of the école principale was responsible for "technical and aerial military instruction directives" in all three levels of the basic flying training system.[15]

After graduating from the écoles principales, students gained specialized training in pursuit, bombardment, or reconnaissance flying procedures at one of several Centres d'instruction. There were two pursuit centers, four bombardment, and three reconnaissance centers distributed among the various air regions. Thus, as students traveled through the stages of flight training in the 1930s, they changed bases at least four times before reaching their first tactical unit as qualified aircrew members.

But aircrew training was not the only type conducted by the Armée de l'air in the years before World War II. The air service needed recruits who could complete a rigorous program of instruction to become aircraft mechanics, civil engineers, radio operators, photographic technicians and interpreters, and intelligence specialists. Recruiting efforts to attract young men to the air service emphasized the practical benefits derived from the sophisticated technical skills gained in the Armée de l'air's training system. A recruiting poster that detailed the procedures for obtaining certification as an aircraft electrician *(mécanicien d'aéronautique, spécialité: aviation—mécanicien-électricien)* addressed "young men who wish to serve the full duration of their legal service" in the Armée de l'air.[16] The poster touted the practical advantages of skills gained in the air service: "Because of the strong scientific culture and the practical professional experience acquired, those young men who hold the Aeronautical Electrician's diploma possess, upon completion of their service, a true profession that embraces mechanics, electrics, and radiotelegraphy as well as greater abilities that will permit them to aspire to higher paying civil positions in their specialty."[17]

In addition to the deferred benefits of possessing a license that granted entrance into a profession, the recruiting poster added that there were "pecuniary advantages" available. Volunteers who signed a four-year contract received a bonus of 3,250 francs, and those who opted to serve for five years received 4,550 francs above their daily pay. Moreover, the service offered the promise of regular promotions with accompanying pay raises, for those who found life in the air service to their liking. Those who adapted well to military life in the course of their technical training could receive promotions to the rank of corporal upon graduation, with an additional advance to sergeant after five months of satisfactory service. Ultimately, the most enterprising recruits could work their way through the enlisted and noncommissioned officer ranks to become officers.

Similar offers applied to potential recruits in the radio operator, gunnery *(radiotélégraphiste* and *mitrailleur),* and pilot career fields. The only exception to the standard recruiting formula for pilots was the addition of a daily bonus, the expansion of the four- and five-year bonus to include recruits who signed on for two or three years, and a separate pay scale that granted higher daily amounts for pilots than for personnel in nonflying specialties.[18] The message that these recruiting advertisements communicated was that the air service needed dedicated recruits who were willing to make a long-term commitment to the Armée de l'air. The service was willing to offer tangible as well as intangible compensation to those who were willing to trade several years of their lives for high-quality technical training.

The goal of the Armée de l'air's training system centered on instilling problem solving and critical thinking skills rather than passing on an approved staff solution to operational and tactical challenges.[19] The organizational doctrine specified five categories of instruction: morale, general, military, technical, and liaison with land and sea forces. Lessons progressed through a series of lectures, demonstrations, and practical problems. Throughout the process, instruction in the training system targeted every aspect of the airman's professional life.

Morale education formed the basis for all other categories of air force instruction. Modern aerial warfare conditions, even in multiplace crew airplanes, tended to isolate the individual. The fear this provoked could intensify with the knowledge that French airmen fought from a position of numerical and technological inferiority. Therefore morale programs sought "to develop among all flying personnel a spirit of unfailing sacrifice, devotion, and discipline, combined with a keen sense of responsibility and thorough comprehension of the mission."[20] When the pressures of combat came, French airmen could rely upon the lessons of discipline, patriotism, and sacrifice, along with a shared sense of purpose to bolster their courage.

The architects of the training system recognized that morale was just as important for nonflying personnel as it was for the flight crews. The *Règlements* pointed to the positive effects gained from a well-defined sense of purpose and mission. The symbols of the nation, national holidays, and significant unit accomplishments instilled a sense of personal connection to the mission and to the greater purpose of national defense. Commanders and subordinates alike shared in the responsibility of cultivating this awareness of the role that their unit and the Armée de l'air at large played in national defense. "The purpose of morale education" for all air force personnel was, therefore, "to exalt patriotism, to inspire confidence, to develop an understanding of the necessity of discipline, and to develop feelings of solidarity and esprit within the unit."[21]

Just as morale education served emotional purposes, general education addressed rational requirements. The two were not, however, mutually exclusive. General instruction focused on developing an understanding among airmen of the nation's strategic and operational circumstances. This related directly to the morale education objective of cultivating mission awareness. In a broader sense, however, this type of training was necessary because of the rather isolated character of the French citizenry.

As Eugen Weber argues, France remained a rather fragmented country until late in the nineteenth century. Even in the 1930s, Frenchmen tended to focus on local rather than international concerns.[22] New recruits brought this worldview to the air service. Therefore the leaders of the air force sought to provide a training system that educated service members on the outlines of geography and European politics, national defense policies, the general principles of land, air, and sea power employment, and the latest advances in military technology.[23] The air force was, thus, not just a military institution; it became an engine of social advancement and change.

For Pierre Cot, the Armée de l'air's potential as an instrument of social progress was one of the most important functions the service could perform for the nation. Cot attempted to accelerate the socializing role by instituting regularly scheduled lectures followed by mandatory writing assignments for the regular officer corps. By forcing the air service officers to encounter and write about stimulating and controversial subjects, Cot hoped to make the Armée de l'air "a laboratory of ideas, technical, and tactical conceptions."[24] He sought no less than to make the French world leaders in aviation thinking; as the airmen fulfilled this role, France would resume her rightful place as the leader of the globe in political, social, and cultural matters.

As the syllabus moved from the affective *(éducation morale)* and the intellectual *(instruction générale)* to more practical forms, objectives assumed characteristics akin to those of traditional military training programs. *Instruction militaire* included drill, specialty instruction, and physical education. Military aviation presented unique physical challenges, and to prepare airmen and support personnel to meet them, air staff regulations specified a complete regime of regular fitness activities. "A physical education lesson, occurring before the duty day begins for all personnel, lasting from thirty to forty minutes will be given each day by qualified instructors. Officers and non-commissioned officers under the age of 35 years will participate."[25]

The goal was to maintain a cadre of airmen that could perform under the stress of fast-paced combat air operations involving aerial maneuvering as well as long-duration, high-altitude flight. For the nonflying specialties, physical education instruction prepared support personnel for long, stressful hours of intense combat operations. Calisthenics, running, gymnastics, and swimming were some of the activities the air staff advocated to ensure that physically capable airmen manned the service.

Physical education was important enough for the air staff to consider creating a specialized training school near Chambéry. According to the proposal, the school would provide "instruction for career officers and non-commissioned officers in physical education and sports." The location, near alpine skiing areas, would afford the opportunity "to form [a cadre] of instructors for winter and water sports."[26] The school's three-month-long winter sports program could accommodate twenty-five officers who, after completing it, would return to their units as *instructeurs d'éducation physique*. The five best officers from each year's course would remain for an additional month and a half of specialized training. The proposal called for a similar four-month program to produce thirty noncommissioned officer physical education instructors.

But lack of money and the limited utility of a school designed to operate only during winter months called the basic premise into question. Thus the aborted proposal for a physical education school at Chambéry illustrated many of the problems encountered in the training system throughout the interwar period. The air staff routinely emphasized the importance of the various elements of the system, but service leaders failed to ensure that it could provide the training the service required to reach acceptable levels of tactical and operational effectiveness.

Technical instruction gave each air service member the requisite skills to perform in his particular specialty. For flight crews, this included special ground courses as well as regularly scheduled flight training. As the authors of the *Règlements* observed: "Preparatory instruction on the ground is the best guarantee of good results in the air."[27] Preparation for technical instruction focused squarely on mission and task accomplishment. There was little room, in either flight or ground activities, for speculation or theory.

Tactical instruction continued to focus on applying the special skills of air combat and combat support to specific scenarios. Airmen began their tactical instruction with a thorough review of relevant air, land, and sea regulations. If necessary, the areas of confusion that arose in this review received clarification in a group discussion of the principles in question, using a historical case to illustrate key points. Map exercises followed the regulation discussion, allowing participants to simulate specific tactical scenarios. The focus was on deploying air resources, tactical maneuvers, intelligence gathering, communications planning, and logistics. This type of exercise allowed unit members to practice all the roles required of air service personnel in wartime with respect to receiving and processing orders, planning air operations, and working with other air, land, and sea combat forces. After each map exercise, the participants convened to conduct a collective after-action review of the unit's performance.[28]

The final category of instruction focused on air operations in concert with land and sea forces. The *Règlements* anticipated some of the difficulties that could occur when the Armée de l'air functioned in a joint service context, and the objective of exercises in peacetime was to allow each service to develop an understanding of how to combine various combat specialties effectively. In reality, the Armée de l'air feared that the army and navy would undermine the authority and the autonomy of air commanders. For this reason, the doctrine specified, "every Air Force element that participates in exercises with cadres, corps, or divisions of the Army shall be represented by its chief."[29]

The five categories of instruction specified in the *Règlements de manoeuvre de l'aviation* provided the framework around which all air service training programs revolved. At the unit level, the air staff divided the calendar year into two training periods. In the winter months (November–April), air education focused on gaining the necessary ground skills to prepare for instrument flight conditions. Any flight training that occurred during this period focused on developing proficiency for individual flying skills and aircrew in-flight coordination. When meteorological conditions improved during the spring and summer months, the emphasis of the prescribed training syllabus shifted to more large-unit combat training. Between May and October, the airmen participated in exercises and maneuvers with other air force units, and in joint exercises with the army and navy. Despite this logical and well-designed training plan, the air staff had trouble producing a consistent level of proficiency among the crews of the regular air force.

Managing the School System

The air staff established optimistic production goals for the various schools in the training system. Students who entered the service through direct recruitment to receive flight training underwent a three-year program, while maintenance specialists graduated from the basic mechanic's course after two years. In 1937, there were 748 students in various stages of training in the Salon-de-Provence region. That same year, an additional 210 students attended various courses that ranged from two weeks to five and a half months. Similar numbers attended courses administered in other regional training centers.[30]

Air service leaders responded to mounting diplomatic tensions in Europe by creating more schools to handle anticipated service expansion. Many of the new schools received minimum staffing billets, along with the minimum essential infrastructure and support required to manage the programs the air staff charged them to execute. For example, Pierre Cot addressed a secret memorandum to the regional air commanders informing them of his decision to create a new Centre-École at Salon in June 1937. The commandant of the school at Istres, near Marseille, received the additional responsibility of commanding it, and for specific administrative support, the new school became dependent on "une Compagnie de de l'Air rattachée au Bataillon de l'Air No. 125."[31] The impression is one of an organization created on paper, without the requisite personnel resources.

The situation of at Strasbourg closely resembled that at Salon. An air staff memorandum, dated 30 November 1937, informed the commanding general of the First Air Region that a new school for mechanics would activate on 15 December—only two weeks from the date of the memorandum. In this case, the air staff specified the number and skill categories of the personnel who would man the school. Administrative support, like the school at Salon, came from an existing *bataillon de l'air*. This time, however, the air staff provided eleven additional personnel billets to help handle the increased workload. Additionally, the memorandum clearly identified the composition of the school staff. Fifty-one permanent staff members made up the faculty and supporting specialists; only fifteen of this number, however, were qualified as instructors. They were destined to teach a student contingent of 150.[32]

Strasbourg proved to be located too close to German territory to function effectively as a center for air service instruction. Shortly after the date for its scheduled activation, the minister for national defense and war inquired regarding the security of the new school. The air staff reply emphasized its temporary character: "I am honored to inform you that the constitution of this Centre-École fills urgent and temporary needs of the Armée de l'Air. It will be dissolved as soon as the shortage of mechanics in the Armée de l'Air is reduced."[33] The author of the reply went on to assure the minister that the air force remained aware of the precarious position of the base at Strasbourg. In the event of an emergency, the resources would evacuate to an airfield near Saverne, some 30 kilometers (approximately 19 miles) to the northwest of Strasbourg—hardly a significant increase in security.[34]

The air staff's tendency to solve increasing personnel shortages with new schools intensified as threats to French security multiplied in the second half of the decade. Archival sources indicate that at least twelve were ordered to form between 1937 and 1940.[35] But the increase in facilities failed to address adequately the shortages in critical specialties. There were several reasons for this phenomenon. The first, and most obvious, related to the availability of qualified instructor personnel. Second, the length of the various courses meant that the air service would only reap returns on investments in new facilities after two or three years of training there. Finally, the threat of war, real and perceived, prompted the air staff to direct changes intended to preserve the training system in the event of an enemy attack. These added weight to an already overloaded system; the effect was a further slowing of production—the opposite of the air staff's intent.

The necessity to have a cadre of competent instructors was perhaps the most critical element of the French training system. The air staff was slow, however, to detect the relationship between their desired student production levels and the shortage of instructor personnel. Moreover, the school system did not have a dedicated instructor school for pilots until the shortage of instructors had reached emergency proportions. An air staff note, dated 8 September 1939, expressed concerns over the magnitude of the instructor shortage: "It seems essential in these conditions to create an instructor school *[une école de moniteurs]* which will provide all instruction for the cadre of instructors, following one proven method."[36]

The first step to correct the problem was to consolidate the available instructors, from both schools and tactical units. On 21 September 1939 the air staff informed commanders of the five air regions and the schools at Versailles, Bordeaux, d'Avord, and Etampes that a new school for instructor pilots would activate on 15 October at the Salon air base. The shortage was so acute, however, that the new school could not meet the immediate needs. Therefore the commandants at Versailles and Bordeaux also received orders to institute training programs for instructors at their facilities. Further, the air staff directed each school to select twenty-five students to participate in the two-and-a-half-month training program. Thus, according to the production plan envisioned by this directive, the accelerated program could produce approximately 360 new instructor pilots per year.[37]

The air staff devoted much of its attention to fine-tuning the system to obtain the best results. The school and depot facilities at Istres illustrate the difficulties encountered in identifying problems associated with training management and devising valid solutions. In May 1937 the air staff issued a call for a review of operations at the depot that served the training school at Istres. The memorandum identified several factors that may have contributed to the inadequate support that the depot had recently provided. All related to a recent reorganization of the school and to an increase in the number of students in the flying training programs. The air staff tasked the inspector general for technical matters (*l'inspection générale technique*) to assess the facilities and management at the depot to determine if the problem was poor management or lack of personnel.[38] At this point in the saga, the air staff was simply trying to understand the problem.

By August they did. The increase in flying hours that stemmed from additional students in the training programs certainly aggravated the stress on the workers at the depot. There were, however, three facts that had not been included in the May memorandum. First, there was "an increase in the Armée de l'air which had not seen a correspondingly equal increase in the assigned effectives."[39] Second, "the 40-hour law diminished the productivity of the civil personnel by 15 percent, with no corresponding augmentation of military personnel."[40] Finally, "there were a great number of multiplace airplanes placed in service at the Centre-École."[41] The combined effects of these changes led the air staff to conclude: "The depot at Istres cannot function with the current personnel."[42]

The air staff could not solve the critical shortage of civil and military workers at Istres by creating new schools. Moreover, the air service budget had no resources for hiring new civil personnel. According to the staff memo: "The Military Air Material Management [Directorate] has arrived at the limit of its budgetary resources for recruiting civil workers."[43] There were, however, inefficiencies in the system—"excess [workers] in certain depots, in particular those at Lyon and Dijon"—that the staff could use to advantage in the effort to reverse the situation.[44] The distance between Istres and the two other depots presented new problems. Lyon was approximately 240 kilometers (or 150 miles) north of Istres, and Dijon was almost twice that distance. Enticing civilian workers to make the move would take time, and it would be difficult.

In order to prevent the problems at Istres from having further negative effects on the training mission, the air staff suggested some temporary solutions. First, the civil work force would gain fifty additional personnel (there was no air staff directive to explain how the depot at Istres would acquire these workers). Second, the contracts for new maintenance hangars and repair facilities would proceed immediately to provide adequate space. Finally, a review of flying operations would reveal inefficiencies in the system. The optimistic view that the staff adopted held that once the training system began to operate more efficiently, all operations at the base would turn to a "more rational utilization of flying at the field."[45] These suggestions did not address, however, the underlying causes of the maintenance, training, and flying problems at Istres.

Fourteen months later, operations had failed to improve; they had grown worse. The air staff characterized the situation in October 1938 as *la crise d'Istres*.[46] By this point, staff solutions fell into one of three categories: "either a decrease in the workload; or an increase in [personnel] resources; or a compromise."[47] None of the alternatives was attractive. Decreasing student output meant delays in augmenting air force combat power. The staff recognized the import of this suggestion; student production was a function of "the needs of the Plan to increase [the strength] of the Armée de l'air. Those needs are imperative; to reduce them would compromise the realization of the Plan."[48] There was, however, a way around the tyranny of the student production goals.

Istres functioned as a joint service base, where both air force and naval aviators received flight training. The air staff acknowledged the legal obligation to provide training for naval aviators, but noted in their memorandum: "It seems that the number of Navy students instructed each year at Istres is out of proportion to the importance of Naval Aeronautics."[49] Therefore the staff recommended a reduction in the number of naval aviation students, along with the transfer of some specialized air force flight training to other bases with similar missions.

The structure of the flying training program appeared to have contributed to la crise d'Istres also. The staff study noted that between 1932 and 1938 the number of flying hours for student aircrews had increased from 125 to 240. This increase had "compromised the functioning of the école and had brought about the current crisis."[50] The staff did not acknowledge, however, that increases in technological sophistication and mission complexity may have contributed to the increase in flying hour requirements. The recommendation called for a comprehensive review of the training program, to identify inefficiencies and to eliminate wasted flying hours that contributed to the maintenance workload.

Adding military maintenance personnel to the work force, according to the second alternative suggested by the air staff, appeared nearly impossible. The assessment revealed a 20 percent shortage of qualified noncommissioned officer mechanics. The problem was that the only way to overcome such a shortage in military personnel was to pull them from operational units. The air staff was unwilling to push this point, noting: "Such augmentation of the effectives would be made at the detriment of the combat formations which are already deficient and would risk compromising the functioning of those units."[51]

In the final analysis, the air staff could only suggest temporary measures to solve the crisis at the southern training base. The real solution would come only after the air force training system could produce enough qualified mechanics to fill the requirements at Istres and the other training bases. The situation was destined, however, to continue for another eleven months before the air minister acted to relieve the pressure.

In October 1939 the air ministry began to take action to repair a training system that had proven inadequate for its assigned task. The situation at Istres prompted the ministry to form a commission to look closely at the entire system. The corrective actions that came from the commission's study would be a product of "the various inspections accomplished in the écoles and instruction Centres for one part, and numerous conferences that had met relative to these same organizations for another part."[52] The ministry optimistically declared that the solutions would address "all questions relative to their [the Écoles and Centres] functioning (Organization, Command, Student recruiting, Infrastructure, Material, etc.)."[53] The crisis at Istres, which had developed over two years, still required corrective action.

In November 1939 the air minister addressed a secret memorandum to the commander of the Fourth Air Region detailing his initiatives to ease the burden carried by the school and depot at Istres. After more than two years of temporary adjustments, study, and discussion, the minister had decided "to reorganize the air base at Istres beginning on 1 December 1939 by reconstituting Air Battalion No. 125 and converting the existing depot and by creating on this base, in the conditions and on the date that you [the air region commander] will ultimately establish, a Group of three pilot schools *[écoles de pilotage]* which will be placed under the command of a superior officer, Commander of the Groupe d'Écoles and the Air Base."[54]

By this point, the crisis at Istres had spread to encompass the Armée de l'air's entire training system. Yet the leaders of the air service continued to focus on incremental stopgap measures. They chose to treat the symptoms rather than the underlying causes. The air ministry asked the air staff to examine instructor and flight leader *(chef de patrouille)* manning levels at the schools, with an eye toward "filling existing deficits, or in the expectation of relieving younger active-duty officers currently functioning in these organizations."[55] In other words, the air minister suggested transferring active-duty and, presumably, more qualified instructor pilots and flight leaders from the schools and replacing them with older reservists.

Late in 1939 the pressures of service expansion began to exert themselves on the entire training system. An inspection of the pursuit school (Centre d'instruction de chasse) at Montpellier, approximately 130 kilometers (80 miles) from Marseille, revealed the system's inability to provide the air force the critical numbers of pursuit pilots. General Vuillemin proposed augmenting the instructor cadres at the Montpellier and Chartres pursuit schools with teachers drawn from certain line units and from the staff at the flight instructor school (l'École de formation des moniteurs de pilotage).[58] Both solutions represented the worst of all possible alternatives.

The pursuit aviation *inspecteur et commandant supérieur,* General d'Harcourt, informed the air force chief of staff that the minister did not fully understand the problem. According to the general, the schools needed instructors, not flight leaders. To remove the young instructors from the school system in favor of older, less-qualified reserve instructors would only exacerbate the problems. Moreover, the pursuit schools that were charged with the mission of forming crew members and flight leaders needed a number of flight leader instructors who, according to d'Harcourt, were then available at flight training bases and other locations. The pursuit commander's assessment was that there remained an excess number of qualified flight leaders in the interior who could transfer to the faltering school system, without necessitating the removal of the best instructors and flight leaders from either the schools or the combat units.[56]

General d'Harcourt's advice apparently did not sway air force chief of staff General Joseph Vuillemin. The chief of staff informed the air minister that it was impossible to transfer any instructors from the schools. It was equally impossible, according to Vuillemin, to "release personnel of the Armées to the benefit of the interior," and finally, "the release of *officiers instructeurs* and flight leader instructors at the schools and centers of instruction could be brought about, in principle, next spring."[57] The air staff had once again failed to address adequately a critical systemic problem that held dramatic consequences for the effectiveness of French airpower.

Removing experienced instructors from combat units deprived those units of the essential leadership required to prepare for their first operational encounters. Similarly, removing teachers from the instructor school guaranteed future shortages in the teaching force. Vuillemin's actions were analogous to those of a farmer feeding his seed corn to the livestock.[59] The animals may survive—just as the pursuit schools would function—but when planting time arrived, there would be no seed to put in the ground. Moreover, in the context of French grand strategy that sought to draw Germany into a long war, the Armée de l'air's ability to produce instructors and pilots would become almost as important as halting the German offensives.[60]

In January 1940 the air minister attempted once again to impose order and efficiency on the Armée de l'air's training system. The minister settled on a new organizational scheme for the instructor pilot school at Salon. Under the new formula, the school would divide into two phases: "a division of instructors from the école principale," and another "division of instructors from the auxiliary and elementary school that will execute the elementary instructor's course."[61] There was no explanation for the division of effort. The only rational reason for this change could be that the air minister perceived a different skill level required by the instructors operating at the different schools. By separating the skills and training objectives, he may have hoped to produce instructors for the various écoles faster than with a combined program. In any case, the January 1940 reorganization would not be the final word from the air ministry on the subject of training system organization.

In April 1940 the air minister focused his attention on the *bases/centres d'instruction*. This time, archival evidence permits insight into the rationale behind the minister's desire to change the system. The essential problem was that multiple types of training activities occurred at a single base. The purpose of the new organization was to "concentrate the maximum available personnel and material at those bases/centres d'instruction which are currently in the best position to give applied instruction."[62] This reform goal contains a telling critique of the training system. The statement amounts to a frank admission that it was operating in an inefficient manner.

The air ministry plan affected seven bases scattered throughout metropolitan France. The changes focused primarily on consolidating training mission assignments to reduce the redundancy that had come to characterize the system. The obvious benefits that the ministry expected to reap stemmed from pooling the available instructor and maintenance resources at common locations rather than distributing the missions, personnel, and resources in small schools throughout the country.[63] Additionally, because of an influx of foreign students, mostly Poles and Czechs who were eager to continue the fight against German aggression, the French training system found itself flooded. The ministry intended for the new organizational framework to cope with this new student population by grouping nationalities at specific locations, under the command of a French training cadre.[64] Although the increase in combat pilots and ground specialists would prove useful when war broke out, the drain on French instructor resources added stress to a system that had already demonstrated significant flaws.

The only solution to the critical shortage of instructor pilots was to draw upon those who formed the core of experienced flyers in the combat units. Consequently, the air staff issued directions for instructors in certain specialties to report for duty at the centres d'instruction. The directive specified that those selected for this duty "would be detached [from their units] for a duration of six months, then reassigned to their original unit."[65] More important, the air staff specified that instructors chosen to serve in this capacity would "be chosen with a preference for those pilots who have already participated in combat to allow the students to benefit from their experience."[66] With less than one month before Germany was destined to invade French soil, the air staff decided to strip the front line units of their most experienced combat veterans.

Preserving the Training System

As war with Germany and Italy became a reality, the air staff began to formulate plans for safeguarding the training system. This proved to be a difficult task, because of the threat posed by enemy aviation. There were few bases in metropolitan France that remained secure from aerial attack. By the spring of 1940, the effects of the *drôle de guerre,* the phony war, had already disrupted training routines at several bases. For example, the air staff modified the airspace available for the Centre d'instruction at Clermont-Ferrand to accommodate increased lookout *(ligne de guet)* operations.[67]

In a more serious incident that occurred after the German offensives began, the bases at d'Avord and Châteauroux came under air attack, prompting an inquest into the "dispersal of personnel without orders."[68] The war disrupted training operations at the Centre d'instruction at Chartres so much that the air staff ordered the *escadre d'instruction de chasse* at that base to relocate to Cazaux.[69] The air staff directed the *centres d'instruction de bombardement* at Toulouse and Châteauroux to turn over their modern airplanes for use in combat operations. The air staff replaced the equipment losses at these two bases with *matériels anciens.*[70] Finally, extremely low altitude flights *(vols rasants)* at the Châteauroux base interfered with DAT operations, prompting the air staff to push the training zones and emergency landing fields further to the west to avoid friendly fire incidents.[71]

The heightened tensions and outright hostilities that characterized the drôle de guerre and the early weeks of combat operations placed severe constraints on the training system's ability to produce combat-ready aircrew members. The air staff frantically sought alternatives that promised to preserve the training system, while simultaneously increasing student production goals—two seemingly incompatible objectives.

Air force leaders proposed the French territories in North Africa as a logical sanctuary for the training system. A system of bases in Tunisia, Algeria, and Morocco would provide the security and airspace necessary to produce combat-ready aircrew members. Unfortunately for the Armée de l'air, the reactive posture in the air ministry and the air staff resulted in delays in the planning process for creating the necessary infrastructure to allow the move to North Africa. The first indication that the air minister, Guy La Chambre, planned to move elements of the training system across the Mediterranean came in mid-October 1939. The drôle de guerre had already assumed its surreal characteristics, and the training system showed signs of buckling under the strain of increased wartime requirements.[72] The air minister's plan called for the creation of three types of schools: ten for pilots, one for observers, and one for a combination of gunnery and radio operators.[73]

La Chambre's overly optimistic program contained an added level of complexity—aside from the move to North Africa, it concealed a reorganization of the established training system. The functions of the écoles élémentaires, auxiliaries, and principales would merge into a single school, under the North Africa plan. To further complicate matters, the air minister's program called for each pilot school to receive fifty student pilots per month for a dramatically reduced pilot training syllabus. Rather than the three-year program that the system had followed in peacetime, La Chambre ordered the duration of the flight training cut to six months. Thus, according to the air minister's calculations, each North African school could accommodate six hundred students per year. This impressive projection, however, did not take into account the duration of the new six-month curriculum. Although the schools could theoretically accept fifty students each month, the term of the training program restricted the production of each school to three hundred students per year.

Regardless whether viewed from La Chambre's optimistic perspective or from the slightly more conservative three hundred per year perspective, the creation of a completely new training system would take time. La Chambre's guidance for implementing the program called for two schools to begin operating in December 1939, with the remaining eight to receive their first student pilots by April 1940.[74] Therefore the first hundred pilots to receive their certificates as graduates of the new école principale would not depart the North

African training system for specialized combat training until June 1940; the first full contingent from all ten schools in the new system would not graduate until October of that year.

The unrealistic figures for student pilot production contained in the air minister's North Africa plan carried over into other specialties. According to the concept, the school for observers planned *en principe* at Oran, Algeria, "could produce 200 students every three months in the beginning."[75] The combined gunnery and radio operator school, planned en principe to activate at Casablanca, "could produce 200 gunners and 150 radio operators every three months."[76] But the air minister had made the mistake of forecasting student production figures for these schools before obtaining a final decision from the air staff on the provisioning and location of the facilities.

As the leaders of the Armée de l'air planned the move to North Africa, they encountered the same problems that had plagued the training system since 1937. A fully functioning system depended on "quality instructors, basic, transition, and advanced trainer aircraft, and sufficient stocks of equipment for the observers and gunners."[77] The pressures of war intensified the shortages of these critical resources for the bases in metropolitan France. The air minister commented: "Henceforth, it seems that the resources at my disposal will be very insufficient."[78] The only remedy for the shortages in personnel was to transfer qualified instructors from the currently functioning training bases in France to the newly operating locations in North Africa. The movement of an entire training system would take time—more time than envisioned in the air minister's proposal.

The North Africa solution was the only choice that promised to preserve the Armée de l'air's ability to reinforce the combat units as the war progressed. But the movement across the Mediterranean was not without risks. Italian air and sea forces threatened French shipping and flights destined for North Africa. Furthermore, Spanish intentions in the conflict were not clear. These considerations prompted General Vuillemin to approve La Chambre's proposal, with the understanding that the new training system would not adversely affect operations at the North African air bases charged with preserving French security and freedom of action in the Mediterranean.[79]

Vuillemin's concern for the operational units resulted in a review of the proposed training system in North Africa by the Fifth Air Region commander at Oran. The conclusion forwarded to the air ministry caused a change in the plans to move the schools. Rather than adapting existing bases in Algeria to the mission, the new plan called for the "majority of the projected schools to be installed in Morocco."[80] This adjustment reduced the projected capacity of each school from 600 students per year to 450. The infrastructure decisions also caused delays in activating the new schools. Those originally scheduled to open in December 1939 could not begin receiving students until January 1940, and those scheduled to open in April 1940 were delayed until May.[81] Despite the ambitious scope of the North Africa school concept, it did not replace the existing institutions in France. The size of the training system, coupled with the logistics requirements that accompanied the task of administering technical and flying training programs, precluded a complete transfer of the missions to North Africa.

By the spring of 1940, the air staff found itself in the unenviable position of having to attempt the impossible. The war threatened vital training bases in southeastern France. La Chambre ordered the leaders of the Armée de l'air to develop plans for moving nine schools from seven bases in the areas under the greatest threat. The air minister directed the staff to examine possible evacuation sites in the interior of metropolitan France, but the best hope for preserving the training capability provided at the most critical bases—Istres and Salon—was to transfer those units and missions to unspecified locations in North Africa. Istres was an especially important facility; it contained three écoles principales (two bombardment schools and one for reconnaissance), with an enrollment of 760 student pilots. The potential disruption of the training program that an evacuation could cause threatened to halt student production for more than three months. La Chambre advised a wait-and-see attitude; rather than urging the air staff to begin the moves immediately, he ordered careful studies of the potential reception sites with an eye toward beginning the moves in the summer. The catalyst for the evacuations would be Italy's initiation of hostilities in southeastern France. Once more the leaders of the French air force surrendered the initiative, in favor of reacting to events that promised to shatter their vital training system.[82]

By May 1940 the leisurely approach that had characterized French preparations to preserve the training system during the drôle de guerre began to cost the service dearly. On the seventeenth, the air ministry ordered the Fifth Air Region commander in Algeria to establish a new pursuit school at Oran.[83] Four days later, on 21 May, the ministry ordered the pilot training schools at Istres to begin evacuation to North Africa.[84] On 1 June the intelligence school (Centre d'instruction de renseignement) at Tours, along with the associated schools at Clermont-Ferrand and Rennes, was to cease training operations and evacuate to Afrique du Nord. Those students who had already completed enough of the training program to remain in France and participate in the nation's defense would receive assignments to operational units.[85] Finally, the instructors at the schools at Versailles received orders to depart for Rabat, Morocco.[86]

By failing to act to preserve the training before their enemies launched their attacks, French air leaders deprived the nation of a reliable source of qualified replacement aircrew members and maintenance specialists. If the Armée de l'air was responsible for the defeat in 1940, as the Vichy government charged, the failure of the air ministry and the air staff to act decisively to preserve the system contributed to the weakness of the service's response to German attacks.

The training system that the Armée de l'air had developed in the 1930s had the potential to produce adequate numbers of qualified aircrew members and support personnel. Tragically, it failed to fulfill its potential, because the air staff's sluggish response to several challenges—the shortage of instructors and trained personnel, inefficient system management, and the lack of adequate stocks of material—left the training system at the mercy of increasing demands to produce students and instructors.

Doctrine provided a logical and carefully constructed design to guide the programs at the various training schools and operational units. The leaders of the air staff had no difficulty identifying the problems that plagued the system. The case of the school and depot at Istres illustrates that the airmen in Paris identified the critical elements of the problems. The leaders of the Armée de l'air failed to take timely, decisive action to eliminate redundancy and inefficiencies in the system. The result was a training system that, like the air force it served, drifted from crisis to crisis, until the tragedy of war caused the entire façade to come crashing down.

Dewoitine D-520 Pursuit (1938/39)
Engine: Hispano-Suiza 12Y-31 (1) 860 hp
Takeoff weight: 2,200 kg (4,850 lbs)
Speed: 560 km/h (347 mph)
Ceiling: 10,500 m (34,440 ft)

Morane-Saulnier 406 Pursuit (1938)
Engine: Hispano-Suiza 12Ygrs (1) 860 hp
Takeoff weight: 2,470 kg (5,445.3 lbs)
Speed: 485 km/h (300.7 mph)
Ceiling: 9,000 m (29,520 ft)

Bloch 81 Aeromedical Evacuation (1934)
Engine: Lorraine 5Pc (1) 120 hp
Takeoff weight: 780 kg (1,719.59 lbs)
Speed: 172 km/h (106.6 mph)
Ceiling: 6,800 m (22,304 ft)

Lioré et Olivier (LéO) 20 Bn-4 Bomber (1929)
Engine: Gnôme-Rhône "Jupiter" (2)
    480 hp
Takeoff weight: 5,060 kg (11,155.28 lbs)
Speed: 196 km/h (121.5 mph)
Ceiling: 5,750 m (18,860 ft)

Lioré et Olivier (LéO) 30 Bomber (1932)
Engine: Hispano-Suiza 12 Nbr (4) 650 hp
Takeoff weight: 14,000 kg (30,864.4 lbs)
Speed: 253 km/h (156.86 mph)
Ceiling: 6,200 m (20,336 ft)

Bloch 200 Bn-4 Bomber-Combat-Reconnaissance (1934)
Engine: Gnôme-Rhône K-14dr (2) 930 hp
Takeoff weight: 6,560 kg (14,462.2 lbs)
Speed: 280 km/h (173.6 mph)
Ceiling: 9,400 m (30,832 ft)

Farman 221 Heavy Bomber (1934)
Engine: Gnôme-Rhône K-14 (4) 650 hp
Takeoff weight: 15,000 kg (33,069 lbs)
Speed: 300 km/h (186 mph)
Ceiling: 7,800 m (25,584 ft)

Bloch 211 Night Bomber (1934)
Engine: Hispano-Suiza 12Ydr (2) 850 hp
Takeoff weight: 7,500 kg (16,534.5 lbs)
Speed: 320 km/h (198.4 mph)
Ceiling: 9,000 m (29,520 ft)

Bloch 131 Multiplace Bombardment-Combat-Reconnaissance (1936)
Engine: Gnôme-Rhône 14No (2) 880 hp
Takeoff weight: 8,000 kg (17,636.8 lbs)
Speed: 360 km/h (223.2 mph)
Ceiling: 9,000 m (29,520 ft)

Breguet 690 Attack Bomber (1936/37)
Engine: Hispano-Suiza 14Ab (2) 680 hp
Takeoff weight: 4,500 kg (9,920.7 lbs)
Speed: 450 km/h (279 mph)
Ceiling: 8,000 m (26,240 ft)

Lioré et Olivier (LéO) 45 Bomber (1937)
Engine: Hispano-Suiza 14 Ha (2) 1,100 hp
Takeoff weight: 11,000 kg (24,250.6 lbs)
Speed: 435 km/h (269.7 mph)
Ceiling: 7,000 m (22,960 mph)

5 Maneuvers, Exercises, and Reactive Doctrine

These exercises have shown the perfect adaptation of the current organization to the needs of the modern battle.[1]

The regular schedule of maneuvers and exercises that occurred between 1933 and 1940 did more to reinforce the Armée de l'air's reactive doctrine than any other institutional mechanism. The service used these mechanisms to refine operational and tactical mission capabilities, to experiment with new force employment concepts and technologies, and to resolve differing conceptions of roles and missions.[2] Rather than acting as laboratories for innovation, however, the various maneuvers that the leaders of the Armée de l'air designed and implemented during the 1930s pushed the service away from a vision of modern war based upon an all-encompassing *lutte aérienne*. Instead, the scenarios presented roles for airpower that left the service virtually incapable of independent action, and highly vulnerable to an enemy's new concepts of modern warfare. The tragedy was not that this deterioration of service autonomy happened; it was that the leaders of the Armée de l'air failed to defend a comprehensive vision of modern aerial warfare. In other words, the leaders became willing participants with the army, navy, and government in the process of stripping their service of its independence.[3]

The archival evidence with which to perform an analysis of the Armée de l'air's exercise and maneuver record in the 1930s forms an incomplete trail in the interwar period. The surviving records consist of air ministry and air staff planning documents and after-action reports. Often these refer to more than one exercise in each year, but the records documenting smaller-scale exercises have disappeared. Additionally, the details of how each exercise unfolded—the on-scene umpire's reports—have not survived. The resulting historical record portrays a rather sterile version of air staff conclusions about the various exercises and maneuvers. Nevertheless, questions that staff members posed and the ways they interpreted results provide valuable insight into institutional attitudes toward specific operational, tactical, and doctrinal problems.

The level of detail that came to characterize the planning orders for each maneuver and exercise communicate the degree of importance that service leaders attached to these events. The surviving planning packages and exercise critiques reveal how the practice sessions of the 1930s contributed to the French reactive approach to airpower doctrine. The degree of continuity or change reflected in scenario development from year to year offers clues regarding operational and tactical maturity. Air staff attempts—or lack thereof—to anticipate conditions of modern aerial warfare show how the service matched doctrinal concepts of lutte aérienne to simulated combat operations.

The degree of realism and unrestrained simulated combat allowed in the maneuvers prepared airmen to fight a particular kind of war. This implies that the air service was ill prepared to fight other kinds of wars, because they failed to anticipate alternatives to their own conceptions of aerial warfare. The important question to answer in this regard centers on how closely the maneuvers conformed to doctrinal precepts.

Finally, the exercises and maneuvers contributed—for good or for ill—to doctrine development. If they failed to reflect published doctrines, what messages did they send to service members, and what effect did those lessons have on operational and tactical effectiveness? Ultimately, these three elements—scenario development, realistic exercise play, and the messages received from the exercises—exerted a dramatic effect on air force combat effectiveness in 1940.

Scenario Development

French perceptions of German strategy, coupled with their own grand strategic visions of a defensive war, colored the scenarios created for every maneuver and exercise in which the Armée de l'air participated during the 1930s.[4] The pervasive influence of defensive postures eroded the importance of offensive aerial warfare in the service, until the eve of the Second World War. But more importantly, the scenarios that air leaders developed relied upon French bombardment units to act as enemy infiltrators. By forcing the bombers to act almost exclusively as targets for French aerial defenses, the annual maneuvers exerted a subtle demoralizing effect among the Armée de l'air's offensive strike forces. Thus, when war came in 1939, the French air force found itself caught in an operational and tactical trap of its own making.

Large-scale air maneuvers and exercises usually occurred during the late summer and early fall of each year. This conformed to the broad outlines of the flying training schedule described in the *Règlement de manoeuvre de l'aviation*.[5] Staging the exercises in the fall meant that the various participating echelons could concentrate on compiling their reports for the air staff during the winter months, when ground training assumed a greater importance. The air staff issued directives by late June or early July that provided the details of the scheduled maneuvers, including dates, units tasked, scenario outlines, deployment schedules, funding authorizations, command assignments, and communications procedures.[6] These directives contained scripts for every aspect of the exercise or maneuver and sought to eliminate any unplanned or unanticipated intrusions on scheduled events.

The scenario for each maneuver or exercise comprised two elements. The first was a statement or a series of statements that described the particular operational or tactical problems that the air staff sought to study in the course of each exercise. These were usually broad declarations that introduced the problems; later in the staff package, or in other memoranda, the details were laid out. The second element of the scenario appeared under the heading *thème général*. Here the staff described the political conditions that would lead to hostilities, the general disposition of combatant air forces, the geographic scope of the exercise, and the anticipated actions of the belligerents.

The *1ère manoeuvre combinée* that occurred in June 1933, barely five months after the government had granted the service independent status, represented the earliest recorded maneuver for the independent Armée de l'air. Although this exercise was relatively small in terms of the units employed, the problem that the air staff studied in 1933 would become a recurring feature of all the exercises and maneuvers for the remainder of the decade.[7]

The exercise sought to determine how French pursuit units could intercept enemy bombers before they reached their targets in French territory. The specific agenda for the 1933 maneuvers called for pursuit units to use a tactic described as *chasse à courre,* which means "to go hunting." The limited numbers of available pursuit crews and planes assigned to *aviation légère de défense* near army operational units along the front forced the airmen to devise tactics to help them cope with the demands for their services. The loose control offered by the chasse à courre tactic promised to allow commanders to organize aerial resources assigned to cover the front in a more efficient manner.

The *inspection de l'aviation légère de défense* staff concluded that pursuit units could use the new tactic to cover an area up to 300 kilometers (186 miles) behind the front lines, with fighters based every 200 kilometers (124 miles). The priority for each pursuit base was to intercept enemy bombers within the first 100 kilometers (62 miles) after they crossed French lines.[8] This approach reflected a use for airpower as airborne cavalry, posted on the lookout for enemy penetrations. The geometric design of the chasse à courre intercept zones also conformed to land warfare schemes for maneuver; in other words, the airmen had not begun to think in terms of three-dimensional combat. Despite the mathematical precision with which the staff report defended the conclusions gleaned from the exercise, several flaws in the scenario invalidate the organization proposed by the inspectorate.

In the first place, the practice scenario forced bomber formations into the pursuit patrol zones. Bomber crews flew prescribed routes and altitudes, without attempting evasive maneuvers. Therefore the enemy aircrews in the 1933 maneuvers were not intelligent, thinking foes; on the contrary, they were little more than target drones for the waiting pursuit attackers. To be fair to the aviation légère de défense staff, the report readily acknowledged this point by stating, "it remains to be seen if the liaison with a control airplane and the assignment of pursuit units can occur in a reasonable time."[9] This indicates the staff understood that pursuit units required some assistance in locating determined, creative bomber formations.

The second major flaw in the 1933 scenario lay in the assumption that the pursuit units would have equal or superior speed and climb performance characteristics, compared with the bomber formations they were to attack. Unlike the erroneous assumption that bomber formations would fly passively into the pursuit intercept zones, the staff report did not appear to evaluate the implications for the scenario or operational concepts if either pursuit or bomber capabilities were to change. The exercise failed to test the validity of either doctrine or tactics, thus making it useful only as a vehicle for small unit training. Despite these serious defects in scenario design, the 1933 maneuvers gave the fledgling air service practical experience and confidence that would carry over into subsequent annual exercises.

Joint war-fighting action with land forces characterized the 1934 maneuvers. This scenario forced aviation units into a subordinate, defensive role alongside their army counterparts. Air leaders focused on developing more efficient coordination procedures with land commanders. From the air service perspective, reconnaissance efforts—the principal mission that required interaction with land commanders—often yielded little useful information, because land commanders were too directive and specific when they tasked reconnaissance aviation to search for enemy units. Aviation performed in this role much as it had in the context of World War I battles: there was little flexibility and initiative outside the scope of land operations. Or, as the exercise report stated: "Instead of indicating the objective and allowing the aviator to conduct the search in an intelligent manner, the orders simply treat the airplane as a machine that goes 'to look at such a point,' to 'investigate such a route'. . . the aviator finds himself left with no initiative."[10]   The relationship evolved in this way, in part, because land commanders failed to understand how the perspective from the air changed reconnaissance missions; they thought of reconnaissance aviation as little more than airborne cavalry.[11] The airmen believed that a more flexible tasking of their units would yield better information for their ground force counterparts, while allowing a more efficient use of aerial resources.

A second element of the 1934 scenario concerned the proper role for the aviation commander in joint operations. Army commanders preferred to have the air leader at headquarters at all times. This arrangement presented several problems of command and control from the air service perspective. Armée de l'air command arrangements left very few field grade officers in the tactical units; captains and lieutenants led squadron-level formations. This meant that senior officers routinely spent time traveling between smaller units to check on operations, give advice to junior officers, pass on orders from the headquarters, and fly with the units as mission commander.

Because leadership meant different things to officers in the two services, the air and land perspectives clashed with respect to the role performed by senior aviators during the course of a campaign. Senior army leaders controlled the pace and scope of operations from their headquarters, whereas the air service valued leaders who maintained a rapport with their men. The best air commanders, according to the air force perspective, shared the risks of aerial combat. By forcing senior aviators to remain at army headquarters, ground commanders isolated airmen from the tactical and operational situation in the air, from their own aerial lines of communication, and from the logistics and support situation at their bases. Airmen hoped to use the 1934 maneuvers to demonstrate to army commanders an alternative, more effective way to lead air force units in the context of joint operations.

By 1935 the scenario used in the fall maneuvers focused on a broad range of issues that pertained to unique aspects of airpower employment. The maneuvers involved units of the regular air force and those of the Défense aérienne du territoire (DAT). The DAT organization served as the first line of aerial defense for the nation. DAT units provided security *(couverture)* for land and air forces during the mobilization and concentration phases of the early days of a war. Additionally, the DAT directorate coordinated with the war ministry for antiaircraft defenses, with the ministry of the interior for passive (civil) defense, and with the ministry of posts, telephone, and telegraph to communicate alerts within the system.[12]

DAT units provided a critical element in the detection of air attacks—against military sectors, towns, and vital industrial areas—and in notifying pursuit units, antiaircraft artillery batteries, and civil defense organizations. As the regular units of the Armée de l'air moved from their mobilization centers to concentration and employment bases, they reinforced DAT forces. Therefore the 1935 maneuvers examined two critical problems for the Armée de l'air. First, the air staff was interested in how DAT units, including alerting networks *(réseaux de guet)* and pursuit aviation (aviation légère de défense), performed in the early phases of a conflict. The second question that helped to shape the 1935 scenario centered on how regular air force units integrated with the DAT system in the context of an ongoing theater-level war.[13]

Once again, however, the air service focused exclusively on defensive operations for the largest exercise that would occur in 1935. Offensive aviation units, under the command of future chief of staff General Vuillemin, found themselves arrayed against larger numbers of defending pursuit units under the combined DAT–air force structure.

The records for the 1935 maneuvers offer the first opportunity to study the thème général for a major air exercise. The pattern established here provided the basis for the political and geographic characteristics for most of the exercises for the remainder of the decade. The scenario described two combatant nations: one the aggressor, while the other shunned all thoughts of offensive maneuver or territorial aggrandizement until after the aggressor's offensive had culminated and friendly forces began to counterattack. The geographic characteristics of the exercise concentrated land and air units of the aggressor *(un état bleu)* along a common border, while the defender *(un état rouge)* waited in anticipation of an unprovoked attack by the enemy.[14]

The operational objectives of the blue force commander read like a page from German plans in 1914. "The intention of the government is to attack the Red country using a surprise attack with the maximum force in order to obtain a rapid decision in the West and to be more capable of acting on its eastern frontiers."[15] The action envisioned by blue air forces proved as unconventional as the overall strategy was conventional. "The Air Forces will seek, in a *massive attack,* launched at the opening of hostilities, to strike the morale of the Red nation, to diminish its war potential, and to disrupt the concentration of its armies."[16] In this vision of aerial warfare, the French attempted to apply the full range of airpower effects, including offensive attacks against operational centers of gravity. Ironically, however, the Armée de l'air was on the receiving end of the strategic, operational, and morale assaults delivered by the blue air forces.

The 1935 exercise area covered the northern heartland of metropolitan France. Blue forces operated east of a line that stretched from Montmédy, just north of Verdun, to the Moselle River, south of Nancy. Red forces defended a vast area west of that line, including the Channel coast from Cherbourg to Dieppe. Although Paris served as an acknowledged vital political, military, and industrial center, the air staff elected to make the city off-limits in the scenario.[17]

The Armée de l'air concentrated on defending the nation against a surprise aerial attack on the entire spectrum of civil and military targets. The scenario called for the maneuvers to last five days, from 30 September until 4 October. On the first day, DAT units provided the necessary cover for air and land forces to move from their mobilization centers to join the battle. By the second day of the exercise, regular Armée de l'air units bolstered the DAT defenses, and by day three, the Armée de l'air carried the brunt of the air war for the red forces. The air staff called for operations on the first two days to occur in daylight only; days three and four involved simulated combat operations during night and day. Red forces used the final night of the exercise to experiment with night intercept operations near Reims, approximately 100 kilometers (62 miles) northeast of Paris. Additional operational exercises included in the scenario involved red forces tasked to defend coastal areas against possible blue attacks. On the surface, this scenario provided a vehicle for realizing the potential of the lutte aérienne, but it failed to recognize the full range of airpower options.

The 1935 maneuvers represented the air service's most ambitious attempt to date to evaluate its doctrine and its capability to defend the nation's vital centers against aerial attack. This exercise scenario, for the first time, paid homage, in a conceptual way, to the full scope of aerial warfare. One of the exercise objectives identified in the air staff scenario included an evaluation of the Armée de l'air's ability to strike targets deep in enemy territory.[18] This served as little more than window dressing that did not detract, however, from the defensive operations that made up most of the objectives. The red forces, representing France, had no long-range aviation component; thus there was no way for friendly forces to achieve the offensive exercise objectives. The air staff had assigned its most up-to-date pursuit units to the defensive role.

Fourteen groups flying a mix of Morane 225 and Dewoitine 500 pursuit aircraft challenged eleven blue bombardment groups flying obsolete *(ancien)* LéO 20, aging *(transition)* LéO 206, and modern Bloch 200 and Amiot 143 bombers. The fighters outclassed the bombers in every performance category, with the Dewoitine and Morane enjoying a 30 percent advantage in speed and a staggering 60 percent advantage in operating ceiling capability over the bombers.[19]

One of the distressing conclusions from this comparison of fighter and bomber performance was the obvious failure of the BCR procurement initiative.[20] The aircraft technologies matched against each other revealed an assumption that remained typical of every aerial exercise of the 1930s. French airmen assumed that opposing forces would attempt to defeat their defenses by applying similar technologies and doctrines. Despite the blue forces' material disadvantage, the opportunity to plan and execute offensive aerial operations kept the vision of the *lutte aérienne* alive.

In 1936 the fall maneuvers strengthened the trend toward improving cooperation between DAT and the regular units of the Armée de l'air. The political and operational scenario fell into the well-established pattern of French forces, represented by the *parti rouge,* attempting to halt an unprovoked attack from the east by the *parti bleu.* The 1936 scenario differed from that of earlier maneuvers in its emphasis on studying the operations of alert and communications networks. If the sessions of the previous three years had indicated the air staff's concern for defensive operations, to the point of excluding nearly all other aspects of airpower employment, the 1936 emphasis on communications and alerting procedures made the maneuvers appear more like a ground exercise than one focused on employing airpower. Twenty of the thirty pages that constituted the scenario instructions for the red forces, the *dossier rouge,* outlined the communications procedures for the six-day drills.[21]

The significant reduction in the air forces scheduled to participate represented another, even more ominous, change for French offensive airpower. Although the basic scenario objective remained similar to the offensive thrust of the previous year, "to conduct attacks against sensitive points and air bases in enemy territory," a subtle shift occurred.[22] The scenario directed blue force bombardment units to assign priority to attacks against enemy air bases. The vision of an air war that only one year earlier had described airpower's ability to reach deep into enemy territory to strike the political, industrial, morale, and military centers of gravity now contracted considerably. Blue bombers restricted their actions to the enemy air forces, followed by attacks against mobilization centers and rail networks that supplied men and material to the red army stationed along the common frontier.

Moreover, the scope of the air forces that participated in the exercise decreased significantly. The 1935 maneuvers saw twenty-five pursuit and bomber groups arrayed against each other, but in 1936, red forces consisted of four pursuit groups, while the air staff allocated blue forces only three bomber groups.[23] With this drastic reduction in aviation resources, follow-on attacks against mobilization centers and rail networks by blue force bombers could not threaten the functioning of either target system—if they occurred at all. The largest combat maneuver for the year became no more than a staff exercise, rather than a laboratory for improving aerial effectiveness.

A second exercise in 1936 stressed logistics support for air operations in the context of simulated combat conditions. The *exercise technique de l'Armée de l'air*, scheduled to occur between 7 and 12 September, focused on the relationship between logistics doctrine *(l'instruction provisoire sur le service de l'air)* and mobilization procedures. Air service leaders recognized that an air war presented different logistics problems than those found in land and naval conflicts. Achieving and measuring combat effectiveness hinged, in part, on the Armée de l'air's ability to sustain its operational forces in the increased pace of wartime. Therefore the exercise technique tested the mobilization, supply, and armaments components of the logistics system under the watchful eye of General Paul Armengaud, former 37th Aviation Regiment commander in Morocco, now a member of the Conseil supérieur de l'air and *inspecteur de l'aviation de défense métropolitaine et des écoles.*[24]

Armengaud directed the units tasked to participate in the exercise to begin reviewing the applicable regulations. On 7 August, one month before the scheduled starting date, he also ordered flying units to begin practicing for simulated combat operations. He urged logistics personnel to pay particular attention to resupply procedures when units moved from their mobilization centers to their initial concentration bases. The key, according to Armengaud, was for the crews to "study the best solutions for obtaining the maximum speed" in generating combat sorties.[25] Armengaud thus predicted that the air force that could generate and sustain the most combat sorties would develop a decisive edge over a slower opponent. This approach encouraged the Armée de l'air to focus on tracking missions flown, rather than on devising procedures for effective targeting.

Night operations presented problems that caused air force leaders to include a significant objective for takeoff, landing, refueling, and rearmament in the dark. Night operations were not as much of a concern at established air bases; during wartime, and especially during the hectic mobilization phase of the early days of a conflict, air service personnel could expect to operate from unimproved fields, with poor lighting and few navigation aids. Armengaud developed part of his scenario to test aircrew skills in night "takeoff and landing using only aircraft lighting."[26]

Additionally, combat operations against a robust enemy air force would result in battle damage to some French aircraft. The exercise technique tasked logistics commanders with establishing emergency airfields to assist those aviators "who find themselves in difficulty during the mission."[27] Finally, Armengaud planned to experiment with offensive airpower tactics during the week-long exercise. He understood the importance of the rail system to French (and German) mobilization plans. Therefore he tasked bombardment units *(aviation lourde de défense)* with studying typical railway components to determine how best to inflict "important cuts" on the system. The epitome of skill in railway operations was to "find the points that are the most vulnerable and the easiest to attack."[28]

Although Armengaud's exercise technique was a minor event compared with the scope of the regular fall maneuvers, it highlighted some serious challenges for the Armée de l'air's future combat effectiveness. The stress that accompanied conditions that approximated combat operations caused severe fatigue among aircrews and maintenance personnel alike. The exercise report identified the following problems:

The numerous hours of alert and waiting imposed upon all personnel, 9 to 10 hours each day on average from Monday to Saturday the 12th . . . often resulted in the absolute impossibility of obtaining suitable meals and rest, rendering the situation of the standby and alert pilots impossible . . . all the personnel of the 1st Group were perpetually in alert status. It is necessary to add that two missions per day and even three, as occurred on Saturday the 12th, resulted in overwork and extreme fatigue. Four pilots of the Group exhibited particularly grave signs of intense fatigue, and one of those four was sent for medical treatment.

The essential functioning of the Group was only assured on the last day by two remaining officers (the Group Commander and the Communications Officer) in the most deplorable conditions and without the slightest possibility of food from 0900 until 1800.[29]

The stoic qualities of French airmen allowed them to rise to the occasion, but just barely. The lessons for actual combat conditions appeared evident, for those who wished to acknowledge them. The line between success and failure in support functions could be very thin; thus the 1936 exercise season rendered valuable data for the leaders of the Armée de l'air.

The 1937 maneuvers marked a departure from the predominantly defensive exercises that had characterized the first three years. The scenario expressed a greatly expanded purpose, compared with the anemic goals of the 1936 maneuvers. The air staff directive that announced the exercise schedule stated that the objective was "to study, in the current organizational cadre of the Armée de l'Air, the conditions for employing, to the greatest possible extent, the Grandes Unités aériennes in offensive and defensive situations."[30] The acknowledgment of such possibilities for airpower represented an expansion of the doctrinal approach that had been absent in earlier fall maneuvers. The defensive objectives that had dominated earlier exercises remained a fixture in the 1937 scenario, but offensive operations opened new prospects for the parti rouge. Bombardment operations were not restricted to daylight hours, but if French forces were to develop proficiency in both day and night bombing

strikes, the airmen would have to experiment with various formation configurations, dawn and dusk attacks, and night navigation procedures to ensure the
bombers arrived at their assigned targets.[31]

The enhanced character of the air service as an autonomous force represented
another interesting feature of the 1937 scenario. For the first time, the air staff
used the term *Grandes Unités aériennes* to describe the conglomeration of air
units that participated in the exercise. Organizing offensive striking power into
a Grande Unité aérienne unified the various categories of French airpower. In
previous exercises, the division of air units according to mission—pursuit, bombardment, reconnaissance, transport, and liaison—had fragmented air service
roles and missions and diluted combat effectiveness. In 1937 the parti rouge,
under the command of General Vuillemin, gathered the various types of aircraft
under a single commander who organized his forces according to campaign and
mission objectives.[32]

This new packaging lent credibility to the possibilities of using aviation as a
dominant, if not the dominant, striking force. This development was not surprising, when considered in light of the offensive goals the air staff had routinely assigned to the parti bleu in earlier maneuvers. It appeared, by 1937, that
French air leaders realized the potential advantages available to an air force that
pursued offensive and defensive goals simultaneously.

Operational and tactical innovation also characterized the new goals. The air
staff used the standard political scenario, adjusted geographically to southeastern France to include a larger maritime aspect, to allow the offensive components of French aviation to attempt the disruption of enemy command and control, supplies, and second-echelon forces. Although largely restricted to attacks
against the enemy army, this vision of aerial action represented a significant innovation compared with the purely defensive maneuvers of earlier scenarios.

But the air staff went further, to include "an experimental combined action
(pursuit, bombers, paratroops) against the rear areas of a land force."[33] The
French paratroops, l'Infanterie de l'air, represented an elite strike force within
the air service, designed for three basic types of missions: "demolition, cover
for an aerial landing, or cover for a terrestrial approach."[34] Thus the 1937 maneuvers witnessed the debut of a new striking arm for the air service.

These maneuvers demonstrated that the Armée de l'air had the conceptual
potential to design operations that could influence the direction of theater-level
war efforts. In 1938, however, the emphasis shifted back to defensive warfare.
DAT and army maneuvers scheduled for August of that year emphasized the necessity of halting a massive enemy air and ground assault. The thème général
included a political twist that had not appeared in previous scenarios. The combatant nations still shared a common border, but several neutral states bounded

BREGUET 690/1
Ground Attack and Light Bomber   Crew–2
Span 50′–6″   Length 32′–1¼″   Height 13′–1¼″

Figure 5. Breguet 690/1 (ground attack and light bomber),
   1936–37
Engine: Hispano Suiza 14Ab (2), 680 hp
Payload: 1,000 kg bombs (2,204.6 lbs)
   Rear gunner, 2
   Fuselage gun, 1
   Front guns (fixed), 2
Weight: 4,500 kg (9,920.7 lbs)
Speed: 4,000 m (13,120 ft.) 480 km/hr (297.6 mph)
Ceiling: 8,000 m (26,240 ft.)
Range: 1,200 km (744 miles)

Issued January, 1939 with A.L. No. 1

BLOCH 131
Bomber

Span 65'-9"   Length 58'-5"   Height 12'-2"

Figure 6. Bloch 131 (bomber-fighter-reconnaissance), 1937
Engine: Gnôme-Rhône 14 No. (2), 880 hp
Payload: 1,000 kg bombs (2,204.6 lbs)
 Rear gunner, 2
 Front gunner, 1
Weight: Loaded 8,000 kg (17,636.8 lbs)
Speed: 4,000 m (13,120 ft.) 400 km/hr (248 mph)
Ceiling: 9,000 m (29,520 ft.)
Range: 1,500 km (930 miles)

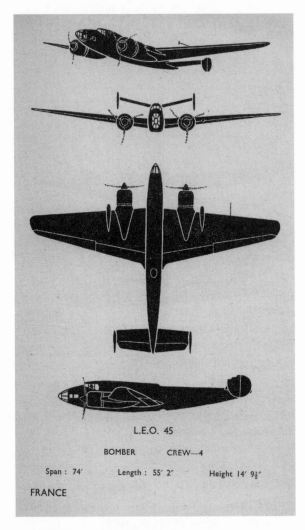

Figure 7. LéO 45 (bomber), 1938
Engine: Hispano Suiza 14Ha (2), 1100 hp
Weight: 11,000 kg (24,250 lbs)
Speed: 4,000 m (13,120 ft.) 483 km/hr (299.4 mph)
Range: 2,600 km (1,612 miles)

the northern zone of the exercise area. Additionally, the scenario departed from the standard designation of the defensive nation as the parti rouge and the aggressor as the parti bleu. The staff directed the parti rouge, now the enemy, to assemble air and land forces east of a line bounded by the towns of Metz, Verdun, Bar-le-Duc, Chaumont, Belfort, and Sarrebourg. The red forces covered their assault on the blue defenders by staging combined air and land maneuvers. War would come unexpectedly, without an official declaration from the red government.[35]

The operational scenario for the blue (defensive) air forces clearly retained some emphasis on offensive operations that had characterized the 1937 maneuvers, despite the overall defensive nature planned for the exercise in 1938. DAT forces received the mission of providing security for land and air forces, as they mobilized and maneuvered into contact with the advancing enemy. This represented the normal role that had been performed by the DAT organization since 1933. The regular Armée de l'air forces were to assume the offensive immediately—a departure from the standard formula, in which the Armée de l'air joined DAT forces to reinforce the defensive effort. The primary mission for the Armée de l'air was "offensive operations, led by bombardment aviation, initially seeking those objectives identified in peacetime with an eye toward attacking the essential sensitive points of enemy aerial and terrestrial maneuver."[36] Thus the autonomous action envisioned in the Grande Unité aérienne organizational structure allowed air force units to restore offensive striking power to French airpower operational concepts, while DAT forces continued to satisfy the army's demands for couverture and reconnaissance aviation.

The possibility that enemy forces would launch a surprise attack with fully mobilized forces caused the scenario authors to include a larger mobilization and logistics component in the 1938 maneuvers. This concern was also a product of problems that had been identified in these systems in earlier exercises. Mobilization procedures focused on developing proficiency among the staff units tasked with processing the large numbers of reservists who would flood the centers when the government placed the nation on a war footing. Additionally, the air staff planned to exercise the air and rail transportation system to evaluate its ability to move personnel and material from mobilization centers to operating areas.[37]

Airpower figured significantly in the logistics component of the exercise. The air staff hoped to experiment with "the rapid resupply of the formations of the Armée de l'Air."[38] This called for placing obsolete LéO 20 biplane bombers at the disposal of the supply depots for aerial transport of critical spare parts. Converted to a transport role, the LéO 20 could deliver limited quantities of parts and fuel to operating bases closer to the front.

This rapid resupply system depended on reliable communications between supply depots, headquarters, and the operational units. The air staff directed two communications units to support the logistics experiment. The headquarters staff would collect requests for material from the operational units, then coordinate with the supply commanders to fill them. A special code established for the experiment ensured that the communications network did not suffer an overload.[39]

A final innovation established in the 1938 scenario involved the use of a radar-like system *(détection éléctromagnétique)* to detect enemy aircraft. The new technology promised to enhance the efficiency of DAT pursuit and antiaircraft units. The plan called for a double line of transmitter-receiver pairs. Overlapping coverage zones for the posts allowed technicians to obtain two independent sources of aircraft course and speed. A central alerting post collected the data and notified by telephone antiaircraft batteries or pursuit units within the overall DAT system.[40]

The 1938 maneuvers clearly represented the most mature and ambitious exercise the Armée de l'air had planned since the service had gained independence in 1933. Unfortunately, the airmen did not have an opportunity to benefit from the full range of activities planned. On 29 July 1938, only one week before the scheduled start date for the exercise, the air minister informed the participants: "The President of the Council, Minister of National Defense and of War has decided that the D.A.T. maneuvers will not be carried out."[41]

Although the defense ministry canceled the full range of maneuvers, the air ministry elected to continue with certain aspects of the exercise. Personnel in the reserves who had received orders to participate continued to their assigned billets, while the DAT passive defense exercises envisioned in the scenario proceeded as planned, along with regularly scheduled DAT training schedules. Certain support units, particularly those that supported field units with communications, photographic services, and fuel, exercised their normal functions.[42] The air service lost, however, its last—and perhaps best—opportunity to prepare for a war against a modern air and land power. After 1938, the exercise pattern reverted to the fragmented application of airpower that had prevailed before the 1937 maneuvers. The Armée de l'air abandoned the offensive strategies that had showed potential in 1937 and in the aborted scenario for 1938.

The way that the exercise scenarios of the 1930s evolved in sophistication and detail reveals that the leaders of the Armée de l'air considered a full spectrum of airpower missions. However, several tendencies emerged: a trend that subordinated air resources to ground maneuver elements, a willingness to "rig" the outcome of the exercises, and the seemingly inescapable tendency to conceive of airpower as another ground reserve.

In spite of these tendencies, the steady increase in complexity demonstrates a level of creativity and innovation not normally credited to French airmen of the interwar years. What the scenarios do not reveal, however, is the degree of realism that the airmen experienced during the course of the exercises and maneuvers. If the aircrews had to conform rigidly to the script established in the various thèmes généraux, the air staff only reinforced institutional policies. If, on the other hand, the scenarios represented a departure point from which airmen could explore the possibilities, the maneuvers filled a vital institutional role in the process of developing French airpower theory and doctrine.

Realism in Exercises and Maneuvers

The progress of scenario development followed a path of increasing complexity and sophistication. Air service leaders gradually pushed the boundaries of airpower employment away from the limited, cooperative roles that were the legacy of the World War I battlefield. The scenarios also pushed the limits of airpower beyond the purely defensive strategies that dominated army employment concepts. By 1937 the leaders of the Armée de l'air successfully incorporated elements of the unified air battle — lutte aérienne — into the annual maneuvers. Scenario design was, however, only one element of the process.

An analysis of how the exercises and maneuvers of the 1930s influenced French air doctrine would be incomplete without examining the relationships between the objectives and the execution of the missions outlined in each scheduled maneuver. As the airmen reviewed the scenarios and their own performance, they provided valuable information for refining their doctrines.

One of the continuing problems that the air staff reports identified related to the lack of proficiency among air force personnel as they performed their assigned duties. In an indirect way, this contributed to a lack of realism in the execution of the exercises and maneuvers. The emphasis on providing basic proficiency training, rather than on rehearsing for operational uses of airpower, corrupted objectives. Staff assessments highlighted this systemic problem in nearly every exercise, for nearly every military specialty, throughout the 1930s.

The combined maneuvers for 1934 revealed "the necessity of developing tactical awareness among [aircrew] observers . . . by making them participate regularly in [map and field] exercises with Army units (Grandes Unités terrestres)."[43] In 1935 the lack of familiarity with aircraft radio equipment and communication security procedures resulted in a flight commander transmitting a message that could have compromised his mission.[44] During a 1936 exercise, a bomber formation made an unscheduled landing because their fuel load was insufficient.[45]

Air service personnel assigned to support specialties on the ground performed as poorly as some of their aviator brethren did. General Armengaud observed that the 1935 maneuvers highlighted "the importance of frequent training for personnel of the General Security Service."[46] One officer reported training-related problems encountered in a heavy equipment company during an exercise, but the officer in charge was not to blame. The reporting officer noted: "The faults committed [by the company commander] do not seem to stem from a lack of zeal on his part, and I believe they are excusable in part for the following reasons: he was designated to take command of the Company only at the last minute—replacing a Reserve Officer who had proved unsatisfactory. He assumed his position with extremely vague notions of his role and almost no information about the exercise."[47]

Therefore, considering these examples of poorly trained personnel, the first assessment of the degree of realism leads to a condemnation of the unit proficiency training programs. To be sure, the same results caused by poorly prepared personnel would have produced unsatisfactory results in combat. In this sense, the sorry state of the Armée de l'air's proficiency training translated into realistic exercise performance. In another sense, however, the consistently poor effectiveness demonstrated by airmen and ground support personnel lent an unrealistic character to the exercises that diverted attention from the air staff's stated objectives and led to erroneous conclusions. In other words, at times the inadequate performance by the aircrews and ground personnel who manned the tactical units prevented the air staff from realizing the goals of the various maneuvers. But the lack of realism was not always the fault of the airmen and ground technicians—often the air staff manipulated the exercise, resulting in less realistic operating conditions.

The state of the French economy, brought on by the worldwide economic crisis, often prompted the air staff to accept circumstances that fell sort of realism in the implementation of exercises in the 1930s. When compelled to limit the forces or situation of a particular maneuver because of economic constraints, the air staff often rendered an honest assessment of how the absence of the resources had affected the outcome of the exercise. For example, in 1934 the fiscal situation precluded full use of pursuit aviation. One consequence of this was that reconnaissance units ranged along the army lines without the normal pursuit escorts. This limitation also applied to the enemy forces, thus allowing friendly reconnaissance aircraft to loiter in their search areas for longer periods. The obvious result was that the information obtained by the observers was of a very high quality. The exercise evaluators emphasized the importance of explaining the constraints that a realistic air war would impose upon reconnaissance units. They expressed concerns that ground commanders would become dependent on rapid, easily obtained aerial reconnaissance and photographic support.[48]

Perhaps the most counterproductive constraint that the air staff placed upon the exercises involved intentionally unrealistic procedures. When this occurred, officers tasked to evaluate often openly criticized the results. In 1935 General d'Harcourt noted: "The operations envisaged for the attacking force directed a one-hour flight over obligatory checkpoints . . . the initiative of the mission commanders was singularly reduced because of these directives."[49] General Armengaud echoed d'Harcourt's criticisms. He commented on the meticulous preparations by pursuit units that had preceded the 1935 maneuvers; the result was a mechanical presentation of this portion of the exercise. In Armengaud's opinion, "pursuit aviation was [for all purposes] only represented by the command airplanes."[50] According to the Armée de l'air's own senior officers, the rigid controls placed on the air forces threatened to degrade the already questionable capabilities of the air service's combat units.

On a more positive note, the air staff's repeated attempts to impose rigid controls often revealed the folly of such policies. As the scenarios unfolded, the airmen began to experience the complex realities of modern air war. And in doing so, they gained proficiency and confidence in performing their assigned tasks. One report noted: "If the experience [using aircraft without radios for pursuit intercepts] failed from a tactical point of view, it was by contrast a success from a technical point of view."[51] Because air service personnel did not have the required levels of proficiency before participating in the exercises, however, they robbed their service of valuable opportunities to test doctrine and force employment concepts.

The alerting network (réseau de guet), a key component of the DAT system, handled large volumes of messages. The exercise reports identified a recurring trend in the network's message-processing function. Invariably, during the first day of each exercise, the communications components of the DAT system handled messages very slowly; by the end of the scheduled activities, however, communications technicians adapted to the pace of simulated combat operations. In the critical areas of communications and warning procedures, the flow of information between alerting outposts and the various intermediate and higher headquarters represented one of the most important measures of effectiveness for the air staff.

As early as the 1934 maneuvers, air leaders realized the importance of improving the communication system on the ground and in the air. Abuses of the network disrupted the aerial reconnaissance effort and caused some crews to land before completing their assigned missions.[52] The 1935 maneuvers revealed ten- to seventeen-minute delays in transmitting to higher headquarters information about enemy overflights of lookout posts. Once messages reached headquarters, the dispatch of pursuit units to intercept the incoming enemy formations required from fifty-four to an interminable one hour and twenty-seven minutes.[53]

In the 1937 *grandes manoeuvres aériennes,* the communications network handled 6,526 messages during the first three days. The average elapsed time required to notify the higher headquarters that enemy aircraft had penetrated the frontier dropped dramatically from six and a half minutes on the first day to one minute and forty-five seconds on the third. The intercept time dropped correspondingly, from an average of twenty-one minutes on the first day to approximately six minutes by the third.[54] This striking improvement demonstrated the validity of the exercise as a training tool. Unfortunately, however, the air staff did not establish training objectives for the exercises and maneuvers. Instead, air force leaders intended for them to be opportunities to assess operational and tactical employment concepts.

Thus several competing trends influenced the degree of realism that the Armée de l'air could impart to the scenarios for the exercises and maneuvers during the 1930s. Economic constraints limited the number and types of forces used. A specific script—using well-rehearsed plans or failing to allow unrestrained combat simulation—directed by the air staff emphasized certain aspects of airpower employment at the expense of others. This tended to make the exercise resemble a play, rather than an operational wargame focused on employing airpower. Finally, the low level of combat readiness on the part of air force personnel exerted the most damaging effect on the Armée de l'air's initiatives.

Although this last trend diluted the intended purpose of the activities, it also gave air force leaders a valuable gauge against which to measure the effectiveness of their training systems, the technical and tactical proficiency of their personnel, and the adequacy of their doctrine. The perceptive critiques provided by officers such as Generals Armengaud, d'Harcourt, and others reveal that service leaders were far from ignorant of the problems that plagued French airpower. The final area to examine concerns how airmen used the information gleaned from the exercises and maneuvers of the 1930s to refine their doctrine.

Exercises, Maneuvers, and Doctrine

French airmen often made honest attempts to use service exercises as vehicles for refining doctrine. The consistent identification of experimental agenda in the scenarios confirms this fact. Just as several trends placed constraints on achieving higher levels of realism, however, there were also propensities that prevented service leaders from translating lessons into doctrine. In some instances, such as the search for a more offensive role for airpower, the service experienced limited successes. In others a host of factors, including interservice rivalry, economic constraints, technological development, and grand strategy, prevented a full implementation of doctrinal changes. Yet the concerns expressed in the scenarios for the aerial maneuvers reveal another clue to the multifaceted nature of reactive air doctrine.

One of the most important doctrinal precepts that characterized the exercises of the 1930s concerned the command and control of aerial resources in the context of a theater-level war. This issue came to symbolize the struggle for service autonomy. Airmen had to choose either to allow land and sea commanders to define the scope and purpose of air service objectives, or to establish patterns that emphasized the ways in which airpower could achieve objectives independent of, as well as in concert with, the other services. Air service leaders argued that even when airpower acted in support of land or naval forces, the most effective use of aviation lay in decentralizing mission taskings.[55]

The law that established the air service compounded the confusion surrounding command relationships. Certain air force units automatically came under the authority of army or navy commanders in time of war. The air commanders in these situations retained administrative authority over aviation assets, but the land or sea officers exercised operational authority over the air units placed at their disposal. To complicate matters further, the Armée de l'air created a wartime command structure separate from that of the peacetime Régions aériennes.[56] General Armengaud used his critique of the 1935 maneuvers to comment on the dangers of this divided command structure:

The Command of the Armée de l'Air in peacetime has the serious defect of being different from that in war. It is necessary, at the very least, to give the Commander of Aerial Defense and each of his two assistants (Heavy and Light Aviation) the opportunity, through the preparation and execution of a general maneuver, to assume command of the units which will come under his authority in the event of hostilities. It is only in this way that these general officers and their staffs can train for the tasks that will befall them on Day J [the initiation of hostilities], when they will be called upon to assume their duties rapidly.[57]

Armengaud did not comment on the loss of service authority to the army and navy commands; rather, he deplored the self-imposed fragmentation of the aerial effort inherent in the air service's flawed organizational doctrine. If air force leaders refused to acknowledge this serious failing in their basic approach, the least they could do, according to Armengaud, was to incorporate the wartime command structure into the exercise scenarios.[58]

In the 1937 maneuvers, the situation deteriorated further for the blue air force commander. By the third day of the exercise, all of the available air units passed to army and navy command authority, rendering the commander of the 3ème Armée aérienne a leader with no forces to lead.[59] The command structure reverted to the pattern established in the days when aviation had served as a combatant arm of the army. That is, the senior aviator received mission orders from the commanders of the Grandes Unités terrestres. Even worse, the air service conformed to army planning procedures. This applied to the extent of requiring orders for air units' operational missions to originate from army headquarters, using army message formats.

Another doctrinal theme that formed a regular feature of the air maneuvers of the 1930s centered on the tension between offensive and defensive uses of airpower. This represented the most important source of reactive air doctrine, because airpower's inherent offensive capabilities clashed with prevailing government policies and army doctrine. But in the intense interservice rivalries that characterized the French military establishment in the 1930s, exercises and maneuvers served as poor laboratories for exploring *both* offensive and defensive applications of airpower.

As French air doctrine matured, the experimental agenda broadened to incorporate a greater variety of operational roles. Consider the limited vision expressed in the 1934 maneuvers, in which aviation performed as an airborne scouting force for the army. The reporting official noted: "This year marked very sensible progress in the 'Information Search Plan' . . . The questions asked were clear and specific regarding the priority of possibilities for Aviation; the times, the places that were necessary to reach were clearly defined."[60] This represented more than a defensive attitude, more than a force that was subordinate to a higher authority. The stance reflected in this assessment conveys a lack of vision for how air force leaders could define objectives outside the context of land warfare. The air service's own critique of operations in the 1934 maneuvers revealed a tentative approach to warfare that failed to consider ways to seize the initiative. Airmen waited for their army counterparts to delegate tactical missions before considering how to use their special skills to achieve theater and national objectives. This marked one of the defining characteristics of reactive doctrine in the context of the exercises and maneuvers. Because airmen depended on army commanders to express the range and scope of campaigns, they restricted to tactical and technical matters their concerns about employing airpower.

In the 1935 maneuvers, exercise evaluators looked more deeply into the consequences of how aerial attacks affected operations. The focus remained, however, on tactical rather than strategic or operational results. This continuing trend is not surprising, considering the recurring problems that the service experienced with technical proficiency. In bombardment operations, evaluators examined how prescribed tactics worked against area targets. Experiments with changes in routes and altitudes revealed that French bomber crews were not ready to adapt to a fluid air war.[61]

Thus another fixture of reactive doctrine began to influence offensive operations. French bomber doctrine began to rely upon mission commanders who directed every aspect of the attack. These commanders became the focal point for successful tactical bombardment operations. And because of the emphasis on multirole aircraft, the same structure migrated into other aviation specialties. The mission commander became the source of creativity and initiative for tactical operations in the Armée de l'air. Aircrews received orders and mission changes from him, and, absent his direction, could only appeal to higher authority for guidance.

The most damning characteristic of the doctrinal lessons that air service leaders pulled from the exercises and maneuvers of the 1930s was the lack of independent conceptions of aerial warfare. The service published a doctrine that expressed a wide range of missions, but strategic conditions in France lent primacy to defensive forms of warfare. Airpower offered the means to halt enemy advances, to strike at second-echelon forces, and to threaten vital centers. French air doctrine accounted for all of these possibilities in the concept of the lutte aérienne. The exercises and maneuvers of the 1930s failed, however, to realize the promise of the doctrine. The scenarios for aerial maneuvers never accounted for the possibility of an air campaign without an accompanying ground campaign.

Thus the doctrinal pronouncements that advocated the primacy of aerial warfare over the battle on the ground never appeared in the exercise and maneuver agenda during the 1930s. Moreover, the ground wars envisioned in the scenarios remained static events, in which armies relied upon airpower to detect enemy attempts to outflank friendly forces. The army's constant demand for aerial reconnaissance quickly consumed the available aviation resources that the Armée de l'air could provide. Consequently, the doctrine and the scenarios expressed in the maneuvers and exercises failed to connect with the actual employment of French airpower.

Because of the wide gulf that existed between doctrinal pronouncements and the actual employment of air forces, the leaders of the Armée de l'air focused almost exclusively on obtaining solutions to tactical problems. Tactical success is certainly an important aspect of measuring military effectiveness, and the Armée de l'air certainly needed a great deal of attention in the tactical arena. The problem came in how French airmen measured success in the context of exercise and maneuver performance. When objectives described a measure of success in terms of providing security (couverture) for air or land forces, it usually applied to sorties flown or to reports transmitted—neither of which translated readily into security.

Similarly, bombardment crews earned high marks for delivering bombs near their assigned targets. Often the evaluators failed to specify how close to the targets the aircrews delivered their ordnance. Even worse, exercise planners never attempted to correlate the type of ordnance with the particular targets; in the French view of bombardment exercises, one size fit all.

The concern for tactical measures blinded French airmen to operational problems. Fragmented command structures represented the tip of the iceberg. The lack of adequate training for regulars and reserves certainly hindered the success of many exercises. This was not a question of regular forces receiving preference for training and equipment over reserve forces—neither regulars nor reserves received adequate preparation for their wartime missions. But the responsible leaders in the air service never seemed to connect the poor performance in maneuvers to potential combat effectiveness.

The vision of aerial warfare appeared to incorporate a rapidly changing air battle. The results of air maneuvers proved this a façade. French airmen were ill equipped to cope with mission changes in any aspect—reconnaissance, pursuit, bombardment, or attack. Rigid command structures at headquarters gave way to inflexible combat applications in the formations. The dependence on mission commanders limited adaptability and initiative, while it created vulnerability in the tactical units.

Unfortunately for France, Armée de l'air leaders approached these deepseated problems from a managerial perspective. Rather than reforming operational procedures, the air staff argued for adjustments to the *tableaux d'effectifs*. Rather than directing changes to unit proficiency training programs, the air staff proposed studies of the system. And, perhaps most harmful of all, rather than evaluating exercise performance against an established doctrinal standard, air leaders failed to apply any standard of effectiveness to the results of the exercises of the 1930s. The true, and only, measure of effectiveness for the Armée de l'air came in the crucible of war in 1940.

6   The Dénouement of French Airpower Doctrine
Mobilization, Offensive Plans, and War

[T]he preparation of an army today seems inseparable from that of a premeditated offensive or from the exact determination of an anticipated attack.[1]

The Armée de l'air's plans for mobilization and war drifted from the needs of national strategy, as French air doctrine assumed reactive characteristics in response to the shifting international political environment and the various missions and tasks assigned to the service in the late 1930s. The result was a mobilization and war-fighting system that failed to meet the demands placed upon it by the government and the army. Much like the maneuvers and exercises, the training system, and the doctrine that spawned them all, mobilization and operational performance in the Armée de l'air focused on procedure, paperwork, and rigid organizational practices, rather than on essential operational and tactical tasks needed to employ airpower against an aggressive foe.

Mobilization presented unique problems for the Armée de l'air, because the service required greater numbers of educated and technically skilled personnel than did the army. Despite their awareness of the problems, however, air service leaders failed to devise solutions that placed trained pilots, bombardiers, gunners, observers, and support personnel in combat units quickly and efficiently. The system failed to provide ample numbers of personnel to meet the Armée de l'air's operational and tactical missions. The mobilization process failed to bridge the gap that existed between war preparation activities and the service's operational war-fighting needs. Consequently, the Armée de l'air failed the test of combat against Germany in the spring of 1940.

A Mobilization System for Reactive Airpower

In many ways, the mobilization problem that the Armée de l'air confronted in the 1930s mirrored the one faced by the army, despite the different missions and personnel requirements that separated the two services. The tragic wastage of the Great War left a male population in tatters. Many who survived the blood-letting of 1914–18 bore the marks of their experiences in the form of missing limbs, blindnesss, deafness, or debilitating psychological disorders. The French birthrate, already in decline before the war, continued its downward trend after a brief recovery in the early 1920s. Politically, as a viable national policy, many Frenchmen saw little future in pursuing war. Agriculture dominated the French economy, with most of the industrial capacity concentrated in the vulnerable north and northeastern sections of the country.

Industrial plants, particularly the aviation industry, hewed to a craftsman ethic in France, where the concept of developing institutions and production practices geared toward competing in modern, machine-age warfare lagged behind the leading industrialized nations. During his second term as air minister (1936–38) under the Popular Front government, Pierre Cot unsuccessfully attempted to persuade airplane manufacturers to adopt mass-production methods. He also pushed aviation firms such as Breguet and Lioré to relocate from the highly vulnerable area near Paris to the more secure southwestern part of the country. When the firms resisted his suggestions, Cot provoked a confrontation by attempting to nationalize the aviation industries. The conflict between Cot and the aircraft company owners exacerbated the aerial rearmament crisis in the late 1930s, while simultaneously complicating domestic policy for Léon Blum's Popular Front.[2] Finally, as national policy drifted toward a defensive posture, the military—in particular the army—approached the mobilization problem in ways more suited to fighting a nineteenth-century conflict, rather than the one in which France found herself in 1940.[3] The Armée de l'air adopted a similar outdated scheme.

The general philosophy that governed mobilization centered on balancing access to national material and manpower resources, gathering them rapidly, and providing a secure environment in which to convert raw materials into effective combat power.[4] The air service inherited the army's regional scheme for mobilizing personnel. As young men entered eligibility for military service at the age of eighteen, they received assignments to regional centers where they reported for basic and periodic training and, in the event of war, for mobilization. The centers performed administrative support functions—they served as conduits for channeling men from their assigned regions (which were not necessarily near their homes or their assigned units) to their concentration centers.

To make the mobilization task more manageable, the Armée de l'air divided the force into categories (echelons A, B1, and B) based upon active-duty or reserve status, military specialization skills, and level of training. In the early years of service independence, air service leaders expected to mobilize 54 groups (26 bombardment, 17 pursuit, and 11 reconnaissance) within four hours of receiving orders from the government or the air staff.[5] Later in the decade these numbers would change, to include 33 bombardment groups, 23 pursuit, and 34 reconnaissance.[6] The remainder of the Armée de l'air would report for duty within fifteen days of the mobilization declaration.

Air staff regulations reflected the assumption that there would be ample time for notifying, processing, and transporting adequate numbers of previously trained personnel to tactical and operational commands. Moreover, mobilization planners assumed that each unit would have the proper equipment assigned in complicated, comprehensive *tableaux d'effectifs de guerre*.[7] Neither condition existed during the interwar period.

As early as 1920, when the air service functioned as a branch of the army, the 9th Army Corps commander reported deficits of 160 personnel in his observation regiment, and 494 in his pursuit regiment.[8] By 1929 General Gamelin, then commander of the 20th Military Region, reported that an inspection of a bombardment unit under his command had revealed that "[i]n its current state, the regiment is incapable of entering a campaign because of the lack of airplanes and engines."[9] In a similar report, Général de brigade Rolland noted: "From the perspective of flying material," the 2d Aviation Regiment, stationed near the strategically important city of Strasbourg, "was for quite a while absolutely incapable of participating in a campaign."[10]

Clearly some of the problems in the 1920s stemmed from overzealous demobilization policies (in the case of the 1920 personnel shortage) and the reluctance of the government to fund procurement and modernization in favor of the debilitating *politique des prototypes*.[11] The solution that the Armée de l'air leadership implemented hinged upon creating a rational, regulation-driven mobilization system that attempted to address both the personnel and material sides of the problem.[12]

In November 1934 General Victor Denain, serving as air minister, issued instructions that established the fundamental precepts for mobilizing the Armée de l'air for war.[13] The service would not depart from the assumptions contained in this regulation for the remainder of the decade. Air staff leaders recognized the serious drain that mobilization would impose on the nation. They noted:

"It is impossible to envisage . . . the *permanent* life of the Air Force in a war footing and in a state of alert."[14] From this perspective, the social, political, and economic implications of maintaining the air service in a state of perpetual alert could potentially traumatize France almost as much as would a war. The air staff rationalized away this scenario by observing that enemy "preparations for a surprise attack will not pass completely unnoticed by the intelligence services, which could provide a few hours' warning."[15] Therefore air service leaders constructed a system that placed force segments in progressively higher alert stages, according to the intensity of international political tensions.

The progressive alerting procedural layers afforded flexibility to the leaders by allowing them to tailor the force in reaction to the immediate threat. Thus they intended to alleviate the negative effects on the French social and economic structure of a prolonged period of alert and mobilization. Alert conditions progressed by stages—*service normal, service spécial, alerte no. 1, alerte no. 2, and couverture et mobilisation générale*—characterized by the time allowed to ready the force for combat operations. Under service normal conditions, echelon A personnel reported ready for duty within eight hours of initial air ministry tasking. This time decreased to one hour for one-fourth of the units under service spécial.

In times of heightened political tension, the regulation required one-half of the units to respond in less than twenty minutes, with the remaining ones ready for duty within one hour of receiving notification from headquarters. Additionally, alerte no. 1 directed units to move from peacetime bases to forward-located combat airfields. Finally, alerte no. 2 represented the highest peacetime alert status. Under this measure, in addition to the provisions contained in alerte no. 1, all units received reduced reporting times. If the government declared general mobilization, the entire force assumed couverture duties to protect the army and sensitive areas from air attack. When war commenced under this mobilization scheme, the service expected orders to defend against penetrating enemy air formations or to launch attacks against enemy cities and critical industrial areas.[16]

The push to modernize the Armée de l'air's equipment and command structures that began during Pierre Cot's first term as air minister (January 1933–February 1934) and continued under his successor, General Victor Denain, disrupted mobilization processes. Consequently, in January 1936 the air staff issued a directive that aimed "to determine precisely the composition of the mobilized Air Force by 15 April 1936."[17] Several force structure characteristics concerned service leaders. First, air staff members feared the changes that accompanied the expansion and modernization programs of the previous two years may have caused confusion among service members as to their assigned roles in a mobilization scenario. Related to this was a feeling that personnel in the active-duty echelon A category were not prepared to fulfill their assigned tasks throughout the year, owing to the infusion of new equipment. On a tactical note, the air staff sought to insert a measure of realism into mobilization exercises by measuring how the various centers functioned under simulated enemy air attacks. Finally, the leaders intended to measure how new ground support and transportation equipment affected mobilization procedures. The report format for this comprehensive snapshot contained eight prescribed sections that exceeded fifty pages for each unit inspected.[18]

From the air staff perspective, the crucial readiness task for managing the system in peacetime lay in carefully prescribing the assignments that each mobilization center performed. Beginning in 1936, after three years of searching for the most effective way to administer the system, the air staff published overarching guidance for inspecting mobilization-related activities. Under auspices of the regulations, reception centers underwent annual two-part examinations. The first included a thorough audit of the records that documented unit readiness. This included inspections of the *journaux de mobilisation,* the unit regulations library, records of authorized unit strength, and procedures for shifting from a peacetime to a wartime footing.

The journal de mobilisation represented the core document for administering and recording mobilization activities. Filling a dual purpose, it outlined activities each unit accomplished (on an hourly basis) when the government announced mobilization, and it served as an audit tool for inspectors when units participated in the annual inspections.[19] The journal consisted of three parts: (1) a listing of unit operations, including the location of material, transportation equipment, the mobilization reception center organization and operation, quarters, meals, and lodging; (2) an hourly chronology of mobilization activities; (3) supporting documents that described the numbers and specialties of assigned personnel, equipment, purchase orders, mission orders, message traffic, and intelligence information.[20] The basic outline of information required for the journal occupied approximately thirty-five pages, and hourly entries that documented mobilization progress caused the volume to grow in proportion to the flow of operational events.

The second part of the annual inspection focused on evaluating procedures for sustaining combat operations. This examination centered on the relationship between the mobilization center, the combat unit, and associated depots or aviation parks. Fuel and lubricant stocks, spare parts, munitions, and land transportation support for travel between support facilities and tactical units also came under scrutiny.[21] As the inspection scenario forced units to deploy from mobilization centers, the examiners measured how well active-duty units integrated mobilized reservists into effective combat forces. When units reached their initial concentration bases, inspectors evaluated how well logistics elements supported the increased pace of combat operations.

Additionally, the onset of action necessitated more stringent air base defense measures. This extra responsibility gradually became part of the dual Armée de l'air–DAT command structure that evolved later in the 1930s. At this point, the unit evaluation depended on the premobilization readiness of reserve personnel. Supplemental training for them delayed movement from mobilization centers to concentration and initial deployment bases. The degree to which the reserve instruction system provided qualified, combat-ready personnel determined the pace of mobilization and, consequently, the Armée de l'air's tactical and operational capabilities.

Assigning reservists to air service duty presented particularly difficult problems for leaders. Aside from some familiarization training in basic flying principles gained in the national flying clubs, the service depended on its training system to provide adequate numbers of pilots and other aircrew specialties; as discussed earlier, this system proved inadequate for its crucial task.[22] The air staff relied on reserve personnel to provide the majority of less technical (but no less important) skills that the Armée de l'air required to field a fully capable force. Managing the recruiting system for this presented complex challenges, as staff officers attempted to fill the noncommissioned officer and enlisted ranks in seventy-three separate skilled jobs, ranging from pilots to meteorological specialists.[23]

Selecting personnel to fill the reserve ranks fell to the commanders of the various air regions. Each year they searched the nation's eighteen-year-old classes for young men with the requisite aptitude for service in the Armée de l'air. Air staff regulations stipulated that the commanders fill their ranks from within their own regions before looking to others for skilled recruits. The process consumed approximately three months, as the regional commanders and their staffs competed for individuals, weighed costs—in terms of money and time—of training and travel to place the recruit in his unit, and compiled the final lists of assignments.[24]

The uncertain nature of the reserve manpower pool, coupled with the French government's persistent refusal to authorize funds to expand the service, forced air staff leaders to rely upon active-duty personnel to provide most of the combat power with which the service would fight a war.[25] For example, regulations specified that nonflying active-duty personnel would assume their duties six weeks after indoctrination, while flying personnel reported to their units upon completing the training syllabus specified for their assigned aircraft and mission. By contrast, the regulations did not establish timelines for incorporating reserves into the force. At best, they could complete the ranks of the echelon B or B1 positions in the mobilization scheme.[26]

The regulations that governed mobilization exercises in the 1930s emphasized the administrative role performed by air service personnel at the regional centers. The 1936 rule specified that exercises could include practice in loading (preparing personnel and equipment for transport), railroad embarkment, alert, dispersal, and complete mobilization of one or more units.[27] In other words, the annual mobilization inspections and exercises represented attempts to fine-tune the processes required to fill air service ranks, rather than relating the ultimate contribution of conscripts and reserves to executing operational war plans.

Mobilization orders represented the crucial administrative link between the individual and the Armée de l'air. The orders described the individual's specialty, his assigned center, the method and route of travel between his home and the center, and the actions he should take when the government placed the armed forces in a heightened defense posture. As one regulation described the mobilization order: "[It] constitutes on the one hand a *transportation order* and on the other a *letter of service.*"[28] Eugenia Kiesling notes that it could qualify certain specialties, especially in the reserve officer corps, for first-class railway passes as incentives for pursuing supplemental training courses.[29] In any event, such simple measures could not rectify the flaws in the mobilization system.

By December 1937 the defects began to manifest themselves to the leaders in the air ministry. One report noted that inspections of "several air bases" had revealed deficiencies in mobilization-related areas. At the most elementary level, the air service—whether the fault lay with the staff or with the regional commanders is unclear—failed to man the critical centers adequately. Given the central administrative role that these centers performed in the Armée de l'air's war plans, this deficiency is puzzling, to say the least. A related personnel issue that impaired effectiveness centered on the training system's failure to provide experienced personnel to fill reserve billets. This should not have surprised the air staff, as the system faltered when tasked to provide fully qualified personnel for the active-duty force. Finally, and most important from the air staff perspective, the mobilization centers lacked sufficient supply stocks for the war preparation programs that service regulations charged them to administer.[30]

The air staff assigned mobilized members of the Armée de l'air to operational units according to the *tableaux d'emploi de l'Armée de l'air dans la métropole.*[31] The original version of this document appeared as Plan E in 1936–37. Beginning in 1938, subsequent modifications appeared under the label Plan E-1. This represented the highest level of mobilization planning documented by the air service in the interwar period. It provided instructions for identifying each unit according to combat specialty, assigned headquarters, and location, and it scheduled time and dates for completing mobilization activities. Plan E and the later variants remained consistent with the mobilization philosophy established

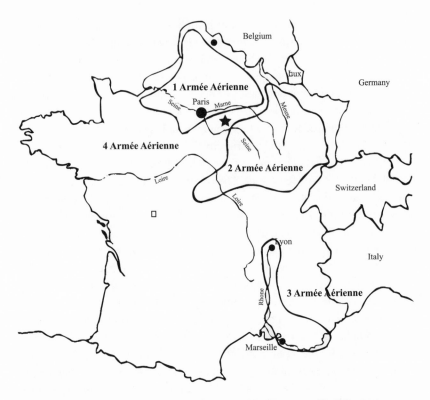

Map 1. Armée aérienne deployment (S.H.A.A., série 2B, carton 23, "Plan E-1: Mobilisation")

earlier in the decade, by requiring the entire force to complete mobilization within fifteen days of receiving orders from Paris.

When fully combat-ready, the Armée de l'air consisted of three air armies headquartered at Paris, Aix-en-Provence, and North Africa. Mobilization times for the headquarters units and their subordinate command centers ranged from two to six hours. Plan E provisions assigned echelon A personnel to these units, to allow them to complete their assigned preparation tasks within the allotted times. The exception to this general rule occurred in aerostation headquarters units that mobilized with the Armée de l'air, outside the DAT command structure. These included echelon B reservists, who reported for duty no earlier than M+3 (three days after the first day of mobilization) and no later than M+13.[32]

To provide mission-oriented taskings, the air staff devised a series of pre-planned orders that directed units to take action in response to increasing international political tension. The regulation that established these procedures described nine groups of orders. Either the air minister or the commanders of

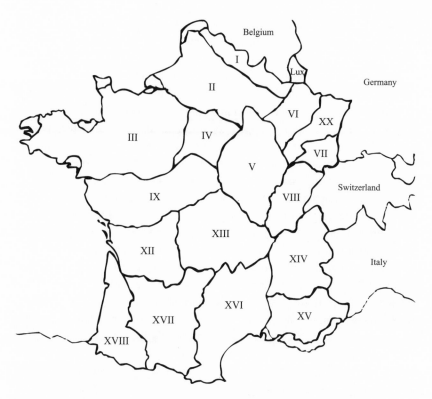

Map 2. DAT air defense regional structure (S.H.A.A., série 2B, carton 23, "Plan E-1: Mobilisation")

the air regions could invoke the prescriptions, if they judged the political situation critical enough to warrant mobilizing all or part of their assigned forces. The regional commanders' authority did not extend, however, to obtaining emergency equipment requisitions—the regulation appeared to grant the authority to protect their assigned areas of responsibility, but not to fight a war without approval from Paris. Alerting messages were divided into nine groups; in all, fifty-four separate communications were available concerning actions that ordered air units to act alone or in conjunction with land or sea commands. Additionally, the message groups included provisions for securing civil aviation facilities that could support air service operational and tactical requirements.[33]

The central administration of mobilization activities provided forces for airpower combat operations by the regional commanders. The greatest complication that air service leaders envisioned involved an unexpected aerial attack against French military and economic centers of gravity. If this occurred, the Armée de l'air relied on existing active-duty or partially mobilized reserves to counter the enemy. Leaders hesitated, however, to commit air forces to combat without unequivocal government permission—even when faced with an enemy strike. General Vuillemin, chief of the Armée de l'air, issued orders in 1939 directing tactical units "to open fire on suspected or presumed enemy aircraft only if the order to do so has been given by the Minister, or by the regional air commanders . . . in no case, even in a pursuit, should Air Force crews cross the frontier before the order to open hostilities has been given by the government."[34] Thus, according to this philosophy, air service commanders and their men walked a delicate line between responding to air attacks on one hand, and respecting air ministry concerns of provoking a war on the other.

Force protection during mobilization further complicated operational readiness for the Armée de l'air. Dispersing tactical units to satellite airfields represented one solution, but in an emergency, this carried some inherent problems that hampered operational and tactical effectiveness. For pursuit and bombardment units, dispersal made force concentration against penetrating enemy formations difficult to achieve. Scattering the force among dispersal fields also introduced complications to logistics a system that already had great difficulty supporting operations. One regulation directed dispersed formations "to use the best local resources, and eventually those of the neighboring air bases . . . to assure their logistical support."[35] Finally, the poor state of communications technology and procedures within the Armée de l'air further complicated the task of responding to rapidly changing conditions when the force spread out.

Armée de l'air personnel tried to create a mobilization system that provided the men and material to fight an international war. They sought to balance the needs of national strategy, social mood, economy, and operational effectiveness, while simultaneously expanding the force structure. All this occurred within the constraints of a flawed recruiting and training system, a flawed logistical support system, and an operational philosophy that placed commanders in the unenviable position of balancing decisions about when they could defend their commands against the risks of starting a major war or widening a conflict in its early stages by escalating the level of violence.

At its core, the mobilization system represented little more than an administrative tool; it allowed the air staff to focus on evaluating processes rather than on employing airpower at the strategic, operational, and tactical levels of war. This does not mean that air leaders failed to consider these subjects. But as the 1930s raced to a close, the schism that prevailed between the mobilization system and French conceptions of how a future air war would progress did not bode well for the Armée de l'air's operational effectiveness.

Offensive Strategies for Operational Warfare

Despite the increasing focus on defensive measures and army support missions that dominated air service attention in the late 1930s, the promise of offensive aerial warfare continued to occupy air staff planners in the Deuxième Bureau, the intelligence service, as war drew near. The statutory precedent for offensive strikes against German centers of gravity had originated in the 1934 law that confirmed the air service's independence.[36] That decree included a requirement for independent air operations, as well as those that supported the army and the navy. The all-encompassing *lutte aérienne* that described a seamless air campaign in basic doctrine manuals represented a vision that merged the independent and cooperative missions into a manageable doctrinal structure. The result, from an offensive viewpoint, materialized in the form of a series of thoroughly developed target dossiers that sought to strike at the heart of several critical elements of the German capacity to wage war.

This aspect of French airpower history does not appear in any other study of the interwar Armée de l'air.[37] The level of air staff analysis that supported these dossiers indicates a conceptual approach to strategic and operational airpower employment equal in sophistication to that of any major nation of the interwar period. Moreover, reviewing the dossiers' contents allows a greater appreciation for the intellectual depth of French theory, as the air staff's conception of offensive air warfare related to the comprehensive aerial battle described in the lutte aérienne. Tragically, however, the plans represented little more than staff exercises, as the Armée de l'air failed to muster the resources to wage a defensive campaign to support the army, while simultaneously pursuing offensive campaigns that remained a fundamental element of reactive air doctrine.

The Service historique de l'Armée de l'air archives contain sixteen cartons with materials related to strategic and operational targets in Germany. Additionally, there are four with similar materials on targets in Spain, and fourteen that provide information on Italian target systems. Documents in these cartons date from the early 1920s through 1940. A clear understanding of how the French planned to wage offensive aerial warfare against their potential enemies emerges from an analysis of these target dossiers and supporting materials. The intensity of the threat resulted in the most comprehensive target packages for an air war against Germany. Packages for Spain and Italy conformed to the general pattern established for the German systems.[38]

The French approach to strategic and operational air warfare stemmed from an understanding of the enemy state as an industrial war-fighting system. This way of thinking resembled characteristics of the U.S. Army Air Corps' high-altitude precision daylight bombardment doctrine developed at the Air Corps Tactical School in the 1930s.[39] Armée de l'air planners reasoned that several critical industries and supporting systems (aircraft production, Luftwaffe air bases, petroleum production and distribution, chemical industries, electric power, transportation networks, and urban areas) sustained civil and war-related production. If such targets suffered accurate aerial attacks, the cascading results could help to shorten a war.

Yet French offensive calculations did not conform exactly to those of the Americans, who tended to emphasize material effects of bombing operations rather than morale consequences. This obtained in large part because American airmen favored a scientific approach to warfare that required measurable, systematic input and feedback. Psychological effects defied such rational, linear calculations. British airmen, on the other hand, led for the first decade of the interwar years by Hugh Trenchard, accepted the premise that bringing civilian populations under air attack would have synergistic material and morale repercussions.[40] The French adopted an approach that resembled elements of both British and American theories, but the French attitude toward targeting evolved along a subtly different path.

The German aviation threat caused French planners in the Deuxième Bureau to place the Reich aeronautical industry high on the target priority list. This decision remained consistent with the lutte aérienne doctrine that envisioned an air superiority campaign as one of the defining characteristics of a future aerial war. Moreover, the theory presented by the Italian theorist Giulio Douhet emphasized the importance of destroying the enemy air forces as a prerequisite for success in future war. Douhet wrote: "Aerial warfare will be intense and violent to a superlative degree; for each side will realize the necessity of inflicting upon the enemy the largest possible losses in the shortest possible time, and of ridding the air of enemy aerial means so as to prevent any possible retaliation from him . . . no reliance can be placed on forces to be activated during the war. One who is defeated will not be able to create another air force."[41] Thierry Vivier argues that beginning in 1933, the ministerial team of Pierre Cot and General Victor Denain institutionalized this Douhetist emphasis on winning the air superiority battle, to allow subsequent concentration on the broader lutte aérienne against the entire range of enemy war-fighting capabilities.[42]

The doctrinal emphasis on winning the initial aerial battle influenced the French analysis of German aeronautical industries. Raw materials, especially aluminum processing plants, represented critical nodes in the aircraft production system. French bomber range and payload capabilities limited planning options for all target systems. Consequently, for the aluminum industry, planners based their calculations on a 300-kilometer (186-mile) combat radius from

French airfields near the Franco-German border (Metz, Strasbourg, Belfort). Of fifteen facilities within this radius, planners in 1938 proposed that "simultaneous destruction of six factories (Höchst, Dölau, Lauta, Greveubroich, Mündenheim, and Ludwigshafen) will result in a long delay in the fabrication of light aluminum alloys."[43] Target dossiers for the critical factories included aeronautical charts oriented to the preferred approach path, detailed analyses of surrounding air defense components, and, in some cases, overhead or ground-level photographs of the factory.

The potential for dispersing component industries caused French planners to concentrate on aircraft manufacturing plants that assembled major components and finished airframes, rather than on smaller component-production facilities. The strategic objective that governed target selection stemmed from a desire "to interdict the material as close as possible to its delivery to the units."[44] The Deuxième Bureau reports appeared reluctant to characterize any single target set as a panacea that would bring about the cascading collapse of German airpower. Supporting analysis in the target packages warned, "the effects [of aerial bombardment] will not last long, because the necessary equipment and facilities could be rapidly reconstituted."[45]

Moreover, the French planners were keenly aware of the limits of their bomber force in terms of numbers of airplanes, range, and payload. Therefore they chose to narrow their target selection to factories that produced carburetors, fuel pumps, diesel injectors, landing gear, and variable pitch propellers.[46] The target package that focused on the aviation industry identified 925 separate manufacturing facilities. Using this assessment of the aviation industry, planners created sixty-six target dossiers, arranged in priority according to intelligence assessments of production potential and the nature of the commodity, the factory's name, as well as geographic coordinates and the nearest town.

The potential for reconstituting aircraft manufacturing centers following air raids caused French analysts to explore possibilities of attacking Luftwaffe air bases to complement the disruption caused by assaults on industries. This set of objectives dovetailed nicely with concerns over establishing air superiority in the event of a German land campaign against French territory. By striking the Luftwaffe in Germany rather than waiting for the German air attack to develop over northern France, the Armée de l'air could achieve independent objectives while simultaneously creating a favorable air superiority balance.

Four general characteristics governed French assessments of the Luftwaffe basing system: distance from the frontiers, number of facilities and their proximity to each other, organization of the installations, and, finally, air defense measures taken to protect them.[47]

The Deuxième Bureau spent a great deal of time analyzing the German air basing organization; German sources helped to inform their assessments. One such source, a census document, *Amtliches Gemeindeverzeichnis für das Deutsche Reiche auf Grand der Volkszählung 1933,* provided detailed descriptions of communities that had local airfield support capabilities.[48] Using such records allowed the air service to compile data, including detailed airfield diagrams, that yielded a relatively accurate intelligence picture of the Luftwaffe's basing scheme.

According to the French analysts, German active and passive defense measures would dramatically complicate the Armée de l'air's attempts to attack the Luftwaffe bases. The report noted, "the care with which every installation is spread out, camouflaged and protected, the important means of air defense placed organically, or as circumstances require, at the discretion of the base commanders, renders the surveillance of these fields difficult, their identification uncertain, and their protection efficient."[49] But the French analysts perceived corresponding weaknesses in the formidable German airfield protection system. According to their calculations, command and control of the dispersed Luftwaffe would prove difficult if central bases suffered accurate attacks. Additionally, raids against fuel, munitions, and other supplies in scattered locations would make operations there difficult.[50]

Therefore the French operational strategy for striking the German aviation system centered on combining attacks: against the industries that supplied airplanes and component parts, and against the airfield basing system. Planners aimed to achieve air superiority to support defensive operations in France, and to advance air offensives against industrial centers of gravity—the essence of lutte aérienne.

Petroleum production represented another important target system that supported German air and ground capabilities. The Deuxième Bureau noted that Germany could operate effectively, using existing stocks and production capabilities, for eight to ten months.[51] Aviation fuels and lubricants, however, presented a less gloomy picture for the potential enemy, according to French analysts. German aviation gasoline reserves, combined with synthetic fuel sources, would allow full air operations to unfold for at least one year. Therefore the air staff concluded that increased fuel requirements for the German land component in a fast-paced maneuver war would hamper flexibility on the ground, while adequate stocks of aviation gasoline would force them to rely upon airpower to achieve major objectives.[52] Regardless of the accuracy of the French assessments and conclusions, air planners identified the petroleum industry as a vital center of gravity.

The intelligence assessment of German petroleum production components divided the system into three categories. Refineries represented the most lucrative target set. Aside from the volatile nature of the products and the ease with which French planners expected their crews to locate and strike the facilities, destruction of the refineries promised to bring about a cascading collapse of the entire fuels industry, as other locations attempted to meet shortfalls by increasing production. If air strikes destroyed enough of the refinery infrastructure, the air staff estimated that it could take from ten months to one year for a return to full capacity.[53]

Fuel depots and handling facilities represented the second priority target set in the German petroleum production system. French planners hoped to disrupt operational effectiveness by interdicting the transport of finished products, and the physical characteristics of the fuel storage and transfer facilities invited aerial attack. Finally, synthetic fuel production facilities completed the list of targets related to the petroleum industry.[54]

Once again, however, planners found themselves having to balance potentially decisive strategic and operational plans against the material limits of French airpower. Analysis of the petroleum system revealed 184 potential targets. Range and payload restrictions prevented French aircraft from striking targets outside a 300–500 kilometer (186–310 mile) radius from the French frontier. Therefore the operational planners developed specific target dossiers for only 49 installations. Within those, the facilities at Hamburg and Bremen received highest priority, followed by the hydrogenation sites in the Ruhr (Gelsenkirchen and Meerbeck) and in Saxony (Leuna, Leipzig, Böhlen-Rotha, and Tröglitz).[55] Because nearly all of these locations were near other industrial areas and important German towns, French analysts anticipated heavy resistance from air and ground defense units.

The German chemical industry supported many war-related activities. The target dossier for this system included six subcategories (sulfuric acid, synthetic ammonia, nitric acid and calcium cyanamide, explosives and munitions, hydrogen, and chlorine and toxic products).[56] In addition to the obvious contribution that these factories made to armaments production, air ministry analysts expressed concern over the contribution that they could make in the form of providing chemicals for use against French troops and civilians.[57] The chemical and munitions factories presented attractive targets for aerial attack, owing to the volatile nature of the raw materials and products located on the sites. French intelligence analysts identified the juncture between concentrated sulfuric acid, ammonia, and munitions assembly plants as the critical nexus for this target system.[58] The assessment of German chemical manufacturing industries revealed 196 separate facilities. Air staff planners developed target dossiers on 73 factories, with a concentration on 22 sulfuric acid, 5 synthetic ammonia, and 20 explosives and munitions plants dominating the lists. Despite the volatility of this segment of the German war industry, French planners once again refused to make overly optimistic forecasts for aerial bombardment strikes against system components. The most definitive statement that air planners would make on the subject promised "at least partial paralysis of the chemical industry."[59]

French intelligence specialists understood that German industry depended on electrical power. Supply facilities (thermal and hydraulic plants, transformer stations) presented inviting targets within the range of French bombers—once again the limiting factor in strategic and operational planning calculations. The strategic objective that attacks against the electrical system would support centered on systematically isolating certain industrial areas. In all, Deuxième Bureau planners identified fifty-one specific bombing objectives in the Ruhr and Cologne area, Baden and Wurtemburg, Hesse-Darmstadt, and the Sarre. But just as in the case of the critical industrial targets discussed above, the air staff expected German defenses to exact a high toll on bomber formations that attempted to cripple the electrical power system.[60]

Transportation networks, the last industry-related target set that French planners identified for aerial attack, held strategic and operational significance. In a strategic sense, all war-related materials passed through various production stages via the sophisticated German rail or canal systems.[61] Thus attacks against the transportation networks threatened to cripple all of the aforementioned industries. From an operational perspective, the German army depended on this network to mobilize and sustain campaigns against enemy defenses.

French intelligence specialists developed nine separate dossiers that identified targets related to the German transportation networks. Attacks against this system aimed to constrict the operational maneuvering capability of German ground forces bound for France.[62] The dossiers conformed to one of four separate hypotheses (North, Center, South, and Center-North). The complete plan for interdicting German land movements divided the rail network into twenty-one attack sectors that stretched in the north from the Dutch border near Bremen in a sweeping arc toward the south, where it terminated near Nuremburg.[63] Bridges, locks, and railroad marshaling yards presented the most vulnerable and important bombing objectives. Aircrews received detailed maps, drawings, and photographs of proposed target areas. With such well-developed plans, Armée de l'air leaders had reason to be confident in their preparation for stifling any German movement toward the west.

If the French planning staff proposed a panacea aerial offensive strategy, it came in the form of reprisal attacks against civilians. The picture that air service analysts painted of the German population described a nation with a brittle moral fiber that could not withstand a prolonged war. The Czechoslovakian crisis of September 1938 indicated to French observers that "the haunting fear of war" had left Germany with "morale inferior to that which sustained it in 1914."[64] Thus, according to this perception, Germany already suffered from a weakness that the hardships of war, including "more or less prolonged dietary restrictions," would exacerbate.[65] Bombardment attacks against civilian populations, especially in those areas dominated by factory workers, would hasten the moral collapse of the German state. According to French assessments, bombing attacks did not even have to be particularly accurate to achieve the desired effects: "repeated bombardment incursions, even when not accompanied by effective destruction, will rapidly render moral results."[66]

The air staff qualified its optimism, however, by recognizing that the efficient German state organization could ease the repercussions of aerial attacks: "It is necessary . . . not to underestimate the effects, in a country like Germany where all activities, at all times, but especially in time of war, are strongly centralized."[67] Because French leaders fully expected Germany to launch bombardment attacks against metropolitan cities, they intended to strike back in kind. Consequently, air service planners identified 109 German towns as valid bombing objectives and developed 53 detailed target dossiers from that list.

The French strategic and operational planning efforts in the 1930s represented a robust attempt to capitalize on the flexibility that airpower afforded. A concentrated air campaign against several interconnected layers of the German war economy promised to allow the Armée de l'air to employ its capabilities offensively, thus granting a measure of initiative that army support requirements denied. By targeting selected economic and military components deep inside Germany, the air service could continue to support, in principle, defensive strategies in the West. Attacks against Luftwaffe air bases and aviation industries supported the air superiority campaign that doctrine and common sense had established as a prerequisite for success.

Petroleum production linked air and ground operations, and French planners understood that Germany depended on synthetic or outside sources for most of its fuel and lubricant needs. Destroying this important target system promised to contribute significantly to land and air campaign objectives. The chemical and munitions industries provided critical materials for all aspects of the German military effort. Additionally, chemical production facilities represented a potent threat to French civilians and soldiers in the field, should Germany choose to initiate chemical warfare. French fears of such attacks elevated the chemical industry on the target priority list. Electrical power production connected all industrial and quality of life systems. And attacks against the transportation network represented an attractive strategic and operational objective that could stall the German attack in the West, while simultaneously interdicting the flow of strategic goods far from the front. Finally, the Deuxième Bureau characterized German morale as weak—possibly *the* center of gravity that would allow France to achieve all of its goals.

Many of the target systems that French planners identified coincided with those subsequently chosen by British and American leaders. The French chose objectives for subtly different reasons, however, that balanced force structure limitations against political and operational constraints. These latter dictated a national strategy predicated on defensive rather than offensive operations.

Unfortunately, the depth and quality of the air campaign plans against Germany never bore fruit. The war did not proceed according to the pattern that French leaders anticipated—the air campaigns against the German war economy would wait for other air forces and other days.

War—Phony and Real

On 3 September 1939 France and Great Britain declared war against Hitler's Third Reich in response to the German attack on Poland. Although France was officially at war, it was a peculiar kind of conflict. Germany, rather than launching across the northeastern frontier in a reenactment of the 1914 attack, remained content to consolidate its gains while securing access to mineral resources in Scandinavia. For its part, France faced the prolonged period of mobilization that air staff planners had dreaded. The *drôle de guerre,* eight months of anticipation, offered the Armée de l'air opportunities to identify obvious organizational and operational flaws before the German attack. However, as it waited for the battle to commence, the air service encountered self-inflicted distractions that confirmed and intensified the firmly entrenched reactive tendencies that had evolved during the interwar years.

The mobilization system failed to fill the ranks as the air staff had designed it to do. Interwar exercises had also not prepared air service personnel to fulfill their duties in combat. One officer reported that the mobilized formations in his command operated with "a deficit of 15 percent enlisted *[soldat]* personnel, 30 percent trained cadres, 20–30 percent rolling stocks, and 20–50 percent miscellaneous material."[68] Some units never received their full complement of personnel. After the armistice, one officer had reported that his command "appeared at the front with a serious deficit in officer ranks and in all specialties . . . In spite of numerous requests . . . these deficits were never resolved."[69]

The personnel problem that confronted the Armée de l'air in 1939–40 had several facets. First was the training system's failure to produce adequate numbers of skilled officers, noncommissioned officers, and instructors. Second, in many instances the tableaux d'effectifs de guerre manned staff organizations to the detriment of line combat units. A Colonel Boucher reported to Général

Prételat at the air staff in December 1939 that "there is an overabundance of overpopulated staffs."[70] From an economic perspective, the long mobilization period exerted a significant drain on French agriculture and industry. In addition to the hardships imposed on French industry that Eugenia Kiesling describes, farm laborers left their fields untended to fill the ranks, only to find themselves sitting idle.[71] Requests for permission to return to the farms inundated air staffs.

Bataillon de l'air no. 136, stationed near Agen in southwestern France, granted forty-seven agricultural leaves between October 1939 and February 1940. Two additional groups of fifty farm workers received thirty-day passes — one group began leave on 2 March 1940, the second departed on 1 April.[72] Balancing operational and economic demands cost the Armée de l'air dearly in terms of raising effectiveness levels. Finally, the poor quality of mobilized personnel, combined with poorly trained and motivated officers, made it difficult to devise solutions for the first two problems. One report described the mobilized troops as "undisciplined, military training insufficient . . . NCOs with no military preparation — having no idea of service, no knowledge of command or obedience . . . knowing perfectly their rights but ignoring their duty."[73] At least one observer recommended a complete reconstruction of aviation.[74] The reorganization that occurred, however, effectively merged the army and the air force.

On 26 February 1940 the Armée de l'air reverted to an operational command system that supported the army's concept of how to fight the war. The order that signaled this decision dissolved the air army structure that had evolved in the 1930s, in favor of separate commands that focused on cooperating with army commanders. The new scheme "placed the air forces and antiaircraft defense forces at the permanent disposal of the land units [Grandes Unités terrestres] on the northeastern front."[75] This system, the product of a series of intense debates among air force, army, and civilian leaders, effectively restructured the air service's approach to war fighting.

Rather than organizing to fight a seamless lutte aérienne under a unified air commander, the Armée de l'air found itself fragmented under theater land commanders, regional air commanders, air defense cooperation forces, and the chief of the Armée de l'air. General Marcel Tétu commanded the cooperation forces that received the lion's share of the air strength. Vuillemin created two zones of operations, one in the north and one in the east, to counter the German and Italian threats respectively. These command reorganizations effectively nullified interwar air doctrine developments, by granting land commanders authority over the objectives and scope of air operations. Thus the Armée de l'air fought in 1940 with an airpower employment philosophy that resembled the one that had been used in the First World War—geared toward the army doctrine of methodical battle—rather than with one that reflected nearly a decade of air doctrine development.[76]

On 10 May 1940, after nine months of waiting, intermittent aerial engagements, false hopes of peace, poorly executed efforts in other theaters, and ineffective attempts to correct operational and tactical flaws, the war that France sought to avoid for two decades erupted. On one hand, France met the war with a sense of trepidation. Germany overwhelmed every strategic device—in Czechoslovakia, Poland, the Soviet Union, and Norway—that French leaders had attempted to use against its neighbor's growing power and bellicosity.[77] On the other hand, war represented an almost welcome respite to the purgatory that the drôle de guerre had represented. One officer reported:

The inactivity of the months before 10 May only charged the pilots, officers and NCOs with excitement for the desire to participate in combat. After 10 May, the Group was thrown into battle; morale remained high in spite of the fatigue of combat and the interminable hours of alert, in spite of, above all, the feeling of the uselessness of a battle engaged against an infinitely superior enemy. Anguish and fear, inevitable in such situations, remained, as they should, secret, and did not influence the action.[78]

Once begun, the fighting led to a conclusion that would redefine the European security environment. In May 1940, however, French leaders remained confident that they could persist long enough for the Franco-British coalition to solidify and stop the German onslaught. Ironically, their confidence nearly proved justified.

The evolution and outcome of the German plan to conquer France are well known, thanks to the thorough efforts of several generations of scholars.[79] Understanding French efforts to counter the German assault remains somewhat clouded in mystery and confusion. Robert Doughty has produced perhaps the clearest analysis of the operational campaign in the critical northeastern region.[80] However, even this excellent work focuses on how the land campaign unfolded, while devoting little attention to the relationship between French land and air organizations.

There is little doubt that in the first two weeks of the campaign, the French air force lost the battle for air superiority over the contested north and northeastern sectors. That failure contributed to the army's inability to halt the German spearhead at critical points along the Meuse near Sedan. However, the army shares the blame for failing to thwart German operational plans. Ground commanders, including General Gamelin and his staff, deployed forces based upon preconceived notions of German strategy.[81] This meant that older classes of poorly trained reservists manned the 9th Army Corps in the critical Ardennes sector, where the early breakthrough occurred—and where the French least expected the Germans to attack.

French reliance on positional strength and artillery concentration, rather than on maneuver and combined arms tactics, further compounded the army's tactical ineffectiveness. Finally, the army failed to adapt to the shifting nature of the campaign, as it became increasingly clear that the Germans had elected to fight a very different war from the one that the French had anticipated. The result was a cascading operational collapse in which the bulk of the French army, despite isolated instances of determined—even brilliant—resistance, found no alternative except in retreat.[82]

On a purely tactical level, the Armée de l'air's performance mirrored that of its land counterpart. French airmen flew patrols to protect the frontier from German reconnaissance, resulting in the first combat experiences for many French pilots. Those ordeals revealed flaws in the Armée de l'air's fighting effectiveness. Pursuit units had become stratified according to flying experience, thus concentrating seasoned pilots in formations rather than using them to guide the less practiced aviators who constituted the bulk of the operational cadres. Pierre Boillot, a sergeant-pilot in 1940 who later retired as a general in the resurrected Armée de l'air, recalled that pilots in his fighter squadron emerged from the training system with approximately 260 flying hours. This apparently high experience level concealed significant flaws. Boillot related that none of his prewar flying had included training under instrument conditions, operations at night, bombing, or gunnery activity. Apparently Boillot's instruction had prepared him for clear-weather daylight flying—under simulated combat conditions. The first time he attacked a German reconnaissance plane, he discovered that the munitions specialists had not equipped his aircraft with a full load of ammunition, and that he could not manage to hit the German. He expended all of his ammunition in futile attempts to bring the enemy down.[83]

The Luftwaffe launched a combined attack against the French deployments, aimed at achieving air superiority by eliminating as much of the Armée de l'air's strength and infrastructure as possible on the ground. Consequently, strikes on airfields characterized several days of fighting. French security measures proved inadequate. Boillot recalled that "on the morning of 10 May . . . the Germans had an absolutely marvelous target in their sights arranged as in peacetime, because nothing had been done to disperse the airplanes."[84] Despite early setbacks, the Armée de l'air struggled to recover and to adapt to the reality of the war that the Germans thrust upon them.

One adjustment the French attempted involved upgrading their pursuit fleet, to field an airplane that could compete on par with the German Messerschmidt 109. The Dewoitine 520 was, by all accounts, equal to the task, but the French manufacturing and logistics system failed the air service as it attempted to increase combat effectiveness by placing this aircraft in the battle line. Boillot recalled a mission to the depot at Toulouse, to take delivery of approximately six Dewoitine 520 fighters during the first week of the war. The new planes would replace the Morane 406, which could not compete effectively against superior German fighters. Boillot and his companions found that the war had not yet reached Toulouse—civil defense measures were not in effect, blackout procedures were absent, and the planes on the airfield were lined up as easy targets for enemy air attacks. According to Boillot, it was like entering a different country. Moreover, the new airplanes were far from combat-ready. They lacked basic instruments, the guns were not sighted or armed, and they were not fueled. The logisticians at Boillot's base had to procure the required materials outside normal logistics channels.[85]

The French air effort centered on providing aerial reconnaissance, superiority, and support for General Gamelin's land forces. When bombers sortied to support ground forces under pressure from the German spearheads, they encountered withering fire from Luftwaffe fighters and antiaircraft artillery. In the battle that raged near the critical Meuse crossings, French Amiot 143s, underpowered products of the BCR program, suffered better than 50 percent losses in futile attempts to stall the German advance.[86] Specially trained ground attack aviation groups equipped with newer Breguet 693 aircraft fared no better, with fifty-eight aircraft shot down and another forty-two damaged by antiaircraft fire during the course of the campaign.[87] This brutal sacrifice was shared by other units; one group lost "nearly 80 planes out of an assigned 52, or 150 percent . . . in personnel, 122 officers or NCOs out of action (82 dead or missing) out of 240 assigned, or 50 percent."[88]

By 17 May, with the German sprint toward the west driving a wedge between Allied forces in northern France and Belgium, Generals Vuillemin and Tétu decided to concentrate the air effort on attacks against German ground forces and Luftwaffe bombers. This decision, while making tactical sense, as it concentrated the French air effort against the most pressing areas in the theater, effectively ceded the long-term air superiority battle to the Germans. Thus the new approach virtually guaranteed that the Armée de l'air would fail to win the operational air war, owing to a loss of air superiority. French air forces fought with renewed vigor and effectiveness for several days and, in doing so, allowed some army units to mount temporarily effective local defenses. By 23 May, however, the Armée de l'air's logistical system's ineffectiveness began to exert a greater influence on the air service's ability to accomplish its mission.

Aside from the normal supply difficulties expected in war, the Armée de l'air logistical system could not keep combat units supplied adequately. This critique

BLOCH 151/2

S.S. Fighter

Span 34′–4¾″   Length 29′–8¼″   Height 10′–1¾″

Figure 8. Bloch 151/2 (fighter), 1938
Engine: Gnôme-Rhône K-14 (1), 880 hp
Weight: Loaded 2,270 kg (5004.44 lbs)
Speed: 5,000 m (16,400 ft.) 510 km/hr (316.2 mph)
Ceiling: 11,000 m (36,080 ft.)
Range: 750 km (465 miles)

Issued January, 1939 with A.L. No. 1

MORANE SAULNIER 405/406
Single Seater Fighter
Span 33'-8"   Length 26'-2¾"   Height 8'-10"

(56703)   B

Figure 9. Morane Saulnier 405/406 (fighter), 1938
Engine: Hispano-Suiza 12Ygrs (1), 860 hp
Payload: 20 mm canon, 1
Weight: 2,240 kg (4,938.3 lbs)
Speed: 5000 m (16,400 ft.) 485 km/hr (300.7 mph)
Ceiling: 9,000 m (29,520 ft.)
Range: 800 km (496 miles)

DEWOITINE 520

S.S. FIGHTER

Span : 33′ 5½″   Length : 26′ 11″   Height : 8′ 6½″

FRANCE

Figure 10. Dewoitine 520 (fighter), 1939
Engine: Hispano-Suiza (1), 850 hp
Payload: 20 mm canon
Weight: 2,531 kg (5,579.84 lbs)
Speed: 4,000 m (13,120 ft.) 530 km/hr (328.6 mph)
Ceiling: 10,500 m (34,440 ft.)

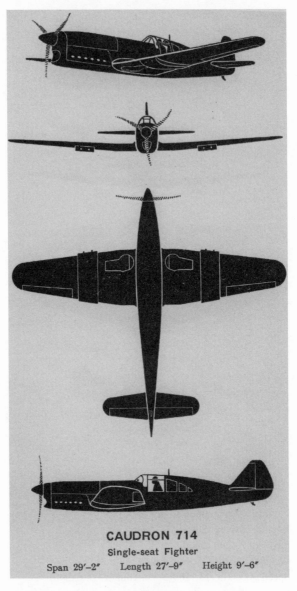

CAUDRON 714
Single-seat Fighter
Span 29'–2"   Length 27'–9"   Height 9'–6"

Figure 11. Caudron 714 (fighter), 1939
Engine: Renault 12Roi (1), 450 hp
Speed: 4,000 m (13,120 ft.) 487 km/hr (301.9 mph)
Ceiling: 9,100 m (29,848 ft.)
Range: 900 km (558 miles)

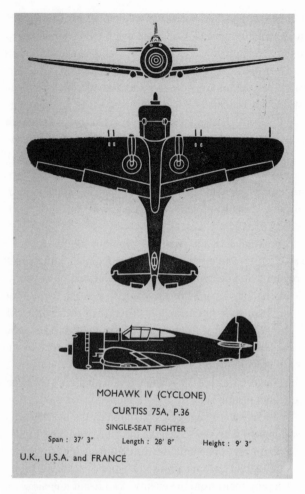

MOHAWK IV (CYCLONE)

CURTISS 75A, P.36

SINGLE-SEAT FIGHTER

Span : 37′ 3″   Length : 28′ 8″   Height : 9′ 3″

U.K., U.S.A. and FRANCE

Figure 12. Mohawk IV (Cyclone), Curtiss 75A, P-36
   (fighter), 1938
Engine: Wright Cyclone R-1820 (1), 840 hp
Payload: 25 lb bombs, external, 10
   50 lb bombs, external, 6
   .50 cal gun, 1
   .30 cal gun, 1
Weight: 2,406 kg (5,304 lbs)
Speed: 386 km/hr (289.3 mph)
Ceiling: 9,700 m (31,816 ft.)
Range: 1,950 km (1,209 miles)

has at least three components. Aerial rearmament efforts begun in 1938 started to bear fruit as war commenced. Consequently, the maintenance depots and air parks, tasked to configure new material for operational use, developed backlogs of airplanes awaiting final configuration. This condition led to a particularly damning critique by senior army officers after the war, because the air service's numerical strength was actually greater when the Vichy government announced the cease-fire than on 10 May. Pierre Cot reported that air strength at the beginning of the war totaled approximately 2,100 planes. After surrender, there were 4,238 planes on the continent, and an additional 1,800 in North Africa— this after suffering nearly 2,000 combat losses in six weeks.[89] Therefore the material problem appeared to center, in part, on the logistical system's inability to deliver mission-capable airplanes to combat units, rather than on the lack of airframes.

A second component of the logistics problem related to the centralized arrangement of depots and air parks within the regional command structure. A peacetime organization designed for economy does not always meet the fast-paced needs of combat. As one officer noted, "it was the fault of the organization, seductive in concept, but incapable of resisting the realities of maneuver warfare."[90] This was the case at the repair depots tasked to keep the Armée de l'air's frontline planes in the air. The depots were not manned or supplied adequately to keep up with the repairs that war demanded.

Finally, the effects of the retreat—which began after only two weeks of fighting and accelerated near the end of May—resulted in central logistics branches having to relocate repeatedly until the end of the battle. Under such conditions, the only possible action was to "conserve the indispensable supplies for use by the front-line air formations while exerting all measures to deny them to the enemy."[91] As the retreat became a rout, the emphasis shifted from conserving resources to keeping them from the enemy. As a result, the air service became increasingly ineffective as German air strength grew.

The Battle of France ended on 22 June 1940. For many French airmen the war was over. France lay divided, literally and figuratively. Germany occupied two-thirds of metropolitan territory, while Marshal Philippe Pétain's Vichy government struggled to maintain an illusion of autonomy under the heel of German oversight and occupation. The Vichy government transformed the national slogan from *liberté, egalité, fraternité* to the less inspiring *travaille, famille, patrie*. On 18 June General Charles de Gaulle rallied all Frenchmen who loved freedom to continue the fight as part of the Fighting French Forces (later Free French Forces). In doing so, de Gaulle erected permanent barriers between himself and the Vichy government, which sentenced him to death in absentia. Vichy leaders launched an investigation into the causes of the defeat and branded the

Armée de l'air one of the chief scapegoats responsible for the disaster. The air service thus ended the war with a burden of guilt that stemmed from its own culpability in failing to execute its assigned missions, and from government accusations that condemned nearly a decade of institutional development.

7 Assessing Combat Performance and Air Doctrine

The total number of forces (Army, Navy and Air) in the unoccupied part of metropolitan territory, including Corsica, will not exceed 100,000 men including officers, medical personnel, and military functionaries.[1]

French forces collapsed in the face of the German offensive, in six weeks of chaotic fighting. Marshal Philippe Pétain assumed the reins of government and appealed to the Germans for an armistice as the Third Republic disappeared in the wake of the defeat. General Charles de Gaulle, the flamboyant advocate of armored warfare, rejected any hint of accommodating the Germans and fled to Great Britain where, on 18 June 1940, he called all French citizens to keep "the flame of French resistance" alive.[2] French society fractured into groups representing the Vichy regime, de Gaulle's Free France, Communist sympathizers who viewed the war as the end of capitalism, and average citizens who merely struggled to survive another European war.

Within weeks of the disaster, with forces reduced to levels mirroring those of the the Versailles treaty, imposed by the Allies on a defeated Germany at the end of the First World War, the leaders of the Armée de l'air began to examine the causes. The air staff, reorganized under the Vichy government, ordered officers who had participated at every level in the war effort to compile reports that reflected their experiences and their criticisms of air force performance during the hostilities. The air staff solicited information regarding organization, command relationships, logistics support, combat experience, technical evaluations of aircraft and other equipment, and doctrine. The directive that ordered this review asked for a frank account of the events: "The authors will assess the related events and will express their personal opinions with complete independence of spirit and with sincerity."[3]

Although reports began to arrive at the air staff offices by August 1940, the final staff study did not appear until March 1942. In the intervening months, the air staff created Commission G, charged with sifting through the reports and arriving at a consensus on the lessons for the future of French airpower.[4]

Commission G operated under severe constraints that stemmed partly from the fact that the Vichy government was overseen by the Germans, and partly from its own duplicity.[5] Because of the German-imposed requirement to reduce armed forces, there were few personnel available to conduct the study. The air staff selected Colonel Jean Carayon to chair the commission, under the authority of the air force vice chief of staff. Carayon later rose to the rank of general in the Vichy air force, where he served on the staff of the Secrétariat général à la défense aérienne (SGDA). He used his position in the SGDA to assemble an effective resistance organization that worked clandestinely with the Organisation de résistance de l'armée to play a dangerous cat-and-mouse game with the Germans.

Carayon hoped to preserve the Armée de l'air's structure and personnel, with an eye toward taking part in the eventual eviction of the occupation forces from French soil. The chairman supervised a staff of four officers and six enlisted men. This small unit operated from a building at the Bordelongue airfield near Toulouse. French authorities feared that German occupation authorities would look unfavorably upon the commission's efforts; consequently, the air staff attached its members to the Service des archives et du Musée de l'air as an administrative cover for their actual duties. The commission began work in October 1941, and completed the effort by publishing a 291-page report in March 1942.[6]

This final report clearly acknowledged the air service's faults, but the authors struggled to maintain a balanced perspective, while simultaneously exposing the numerous and obvious shortcomings that had characterized the Armée de l'air's operations in the spring of 1940. Commission members resisted the temptation to recommend scuttling the French system in favor of the apparently successful German organization and methods. Thus the recommendations often followed a conservative path that emphasized reforming or even retaining the institutional structures of the 1930s, rather than urging wholesale structural and doctrinal change. This conservatism prompted the authors to analyze the character of the air operations that continued in the war between Germany, Great Britain, and Russia, to discover trends of aerial warfare both in the present and for the future. The report remains a valuable resource for examining how French airpower doctrine evolved after a disastrous defeat. Yet to read it without referring to the reports submitted by the officers who had participated in the *tourmente* of 1940 would reveal only part of the story.

Commission officials separated into subject-related categories many of the reports submitted by air service officers. Ultimately, members identified twenty-seven separate subjects that touched on every aspect of the Armée de l'air's war effort.[7] To save time and to facilitate handling of the materials, the commission cut the original reports into strips, sorted these according to subject, and glued them onto large sheets of paper. The resulting archival record yielded a meticulously organized but fragmented series of comments. Members annotated many of the strips to indicate which unit had submitted the original report, but the mutilation made it impossible to reconstruct them. Fortunately, several originals still exist in their initial form.

They reveal that the officers who served in the French air force approached their duties in a serious, professional manner. Their comments indicate an understanding of interwar doctrines, tactical employment principles, and the shortcomings of their prewar preparation. The officers who wrote the after-action reports also remained true to the air staff directive to render honest and sincere opinions. The comments penned by lieutenants to colonels openly reveal the frustration and agony that plagued the Armée de l'air's officers as they tried in vain to defend their nation. The appraisal that commission members produced from all this purged the emotions expressed in the original reports; the result was a sterile, objective account of lessons learned from the war. Thus a more comprehensive impression of the Armée de l'air's effort to learn from the defeat emerges from a comparison of the strips, the surviving complete reports, and the commission's final report.

The Nature of Modern Warfare

To many observers, the war of maneuver that the Germans visited upon France in May and June 1940 represented a new revolution in warfare.[8] The commission devoted considerable attention to analyzing whether the nature of war had, indeed, changed as a result of new tactics and technologies. If the events of 1940 heralded a new form of warfare, the French air force of the future needed to adapt. On the other hand, if the Armée de l'air had performed poorly in 1940 because of flawed leadership, policies, or technology, future service leaders could retain the fundamental doctrinal assumptions that had prevailed previously. Before arguing for abandoning the fundamental principles of the 1930s,

must to determine actual cause. when making changes

to correct

the commission carefully examined each possibility to detect how the air service had contributed to the defeat.

The tension between offensive and defensive forms of warfare presented a logical starting point. French strategic calculations throughout the 1930s assumed that the inherent strength of defensive preparations would thwart German hopes for a sudden victory. This assumption constituted one of the fundamental doctrinal breaks between the air and land services during the 1930s. By 1940, however, the land service successfully imposed its vision of how to wage war upon the Armée de l'air.

As war, both phony and real, descended upon the French, airmen experienced two major service reorganizations designed to achieve closer integration with the army's views of how to conduct a defensive theater-level war. The first, in September 1939, aligned the air units with the major army zones of operations; the second, in February 1940, established a command structure that divided responsibility for air operations between the applicable army zone of operations commanders, the newly established Forces aériennes de coopération (FAC) commanders, and the air force commander in chief.[9] The new arrangements forced the air service to jettison its fundamental precepts of *lutte aérienne,* in which airpower could play an independent, primary role, while land forces supported aviation with maneuver and land-based antiaircraft defenses. Confronted with army demands for greater control over air operations, the Armée de l'air dismantled its Grandes Unités aériennes and air regions. The French air force fought the Germans with its combat power dispersed among the army commands.

The process of subordinating the air forces to army zone of operations commanders, begun in September 1939 and completed by February 1940, affected airmen from the declaration of war until the cease-fire. One of the most dramatic effects that the new command structure exerted on air service tactical employment was the isolation of air groups from higher echelons. Between September 1939 and June 1940, individual flying unit commanders reported receiving orders to relocate as many as eighteen times.[10] For the aviators, this meant little more than flying to a new landing field. However, for the essential support units—mechanics, services, administration, communications, and air base defense—that remained attached to each flying organization, the moves involved chaotic journeys using rail and road routes. Often support units arrived at newly assigned locations to find their parent flying organizations had moved once again. This separation of combat and combat support units affected flying operations. Lieutenant Colonel Demery, commander of the Groupement d'aviation d'assaut no. 18, observed that "from the unleashing of operations the groups were, and remained thereafter, totally isolated from resupply organizations, depots, and technical organizations."[11] Even during the relatively benign phony war, the defensive positional warfare that the army anticipated became a constantly shifting war of maneuver for the Armée de l'air.

The failure of army leaders to comprehend that defensive operations in the air could not remain tied to maneuver schemes conceived for land units deprived the airmen of the ability to mass their forces to defend critical points. As for attaining unity of effort, the airmen labored under an unfamiliar and unwieldy command structure that often left them ignorant of the intentions of the commander of the zone of operations. The commander of Bombardment Group 2 noted: "The difficulties encountered in the exercise of interior command resulted principally from the mediocrity of the means of communication that prevented sure and rapid liaison, which is of capital importance in the execution of missions against mobile and intermittent objectives."[12] Therefore the airmen, divorced from strategic and operational vision by the new command structures and unable to develop a coherent tactical perception of the battlefield, reverted to a reactive posture, characterized by the grim determination to contribute in the most effective ways possible.

Ironically, the commission concluded that the type of war that had occurred in 1940 fit well into French conceptions of airpower. Flexibility and initiative at all levels of command would characterize future operations, according to the commission's final report. The most deficient area for French operations lay in the fragmented command relationships that had existed between the army, the air force, and the national political-military command authorities. Although General Gamelin, and later General Weygand, had guided the war effort in principal, their efforts had proved woefully inadequate to the pace, scope, and complexity of modern war.[13] The military establishment of the future—and, by extension, the future air force—required a *commandant du théâtre d'opérations* who could effectively control the combined air, land, and naval operations that would represent the rule, rather than the exception, in operations.[14] The commission argued that the absence of such a commander, one who was morally, intellectually, and materially adapted to his mission, could only result in renewed disaster.

For all combat forces, but especially for air forces, the commission advocated a reformed organization to support the theater commander. It had to be rational, decentralized, equipped with modern, high-speed communications, and prepared intellectually to cope with the forms of modern war.[15] Tactical experience confirmed the commission's conclusions. Lieutenant Colonel Castet, commandant of the Groupement d'aviation d'assaut no. 19, had reported in August 1940:

The existing organization permitted:

— neither the rapid execution [of missions] that would allow the delivery of a stopping blow against the enemy advance, because of the delays in the conception and transmission of orders;

— nor massing of assault aviation, because of the very small number of assault units, the scattering of the commands, and the large number of objectives attacked simultaneously;

— nor the effective protection [of assault units] by friendly pursuit, because of the impossibility of personal liaison between assault and pursuit.[16]

Castet criticized the organization for its tactical flaws. Another author echoed his observations, writing: "Our ties with the Zone of Aerial Operations were completely broken."[17] The commission interpreted the problems that had prevented the Armée de l'air from achieving mass and unity of effort as symptoms of a higher-level organizational issue.

The theater command philosophy—in effect, a joint force command structure—that the commission advocated relied upon the primacy of land warfare. In response to accusations that the French air force had been weak in 1940, the commission responded: "In May 1940, a [more] powerful French aviation could only have delayed defeat, not prevented it."[18] According to this view, land forces provided the war-winning element—air and sea forces only helped to establish the conditions for victory. Thus airpower, properly applied, supported the joint force commander's theater objectives.

The dramatic contribution that German airpower offered to the ultimate outcome of the Battle of France presented French airmen and the commission members a paradox that led to a corollary to the principle that asserted the primacy of land forces. The experience of the *tourmente* revealed that no nation would seriously attempt to wage war in the future without considerable aviation assets. In other words, land forces could not win the campaigns of the future without air support—the commission even went as far as to conclude that air superiority set the essential conditions for victory on the ground.[19] This symbiotic relationship between air and ground power helped the commission to define future organizational and force structure requirements for the Armée de l'air.

The difference between French and German approaches to employing airpower in the war of 1940, according to the commission, lay in the contrast between the German combined arms team and the fragmented French command structure. This adjustment had allowed the Germans to conceive and execute offensive operations, while the French had remained paralyzed and incapable of adapting at the operational or tactical levels to counter enemy air-land thrusts. As the authors observed: "In 1940, the French military forces were defeated by an adversary that had created, focused, and applied a doctrine of offensive combat, based upon massive action and on the direct collaboration of an independent Air Force and armored formations engaged simultaneously in battle."[20] The innovation achieved by the Germans had stemmed from their use of airpower to support offensive operations on the ground—not from their use of armored forces. Therefore the commission proposed a strong defensive air arm designed to cooperate intimately with land forces to break the cohesion between enemy air and land forces.

The principle of cooperation between air and ground forces had existed in French air service doctrines throughout the 1930s. Several reports emphasize the clearly defined doctrinal axioms that outlined how air forces should cooperate with land forces.[21] Air service experiences indicated that the fault in 1940 lay in the absence of procedures, equipment, and training that made coordination and communication possible between air and land units. By gaining air superiority, airpower, properly applied in the context of the land battle, assured the freedom of maneuver for land forces. It also guaranteed their security, by finding and fixing enemy mobile forces so that friendly land forces could concentrate against them. Finally, airpower could constrain enemy maneuver possibilities, by depleting follow-on strength through attacks against supplies and transportation networks.[22]

The commission struggled with a vision of airpower that remained tied to the terrestrial battle. The same characteristics that allowed airpower to guarantee the security of friendly land maneuver forces also offered expanded possibilities for attacks against operational centers of gravity. The commission authors argued: "The initial action aimed at totally paralyzing the enemy organs of command, from the outset, could cause them to lose all freedom of action on the battlefield. It seems that, in general, this initial action has been established a priori, and *regulated according to an hourly precondition.*"[23] The commission noted, thus, that effective operations in maneuver warfare required reliable communications between maneuver elements and the operational command echelons. Airpower could halt enemy offensives by breaking the links between tactical units and the operational commanders. Despite the obvious benefits gained under the joint command structure in terms of unity of command, the commission members could not escape the wider possibilities that three-dimensional warfare offered modern commanders.

As Colonel Carayon and his team struggled with issues of command relationships between air and land forces, they found themselves returning to the structures contained in lutte aérienne doctrines of the 1930s. The authors concluded that the development of mechanized and motorized forces in land warfare had resulted in the possibility that offensive and defensive battles would occur simultaneously, in the same theater. Similarly, the addition of airpower to the modern battle forced theater commanders to consider offensive and defensive objectives in the air war. As they wrote in the final report, "it is no longer adequate to speak of the terrestrial battle, but instead of the aero-terrestrial battle in which the actions of land forces and those of the air forces, directly combined, are pursued normally during the entire duration of the battle."[24] This expression of the characteristics of modern war reflected little change from the descriptions contained in the prewar doctrine; in the 1930s, however, French airmen had speculated about the primacy of airpower and about the possibility that land forces would support the aerial fight. Now they rejected, or at best only hinted at, the possibility that airpower could dominate the war effort.

The leaders of tactical units who critiqued air force performance did not provide clear evidence upon which the commission could base its conservative conclusions regarding the relationship between air and land forces. The reports were virtually unanimous in their condemnation of the lack of communication within the air service and with the army units they supported. None of the surviving original reports, however, contained opinions that supported a permanently subordinate role for the Armée de l'air. At the tactical level, the airmen expressed frustration over inadequate equipment: "[A] single Potez 63, capable of 400 km [248 miles] per hour with only one machine gun mounted in the rear for defense with a 30-degree field of fire, could hope neither to attack the German pursuit planes capable of 500 km [310 miles] per hour, nor to resist alone against a patrol of two or three such pursuits, each equipped with four machine guns."[25] They were frustrated as well by the poor quality of communications support: "The radiotelegraphic liaison never worked between the Forces Aériennes du Corps d'Armée, despite all the efforts of the command."[26] But French airmen rarely questioned the assumptions of their fundamental doctrines.

The joint theater command that Colonel Carayon and the other commission members advocated reinforced the institutional trends that favored reactive doctrine within the service. The structure of the joint forces command forced senior aviators into roles as technical advisers to the joint force commander (who would always be an army general). Commission members argued: "It remains, then, for the aerial commander to adapt the activity of his forces constantly, within the context of the assigned mission, to the unfolding operations. It is necessary for him to *live the battle,* to take daring initiatives at the right time, and to respond to and even anticipate the desires of the land forces."[27]

The attention of the air force commander remained limited, in this characterization of future war, to the pace, scope, and time constraints of land warfare. But more important, the commission's formula restricted the airmen's exercise of initiative to the unfolding land battle. This limited vision guaranteed that

French airmen would continue to react at the operational and tactical levels of war. The airmen could not develop and articulate alternative visions of how to accomplish strategic or operational objectives, because they owed total allegiance to the land commander.

Defining the Characteristics of Airpower

The approach that the members of Commission G adopted to define modern warfare led to a narrow emphasis on the tactical details of aerial warfare. To a certain degree, this focus stemmed from the commission's mandate to derive lessons for improving effectiveness of the air force. If the Armée de l'air of the future should depart from the institutional structures of the past, the service's tactical composition would necessarily change, to conform to new fundamental and organizational models. The joint theater command that the commission advocated as the model for a revised fundamental and organizational doctrine, however, preserved the categories of aviation that had dominated French airpower thought since the First World War. Airmen perceived only one revolutionary application of airpower in the campaign of 1940—airborne assault and its corollary, aerial transport. The remaining missions conformed to old formulas that relied upon aviation to contribute bombardment, pursuit, and reconnaissance to support the ground battle.

The German use of air transport and airborne troops opened new possibilities for the marriage of air and land power. The French, largely at Pierre Cot's urging, had experimented with airborne troops, l'Infanterie de l'air, in the 1930s. The leaders of the Armée de l'air had published tactical doctrine manuals, provided training, equipment, and personnel to create a force similar to the German paratroop force that caused such havoc in Holland and Belgium in 1940, and in the assault on Crete in 1941. The results that the Germans achieved with lightly armed paratroops and glider-borne assault forces surpassed French expectations for such methods.

The commission's final report contained the observation that airborne operations "suddenly opened distant theaters through combined operations in which aviation played an important role"; the authors concluded that such operations "constituted one of the interesting lessons of the current conflict."[28] German airborne assaults and the collapse of the Belgian fortress at Eben Emael shocked the French into an awareness of new possibilities for vertical envelopment and strategic effectiveness.[29]

Commission members chose to use the lessons gleaned from the German successes with airborne troops to argue for a greatly expanded air transportation arm in the Armée de l'air of the future. The authors settled upon the phrase *avia-*

tion de débarquement to refer to a wide range of activities.[30] The first characteristic of the new arm conformed to the model established by the Germans. French airmen could deploy in force, using parachute or landing assaults, deep in enemy territory. These missions would meet stiff enemy resistance and would require close coordination and cooperation between air and ground commanders, to ensure the survival of the airborne force.[31] Ironically, the assumption was that French military and political leaders would pursue offensive strategies predicated upon a war of movement—the antithesis of interwar policies.

The second category that commission members outlined for aviation de débarquement represented a more traditional support role. Transportation aviation offered new possibilities for supporting air and land forces. France had lacked this capability in the 1930s for several reasons. The most obvious centered on nonexistent clearly defined military requirements for such aircraft.[32] The Armée de l'air relied upon converted or obsolete bombers and light transport airplanes to deliver the small volume of cargo required by interwar operations and maneuvers. The pressure brought on by the worldwide economic crisis provided another brake on French transport aviation development.[33] Finally, the confines of Western Europe, coupled with the absence of power projection strategies among French politicians and generals, restricted air transport development. The dominance of defensive strategies encouraged French military leaders, including those in the air force, to rely upon the railroad network to provide operational and tactical support, rather than developing aerial transport. But the war changed French perceptions regarding the utility of strategic and operational air cargo movement.

The final aviation de débarquement category that commission members identified represented the only element that had existed in significant numbers in the French air service of the 1930s. Liaison aircraft provided a solution to at least one of the problems brought on by dispersing air units among army theater commands. By operating in a tactical airlift role, liaison aviation could deliver personnel and cargo to combat units that became isolated from the air force support infrastructure. Conceived in this way, such a use of aviation provided the joint theater commander with a flexible means of reinforcing tactical units, as well as a tactical reserve that could help to keep units in the fight longer. The problem in 1940, as the commission understood it, was that too few of the liaison aircraft and crews had been spread across the air service to function effectively.[34]

Colonel Carayon and his team of analysts departed from their usual conservatism when describing the potential importance of aviation de débarquement missions. For the first time in the final report, the authors did not couch their arguments in terms related to the joint force command structure, or how the air service could contribute to accomplishing joint theater objectives. The commission report stopped short of making an overt declaration of an independent role for airpower and airmen. But the authors clearly implied that the complexity of transport missions, the cost of the planes, the speed with which such charges unfolded, and the risk to personnel meant that airmen should take the lead role in planning and executing these new tasks. According to the commission's report, "a transport operation should not be improvised but should be meticulously prepared . . . the general direction of the operation should be assumed by a specialist acquainted with the difficulties of the enterprise."[35] The airmen had witnessed the operational successes achieved by German aerial assault forces in the campaign of 1940; through their analysis of the lessons from the defeat, they now expressed a desire to control this apparently important weapon in the Armée de l'air of the future. Curiously, however, the commission members elected to frame their analysis of traditional missions (bombardment, pursuit, and reconnaissance) within the context of the joint theater war.

As a weapon against their enemy, bombardment aviation failed to supply the shock, stopping power, or material destruction that French strategists had demanded in 1940. This happened, in part, because bombardment units had little experience with executing attacks against mobile ground combat units. Interwar training and exercise opportunities had focused on using bombers to attack preplanned, stationary targets. During the 1930s, enemy industrial areas and communication nodes had occupied first priority in French bombardment plans. When the army had called for attacks against enemy land forces in the interwar years, the typical targets had been supply depots, marshaling areas, and communications networks—all readily identifiable and stationary objectives. The target sets conceived in the interwar bomber plans had required precise information about the area. Moreover, successful attacks had required nearly perfect flying conditions en route to the target area, along with good visibility over the mark, because of the lack of proficiency among French bomber crews.

They encountered a war that differed from the one for which they had planned. The hard-pressed army units demanded rapid response from the bomber *groupements* to help slow the German advance—bomber crews proved inadequate to the task. General Pastier, the bombardment inspector general, observed, "bombardment [aviation] could only intervene after serious delays, in some cases on the order of four hours after receiving information from reconnaissance airplanes: it is fully evident, in these conditions, that the fleeting objectives indicated could not always be located by the aircrews."[36] Pastier blamed the convoluted command structure for many of the delays that he witnessed. He also observed that the French failed to maintain air superiority over their territory. The presence of enemy pursuit planes over the battlefield prevented the French bombers from influencing the contest on the ground.[37]

The airmen complained that the published tactical doctrines of the interwar years had failed to anticipate the circumstances of the German assault. One officer observed: "The employment doctrine learned before the war was not confirmed by experience. . . . In effect, the conditions in which Bombardment [aviation] was employed could not be made the object of any regulatory prescription."[38] The departure from published doctrine, the fluid nature of the battle, the effective employment of German pursuit and ground-based defenses, and the fragmented French command structure prevented the Armée de l'air's bomber fleet from achieving any semblance of cohesion or effectiveness in the Battle of France.

Colonel Carayon and the other commission members acknowledged that the mobility of land forces on the modern battlefield made bombardment operations more complex than interwar airmen had anticipated. According to the report, the joint theater command could solve the coordination problems that had afflicted bombardment efforts in 1940. Training and specialization would remedy many of the other tactical problems that had hindered the bomber crews. Commission members readily acknowledged the sorry state of bombardment—and air force—instruction before the war. Captain Meiffren of Groupe aérien 1 of Bombardment Group 23 reported, "certain reserve maintenance company commanders and flying personnel expressed a certain repugnance at times for tasks for which they felt, with good reason, ill-prepared to perform or that could not be done."[39] The commission assumed that future government and military leaders would ensure adequate funding and material to provide realistic and effective combat training. Consequently, the final report focused on defining future specialized mission requirements for bomber forces.

Bombardment represented the most deadly and flexible arm available to French airpower. However, interwar airmen had exaggerated the destructive potential of bomber forces. The commission now advocated changes, to ensure that future doctrines would not make the same mistake. Strategic targets, those that sustained the enemy material or moral capability to fight, were difficult to attack successfully. The authors of the final report noted, "destruction cannot be obtained definitively in a single blow: either the numbers of projectiles dropped are insufficient to achieve it, or the objective can be rapidly repaired."[40] Because of the delays inherent in realizing the effects of such missions, the commission cautioned against launching attacks that did not relate directly to the outcome of the land battle. Moreover, the direct effects of aerial bombardment upon enemy fielded forces contributed in measurable ways to the joint force commander's campaign goals. Thus, for future operations, the authors argued that the joint theater command should receive first priority when assigning bombardment objectives.

The requirement to support the theater commander's efforts helped to define tactical categories for bombardment aviation. Dive bombing, used so effectively by the Germans in the campaigns of 1940, received first consideration in the commission's tactical recommendations. Ironically, the Armée de l'air had conducted extensive experiments with dive bombing tactics in the 1930s, before choosing to abandon the procedure. Airmen at the Centre d'expériences aériennes militaires at Reims had used the tactic in several experiments against objectives including railroad lines, tanks, and fortifications. Although the tests had revealed that the tactic promised to increase accuracy, airmen concluded that the maneuver was too difficult and dangerous for French pilots to perform. The Armée de l'air training programs did not prepare bomber aircrews to perform the tactic; existing French airframes could not sustain the g-forces required as pilots pulled the airplanes out of the dive.[41] Therefore, as they prepared to fight Germany in the 1930s, the French had elected to rely upon traditional level-flight bombardment tactics. The commission now saw this as a mistake that had cost the French dearly in the Battle of France, because it had robbed the Armée de l'air of the ability to strike German armored forces accurately.

The authors of the final report divided bombardment targets into two broad categories: those on the battlefield and all others. These classifications conformed nicely to the commission's focus on the terrestrial battle. But the emphasis on restricting the mobility of enemy forces by using aerial attacks was not new to French airmen. Pierre Cot had correctly assessed the outlines of German strategy in the late 1930s. He had argued that airpower represented the only way for France to thwart German hopes for a short war.[42] The most aggressive and innovative aerial exercises of the 1930s, particularly the 1937 maneuvers and the aborted ones in 1938, had sought to develop methods for the Armée de l'air to use against mobile land forces.[43]

Then, in actual warfare, army commanders had used bombardment units as airborne artillery platforms. One officer noted that "medium bombardment units were used solely to overcome the weaknesses of artillery and to give the infantry the impression that our aviation was present in the battle."[44] Commission G proposed a bombardment force dedicated to attacks against enemy armored formations, motorized columns, troops, entrenched personnel, cantonments, bridges, boats, fortifications, and supply depots.[45] This prioritization scheme promised to guarantee that bombers would remain at the beck and call of land unit commanders for the duration of operations.

The airmen offered the catchall category of "other objectives" in the unlikely event that the aircraft destroyed all of the targets designated by army commanders. Yet these other objectives remained limited to those that contributed to the unfolding terrestrial battle. Bombers could reach behind enemy lines to attack rail lines, roads, marshaling yards, repair depots, warehouses, towns, and air bases.[46] Conceived in this way, bombardment aviation conformed to the restricted vision of airpower that had prevailed among army leaders in the interwar years. The effectiveness of the German combination of air and land power in 1940 discouraged French airmen from articulating a vision, similar to the doctrines established in the Royal Air Force and the U.S. Army Air Corps, of how airpower could achieve strategic objectives independent of theater land goals.

By accepting directions from land commanders for bomber targeting, the Armée de l'air rejected the possibility of using its most potent offensive force to influence a wider range of objectives. The philosophy that restricted bombardment aviation to tactical, or at best lower-order operational, objectives promised to prevent airmen from having a voice in formulating theater strategies. A cardinal principle for French airpower in the 1930s had asserted that there would never be enough aviation resources to fulfill strategic, operational, and tactical requirements. The commission's report accepted that this condition would continue to prevail in the future.[47] Essentially, Commission G advocated placing bombardment groups in an on-call close air support role—this meant that the air service would conduct future bombing operations using an inherently tactical approach.

Pursuit aviation fared no better in the post-debacle critiques submitted by tactical unit commanders. The problem for the fighter forces centered on personnel, organizational, and technical issues. Colonel Boucher, a veteran fighter pilot who had commanded aviation units for the IV Army in 1918, predicted disaster as early as December 1939, when he described the pervasive problems: "The shortage of pilots in the pursuit and reconnaissance groups is flagrant. The IV Army pursuit group, which is authorized 34 single-seat planes, has, in reality, only 23 available, along with only 17 pilots."[48] But air service leaders failed to take effective measures.

As the German attack unfolded in May 1940, French fighter pilots discovered that their equipment placed them at a technical disadvantage. The air staff, on the other hand, had known this for some time. The same report that had warned them about the personnel shortage had also drawn their attention to technical deficiencies in the French fighter force: "The current material, excellent against the Messerschmidt 109, seems to be clearly dominated by the enemy single-seat planes which are appearing. The Dewoitine 520 and the Bloch 152 seem equally destined to be outclassed by the new airplanes. It is necessary, then, to obtain without delay material capable of 560 km/h [347.2 miles per hour], strongly armed (1 cannon, 4 machine guns), with a greatly reduced minimum speed to allow takeoff and landing on relatively short fields."[49] Reports from pursuit aviation units after the French capitulation echoed Colonel Boucher's themes, citing the inferiority of fighter speed, armor, and armament.[50]

Despite the flaws in pursuit organization and equipment, Commission G's final report indicated that this category of aviation performed better than any other in French airpower. The authors claimed that fighter pilots had scored nearly 1,000 aerial victories while suffering only 362 losses to German fighters.[51] The ensuing "myth of the 1,000 victories" provided airmen with evidence to counter the accusation that the Armée de l'air had abandoned the nation in its hour of greatest need.[52] The commission attributed the apparent success of the fighter forces to solid preparation and doctrine during the interwar years. Yet the achievements of air-to-air combat concealed troubling problems in other pursuit mission areas. Rather than tarnishing the reputation of this arm by simply listing the shortcomings of the fighter force, the commission members packaged their critique to emphasize minor recommended adjustments to tactics and procedures. The resulting report advocated few changes to the pursuit doctrines and organizational structures of the 1930s.

With its inherent ability to do battle for air superiority, pursuit represented the most important organizational air component, according to the commission. Tactical commanders agreed. One bombardment group commander related that German pursuit planes had appeared to shadow French bomber formations to notify ground-based air defense units of their speed and altitude. The French airmen had subsequently encountered deadly and accurate antiaircraft artillery barrages.[53] Colonel Dumemes, commander of Groupement de chasse no. 22, condemned the inferiority of French pursuit planes as well as the fragmented command structure that had resulted in the dispersal of French air superiority efforts against the Luftwaffe. Dumemes argued forcefully for a single commander for all pursuit operations.[54]

The commission adopted a more conservative path, however, that conformed to the joint theater command structure and the primacy of land warfare over other forms. Rather than arguing for a single pursuit command, Commission G proposed to "organize the operational Air Force into *grandes unites aériennes mixtes* which will always contain pursuit aviation formations as a minimum."[55] The influence of the joint theater command structure discouraged arguments for a stronger, more independent organization in the future for the Armée de l'air.

In these ways, the commission's approach prevented considerations of organizational alternatives in which the Armée de l'air could assume an equal role, or even a more important one, than the joint force commander's. In other words, in the commission's view, the possibility of planning or executing air operations apart from the joint operational context did not exist. The authors argued further: "Because of the permanence of the danger from the air, every unit of the Army, the Navy, and the Air Force should possess its own organic means of defense against air attacks to guarantee security."[56] This amounted to an assertion of the principle of unity of command for pursuit operations, while denying the means to achieve it by dispersing resources among every unit in the French military establishment.

The loss of local air superiority had represented one of the greatest concerns for French airpower during the campaign of 1940. Bombardment and reconnaissance units had felt this loss to a greater extent than any other air arm. Yet the commission chose to de-emphasize the attrition of unescorted or poorly escorted bombers and reconnaissance airplanes. The problem, members argued, revolved around how to provide security for other aircraft in a rapidly changing air war. The bomber community preferred close escort operations that ensured pursuit formations could provide protection whenever and wherever enemy aircraft challenged the formation along the projected flight path. But commission members rejected this option, in favor of "free pursuit that has the aim of inflicting sensitive and repeated losses on the enemy."[57] This tactic, they argued, had produced the positive results achieved by the pursuit units in the Battle of France. Moreover, the free pursuit organization allowed the Armée de l'air to operate effectively with fewer pilots and airplanes across a wider theater of war. Providing escort fighters for every bombardment or reconnaissance mission would involve prohibitive expenses in both men and material.

The flexibility inherent in the free pursuit tactics would allow those units to gain a measure of autonomy not afforded to the other air arms, in the context of the joint theater command structure. Such freedom stemmed from pursuit's unique aerial mission. While bomber and reconnaissance units provided combat support to terrestrial commanders, pursuit acted directly against enemy airpower. The airmen argued that the joint theater commander would have little interest in controlling the details of these operations, as long as the aviators maintained air superiority over the army corps areas. The authors noted, "the free disposition of the pursuit groups is an evident necessity for the air division command."[58] The most effective relationship between the joint theater commander and the pursuit units involved a loose form of coordination, rather than the control envisioned for the other aerial arms. Close control by the theater commander would only hinder the rapid and spontaneous interception of enemy formations. This argument amounted to a declaration that only an airman, a specialist in pursuit employment, could plan and execute effective fighter operations. Here was a departure from the standard joint theater command structure that dominated Commission G's final report.

The complexity inherent in modern operations allowed both offensive and defensive battle to occur simultaneously. Pursuit aviation could adapt rapidly to the needs of this type of warfare. When the dominant theater strategy dictated a defensive posture, fighter units could provide cover and security for the combined air and land movements. Although defensive operations prevailed on the ground in this scenario, pursuit could offer the means to seize the initiative by conducting offensive sweeps against enemy air forces. Employed in this manner, pursuit set the initial conditions for the joint theater commander to transition from a defensive to an offensive posture. Then, when French strategy dictated a shift to the offensive, pursuit could support the new approach by combining offensive sweeps ahead of the advancing land forces with defensive security and air superiority missions.

The commission members articulated a vision of a robust pursuit arm that would operate in a semiautonomous, but coordinated, manner with the joint theater commander. This characterization of pursuit aviation did not significantly differ, however, from the prescriptions found in the doctrines of the 1930s. Pursuit missions remained reactive at the tactical level, while French strategy remained oriented toward defensive operations. Commission members used the lessons from the war to describe ways to combine offensive and defensive roles for pursuit aviation; in doing so, they aligned themselves with the traits of *lutte aérienne* that air force leaders had articulated in the interwar years.

The characteristics of modern war, as the campaign of 1940 revealed to French airmen, erased the formulas that had relied upon reconnaissance aviation ranging near the lines of two relatively stationary armies. Yet rather than diminishing the importance of such roles, the Battle of France drew attention to the need for an updated conception of how to process into useful information for operational commanders data obtained with airpower. The commission's report noted the consequences of operating with outdated ideas and methods: "Tied for the most part to conceptions of land combat that differed little in their essence from those of 1918, reconnaissance found itself surprised by the new procedures of modern war."[59]

In Commission G's view, the dawn of the Second World War had heralded the end of days when reconnaissance aircraft could loiter over the enemy armies to take photographs that appeared at headquarters hours later. The old paradigm had worked because the tactical and operational situation had changed slowly. Mobile warfare, however, required accurate and timely reports of enemy activities. Viewed in these terms, reconnaissance suffered from the same ills that had afflicted other forms of French aviation in 1940. The formulas to correct problems in other areas of airpower employment also applied, according to the commission, to the mission of battlefield reconnaissance and surveillance.

Organizational problems existed at the tactical level as well as at the operational level. One group commander complained bitterly: "If we now examine the group organization, we are struck by its complexity. Upon mobilization the group possessed one heavy aviation section, one autogyro section, one section of courier airplanes, a weather detachment, followed by a photo detachment."[60] The commander further observed that the diversity of resources and missions, coupled with the lack of effective maintenance and technical support, decreased his unit's combat effectiveness.

Another air commander, Commandant Lanson, revealed the disastrous effects that had stemmed from the ill-conceived command structure, resulting in his group becoming separated from higher command echelons. "During the period 26 May–25 June," he reported, "I only exercised my command under abnormal conditions, and I had practically lost all contact with the terrestrial and air commands after 13 June."[61] Lanson related that the V Army headquarters to which his unit reported had shifted locations without informing him. He acted on his own initiative to move his unit to Dijon, where he hoped to join air and land forces as they regrouped to form a new defensive front. Lanson neglected to mention, however, that in this month of "abnormal" operations, during half of which he admitted to losing all contact with higher echelons, his unit could not have provided effective reconnaissance support to his superiors anyway, because of the disruption in the chain of command. Thus the poorly conceived reconnaissance organization affected operations—subtly at first, through the inefficient flow of aerial intelligence and information, then more dramatically, as headquarters personnel failed to manage the increasing flow of information after the German breakthrough.

The primary solution to the problems encountered by French air forces, as they attempted to provide aerial reconnaissance, centered on devising an appropriate command structure. Reconnaissance units delivered critical information to their command posts, but often it failed to reach the proper echelon, or else the higher commands failed to act upon the data that had been provided by the airmen.[62] Two features describe the information management problem: first, the operational command structure did not allow for effective use of the available reconnaissance units; second, the organization did not have an intelligence processing component. As the intensity of the battle brought increased pressure on French air and land forces, these two characteristics complicated reconnaissance operations.

Commission members hewed to their conservative path when they outlined changes to correct the faults that had been encountered with reconnaissance aviation. The requirements for aerial intelligence gathering did not decrease as a result of the war; on the contrary, mobile warfare only increased the need for timely and accurate information. Airmen would continue to reconnoiter the battlefield in search of enemy forces, they would continue to adjust artillery fire, and they would still range ahead of friendly mobile forces as an aerial screening and protection force. While fulfilling these primary tasks, reconnaissance units could also search for information to pass on to pursuit and bombardment units. Aerial reconnaissance, in the commission's estimation, should receive the highest volume of mission taskings in future wars.[63]

Centralized command structures, combined with concentrated force deployments, described the commission's formula for eliminating the flaws in the use of reconnaissance aviation. As in other aviation areas, a centralized command structure would ensure that reconnaissance remained responsive to the joint force commander's needs. Concentrated force deployments could prevent the dispersal and dislocation of tactical units as the land battle unfolded. At the tactical level, concentration also promised to facilitate the flow of information from airmen to the proper command echelon.[64]

Commission G accurately described the changes in operational warfare that the German attack in 1940 had revealed. The authors of the final report remained reluctant, however, to urge the leaders of the Armée de l'air to abandon doctrinal prescriptions that had guided the service throughout the 1930s. They concluded that combined arms warfare established a permanent place for airpower in operational strategies, but that airpower should serve the needs of a theater land commander. The Armée de l'air had not been able effectively to support efforts to repulse the German offensives in 1940 because the existing command structures had not allowed air and land commanders to unify their efforts. A more effective theater command scheme, in which the senior aviator served as a technical and tactical adviser to the joint force commander, promised to allow future leaders to correct the organizational problems of the French military in the Battle of France.

Under the unified theater command structure that commission members proposed, aviation units could retain traditional roles and mission tasks. Pursuit proved the soundness of prewar tactical doctrines, in the eyes of Commission G. The necessity of gaining and maintaining air superiority meant that pursuit should have a dominant tactical role. At the same time, the airmen realized that army commanders would want to dictate pursuit—and, indeed, all—aviation activities in their operational areas. Therefore the final report asserted that every unit in the military establishment should possess the means to defend itself from aerial attack.

Bombardment and reconnaissance aligned more closely with the needs of the land battle, in the commission's assessment of future needs. The failure to detect and stop, or at least slow, the German advance had seared into the pages of the final report the importance of providing timely intelligence, close air support, and battlefield interdiction. During the time the members worked on their study, massive strategic bomber attacks against enemy towns and industries did not occur on a large scale; thus they apparently could not convince themselves to argue for a bomber force that contained both specially trained close air support and strategic components.

The humiliation and agony of the defeat caused leaders of the Armée de l'air to examine their operations and doctrines in detail. The natural tendency, under such conditions, would be to argue for abandoning formulas that had failed the test of combat. Surprisingly, however, Commission G suggested few substantial changes to the fundamental and tactical doctrines that the air service had developed in the 1930s. The most significant flaw, the barrier to combat effectiveness that emerged from the commission's efforts, centered on organizational doctrine.

The principles of lutte aérienne and the tactical employment concepts of the interwar years required little change to meet the needs of modern, mobile warfare on land. The joint theater command organization that tied the conceptual applications of airpower to the tempo and scope of land warfare would keep airmen focused on tactics. This limited vision had also applied during the 1930s. The result, then, was an air force that remained unable to seize initiative at any level of war—strategic, operational, or tactical. Consequently, the Armée de l'air reacted to every demand for aviation—it could do little else.

8   Neither Decadent, nor Traitorous, nor Stupid

The airmen and politicians who led the Armée de l'air as it served the Third Republic worked diligently to create a military institution that they believed met French defense needs. They encountered difficulty when airpower theory clashed with established notions of how to employ air forces. As competing opinions about the proper role emerged, airmen changed their ideas and methods to accommodate army and navy leaders. While they were altering their arguments to conform to prevailing notions of warfare, gradually they lost sight of the unique characteristics that set airpower apart from land and sea power. Reactive doctrine crept into every aspect of the service because the airmen failed to argue effectively for a distinct vision predicated on the flexibility, range, and initiative that airpower theory described as fundamental characteristics of air warfare.

The historical experiences of the First World War and the 1925 Rif War in Morocco established a tradition of cooperation between air and land forces. Air operations in the Great War derived guidance from army commanders, but late in the war, airmen began to propose and experiment with concepts of strategic bombardment that promised to liberate the air arm from the constraints of a land-based operational philosophy. Limited opportunities to apply airpower against strategic targets laid the foundations for French airmen to consider the potential for independent air operations during the interwar years.

In the Rif War, aviators faced a dramatically different tactical and operational context. Airpower fulfilled many of the traditional roles that had been established during the European conflict, but in ways that stressed the flexibility and initiative for the air forces, rather than the traditional dependence and subordination to land commanders. The airmen of the 37th Aviation Regiment earned the respect of their army brethren as they responded to the operational and tactical situation in a fluid colonial war. The doctrinal legacy of the Rif War was a new definition of how forces should work in concert to achieve common goals. Airmen proved themselves able to formulate operational strategy that capitalized on the unique characteristics of the aerial weapon. By Resident General Lyautey's admission, airpower preserved French authority in Morocco until his ground forces could deploy to counter Abd-el Krim's advances. The relationship that proved so effective in the Rif conflict did not survive, however, as the French government moved to create an independent air service.

Pierre Cot influenced the shape of the Armée de l'air's fundamental doctrine more than any other public figure. Cot recognized that French society would not support aggressive land warfare strategies. He also realized that France would require a military force that could support diplomatic initiatives if the nation was to avoid war with Germany. The air force offered attractive advantages over army forces, because aviation could threaten German strategic and operational centers of gravity while theoretically avoiding costly land engagements. Cot urged airmen to develop a doctrine and a force structure that fulfilled the strategic roles that he believed the nation required to compete effectively against a resurgent Germany.

In his first term as air minister (1933–34), Cot and his colleagues in the air ministry devised a fundamental doctrine that sought to capitalize on the offensive potential available in aerial warfare strategies. He also laid the foundations for an organizational structure, the independent air regions, tailored to the potential strategic and operational effectiveness that airpower could bring to bear against a continental adversary. The concept of *lutte aérienne,* a unified aerial battle, concisely expressed the air minister's ideas about independent operations. The fundamental doctrine grew to include a vision of joint battle, a concept containing the proposal that air forces could bear the responsibility for conducting the war effort, while land forces supported the Armée de l'air. Lutte aérienne also represented a compromise that sought to accommodate the defensive doctrines and strategies that dominated army plans before the Second World War. But aligning fundamental air doctrine with army plans represented only one reason for expanding the boundaries of lutte aérienne.

The law that established the Armée de l'air as a separate service directed the air force to develop capabilities that allowed it to cooperate with land and sea forces. This legal requirement forced French airmen to describe lutte aérienne in terms of simultaneous terrestrial and air wars. The defensive component of the land war introduced a defensive aspect to the aerial effort. This modification was not harmful when considered in the context of an evolving theory of airpower. French strategic calculations certainly emphasized the primacy of defensive operations throughout the 1930s—the Armée de l'air had a moral and a legal obligation to devise a concept of war that served the national strategy. But the combined effects of defensive and cooperative missions, along with bureaucratic politics, allowed entrenched army and navy institutional biases to reduce the authority available to operational air commanders.

The failure of the Armée de l'air's leaders to establish a satisfactory organizational doctrine that preserved the service's role in joint operations added another facet to the reactive approach to aerial warfare. Airmen found themselves moving from positions of nominal equality in joint command organizations to positions that decreased their authority vis-à-vis army and navy commanders. The final insult, in organizational terms, occurred in September 1939 and February 1940, when the illusion of an independent air service evaporated in the wake of the dramatic organizational changes that made the air units subordinate to army corps and theater commanders. Leaders found their airpower dispersed among army units, while they became little more than technical advisers for the army commanders.

As their fundamental and organizational doctrines came under increasing bureaucratic attack from the land and sea services, airmen turned to the process of developing tactical doctrine. This, however, guided the Armée de l'air further down the path toward reaction and compromise, because tactical plans placed the service in a defensive, cooperative posture. The tactical formulas contained in published regulations failed to describe how the Armée de l'air could seize the initiative to accomplish operational objectives that would contribute to winning a war against Germany.

Theories and doctrine manuals accounted for only part of the process that resulted in a reactive posture in the French air force of the 1930s. The training system that provided aircrew members, technicians, and support personnel reinforced the tendencies established in the fundamental, organizational, and tactical doctrines. Air force leaders expected the instructional system to prepare service members for war while it also educated them about the intricacies of European international relations. One of the implied goals of regular training syllabi focused on building a common understanding among airmen of the political, economic, and military causes of European conflicts. The Vichy High Court of Justice used the Armée de l'air's social-education agenda and the influence of Pierre Cot to tar the air force with the brush of Leftist treason. Regardless of the inaccurate Vichy characterization of Cot and the air service, the structure that the regulations prescribed never met the requirement of preparing French airmen adequately for modern war.

The training system never gained enough institutional strength to function effectively as a vehicle for developing air doctrine. The air staff's poor management contributed in a significant way to the abysmal results achieved during the 1930s. Air staff personnel often directed school commanders to create new schools to meet steadily increasing requirements for trained personnel. Yet they failed to ensure that adequate facilities, personnel, and equipment reached the new schools, which consequently only increased the burdens on the system. Growth and inefficiency characterized the decentralized training system that consistently fell short of the Armée de l'air's goals. The strategic emergencies of the second half of the decade caused the air staff to intensify its efforts to improve productivity—with no amelioration of its methods.

By the late 1930s the training system operated in a state of perpetual crisis. Tactical units clamored for trained mechanics, pilots, instructors, and other technical personnel. The schools could not increase production quickly enough to meet operational demands. A severe shortage of qualified instructors in all specialties guaranteed that the situation would take years to remedy. The air staff responded in its usual bureaucratic manner: staff directives ordered the creation of new instructor schools, while simultaneously removing trainers from tactical units to perform school duties. Neither measure solved the air force personnel shortage problems.

The air staff became increasingly concerned, as war loomed, that the schools would fall prey to enemy air attacks. After much debate, the air minister and his staff ordered certain elements of the training system to plan for evacuation to North Africa. This decision, like so many in the Armée de l'air of the interwar period, came too late to provide an effective counter to the threat posed by enemy aerial bombardment. Moreover, the move exacerbated the personnel shortage, by decreasing student production at a time when the system needed to run at full throttle.

Maneuvers and exercises only increased the Armée de l'air's inclinations toward reactive doctrine. A regular schedule was maintained from 1933 to 1938, after which the wave of political crises that swept Europe caused service leaders to suspend large-scale exercises in favor of more focused preparations for war. The annual maneuvers included political scenarios that accurately depicted the outlines of a possible war with Germany. But the operating vision for airpower rarely conformed to the prescriptions of *lutte aérienne*.

Instead, the air staff's scenarios and exercises forced the Armée de l'air to operate from a defensive posture, in support of army ground units. This failure to employ bombardment and pursuit forces in a manner consistent with the precepts of lutte aérienne damaged the Armée de l'air's offensive potential. Bombardment units habitually acted as target drones, while pursuit aviation grew accustomed to scripted combat scenarios.

The exercises served one useful purpose—they highlighted the poor levels of proficiency among air operations and support personnel. Like so many other flaws that came to light in the French air force of the 1930s, this realization proved to be a mixed blessing. Because of it, service leaders began to use the exercises to provide training for personnel who failed to demonstrate proficiency in their assigned specialties. Yet this deviation from the scenario also prevented the accomplishment of the stated exercise objectives. The exercises became training opportunities rather rehearsals for theater-level air warfare, as the air staff intended.

Mobilization and operational war plans reflected the flaws of other structures in the interwar Armée de l'air. Mobilization efforts centered on managing processes, rather than on accurately identifying personnel and material requirements for moving the nation from peacetime to a wartime posture. More important, air service leaders never acknowledged that the mobilization system could not provide adequate numbers of combat and support personnel to maintain operational and tactical effectiveness.

Operational planning against military and economic targets in Germany, Italy, and Spain represented one of the most sophisticated elements of French air doctrine development. The air staff produced rigorous analyses of the war economy of France's principal adversary. After careful study, the staff created comprehensive target dossiers that reflected the complexity inherent in the Armée de l'air's fundamental doctrine, while preserving the flexibility to react to German offensive moves toward the west. The reactive tendency was so pervasive, however, that the offensive component of the French air arm never gained an opportunity to realize its potential. Government economic policies produced a flawed force structure, while interservice conflicts restricted the purposes and scope of aerial operations. In the final analysis, French offensive plans were never more than staff exercises that provided the illusion of operational effectiveness.

The air force suffered, along with the army and the rest of the nation, in the defeat of 1940. The reactive nature of the Armée de l'air's approach to air warfare forced the service into a tactical role, while German airpower conducted a successful operational and tactical campaign. French airmen could only achieve temporary local successes against the better organized, equipped, and trained German air forces. Yet surprisingly, after closely examining the experience of the defeat, air service officers retained the broad outlines of the reactive doctrine that had prevailed during the 1930s. The commission that analyzed the Armée de l'air's performance concluded that French military strategy should adapt to new operational conditions. But the prescriptions for air warfare remained focused squarely on the tactical roles that the service had performed in 1940 and throughout the interwar years.

During the 1930s the leaders of the French air arm had tried to create a service capable of contributing to a fundamental change in the philosophy and practice of war. Doctrine represented one of the primary structures that defined the purpose of the air institution within the larger defense establishment. It outlined the parameters for how the air force interacted with the government, army, and navy. Ultimately, doctrine described how the Armée de l'air intended to perform its primary function—wielding airpower to support national offensive and defensive strategies against various known and unknown enemies.

The failure of the French air force in the 1930s was not an intellectual failure: airmen developed sophisticated doctrines that portrayed the full potential that airpower could bring to bear in a modern war. Nor did the air force fail to develop structures that supported national strategies. The Armée de l'air created institutions designed to promote thinking about how to use airpower in concert with other methods of war. But in the face of competing claims for air resources, the failure lay in the absence of a strong air organization capable defending a vision of airpower that preserved its unique capabilities.

Taken as a whole, Armée de l'air leaders were neither decadent, nor traitorous, nor stupid. They faced the complex task of constructing a more complete theory of airpower, while simultaneously fulfilling strategic and operational missions within an air force that had not yet attained a mature institutional identity. The task became more difficult because war remained a threat throughout the decade. Until 1938, strategists and diplomats in France viewed airpower as an effective deterrent that could protect the nation while it concealed the army's weaknesses. But the defensive strategy that governed France's military policies afforded her adversaries the initiative regarding the timing and character of a future war. Airmen found themselves tasked to create an institution, support active deterrence strategies, and develop comprehensive force modernization programs, all in a context of constant pressure from army leaders to abandon the fundamental premises of their doctrine.

The leaders of the air service could not develop their theory and doctrine free from competing institutional influences. The French air arm struggled with constant demands for support from the army and the navy. The pressure of that pull gradually altered air service priorities, to emphasize the limited vision of land warfare. Accompanying the tempo of this shift, air service capabilities increasingly conformed to the scope of the ground battle.

But the land warfare that the Armée de l'air prepared to support followed principles of fixed fortifications and firepower. In this view of war, airpower performed most effectively in reconnaissance and air superiority roles. Airmen failed to examine and change their doctrine in light of the altered operational priorities. The French realized—too late—that they needed a more potent offensive form of airpower to complement the land and air defensive forces.

French air doctrine became more reactive as the Armée de l'air struggled with conflicting strategic and operational issues in the 1930s. Reactive practices evolved as a function of theory, but philosophy alone could not have been responsible. Political, strategic, and operational influences were also at work. The shifting political and strategic circumstances in the interwar years kept French airmen in a reactive posture, while the pressures from the army and the navy kept the Armée de l'air off balance.

Finally, reactive doctrine was a product of the service's focus on tactical matters: the French air force's ability to promote a doctrine for strategic and operational air warfare remained stillborn in the 1930s. The failure to resolve the conflict between army and air force perceptions of how best to use airpower doomed the Armée de l'air to conform to the pattern of the Armée de terre's strategies. The decision in February 1940 to place the air commands under the authority of land commanders effectively dismantled the independent service. When war came in 1939 and 1940, the airmen could not articulate a unique vision—the perspective from the air—of how to counter the German attack. Their inability to defend their service became the essence of reactive doctrine, the legacy of the Armée de l'air of the 1930s.

Notes

1. Introduction

1. Service historique de l'Armée de l'air (hereafter S.H.A.A.), série 3D, carton 477, état français, secrétariat d'état à l'aviation, "Enseignements aériens de la guerre, 1939–1942, Commission 'G,': Première partie, les conditions de la guerre moderne," March 1942, 10. Unless otherwise indicated, all translations are my own.
2. For a survey of European approaches to airpower doctrine see James S. Corum, "Airpower Thought in Continental Europe between the Wars," in Phillip S. Meilinger, ed., *The Paths of Heaven: The Evolution of Airpower Theory* (Maxwell AFB, Ala.: Air University Press, 1997), 151–81.
3. Geoffrey Till discusses the role of airpower in the Imperial Japanese Fleet: see "Adopting the Aircraft Carrier: The British, American, and Japanese Case Studies," in Williamson Murray and Allan R. Millett, eds., *Military Innovation in the Interwar Period* (Cambridge: Cambridge University Press, 1996), 191–226.
4. Richard J. Overy suggests that operational effectiveness results from performance in five areas: strategic conception, economic capability, scientific and technical mobilization, political and social reception, and combat effectiveness. See "Air Power in the Second World War: Historical Themes and Theories," in Horst Boog, ed., *The Conduct of the Air War in the Second World War: An International Comparison* (New York: St. Martin's Press, 1992), 7–28.
5. Robert J. Young, *France and the Origins of the Second World War* (New York: St. Martin's Press, 1996), 49.
6. See Robert A. Doughty, *The Seeds of Disaster: The Development of French Army Doctrine, 1919–1939* (Hamden, Conn.: Archon Books, 1985). See also Robert A. Doughty, *The Breaking Point: Sedan and the Fall of France, 1940* (Hamden, Conn.: Archon Books, 1990); and Eugenia C. Kiesling, *Arming against Hitler:*

France and the Limits of Military Planning (Lawrence, Kans.: University of Kansas Press, 1996).

7. See Thierry Vivier, "La coopération aéronautique franco-tchécoslovaque, janvier 1933–septembre 1938" *Revue historique des armées* (March 1993): 70–79. See also Thierry Vivier, "L'aviation française en Pologne, janvier 1936–septembre 1939," *Revue historique des armées* (December 1993): 60–70.

8. Thierry Vivier studied the Armée de l'air's assessment of German intentions and the effects of that evaluation on procurement decisions in the mid-1930s. See *La politique aéronautique militaire de la France, janvier 1933–septembre 1939* (Paris: Éditions l'Harmattan, 1996), 183–238.

9. Robert W. Krauskopf, "French Air Power Policy, 1919–1939" (Ph.D. diss., Washington, D.C.: Georgetown University, 1965).

10. For the most recent example of this genre, see Vivier, *La politique aéronautique militaire de la France.*

11. "The code of responsibility is drummed into officers from their first days as subalterns. Their right to command rests, ultimately, not only on their acceptance of greater risk and hardship than those under their command, but on their willingness to accept responsibility. To say that a spectacular failure is either nobody's fault, or everybody's, or indeed the consequence of a complicated chain of events and decisions, is to undermine the moral order an army requires in order to be able to fight." Eliot A. Cohen and John Gooch, *Military Misfortunes: The Anatomy of Failure in War* (New York: Vintage Books, 1991), 33.

12. Kiesling, *Arming against Hitler,* xii.

13. Thierry Viver comments, "the history of French military aviation has remained a minor genre, far at the margins of the French Academy." Vivier, *La politique aéronautique militaire de la France,* 15.

14. See J. Néré, *The Foreign Policy of France from 1914 to 1945,* translated by Translance (London: Routledge and Keegan Paul, 1975).

15. Two notable exceptions are Thierry Vivier, "La commission G: Entre la défaite et l'Armée de l'air future, 1941–1942," *Revue historique des armées* 3 (1989): 113–21; and Claude d'Abzac-Epezy, *L'Armée de l'air de Vichy, 1940–1944* (Vincennes: Service historique de l'Armée de l'air, 1997), 363–72.

2. Sources of Reactive Air Doctrine

1. S.H.A.A., série 2B, carton 109, ministère de la guerre, "Instruction sur l'emploi tactique des Grandes Unités" (Paris: Imprimerie nationale, 1936), 17.

2. Although there were no airborne operations during the war, in 1918 the American airpower pioneer William "Billy" Mitchell proposed a division-level parachute assault behind German lines. See Mark A. Clodfelter, "Molding Airpower Convictions: Development and Legacy of William Mitchell's Strategic Thought," in Meilinger, ed., *Paths of Heaven,* 79–114.

3. "Avant-propos," *Revue de l'aéronautique militaire* 1 (January–February 1921): 2.

4. See Robin Higham, "Air Power in World War I, 1914–1918," in Alan Stephens, ed., *The War in the Air, 1914–1999,* proceedings of a conference held by the Royal Australian Air Force in Canberra (Fairbairn, Australia: Air Power Studies Centre, 1994), 23–45.

5. The authors of the Treaty of Versailles attempted to guarantee Allied sovereignty in aviation matters. Part 5, Article 198 stipulated, "the armed forces of Germany must not include any military or naval air forces." But Article 201 promised to be more important than the demobilization of the air forces, stating: "During the six months following the coming into force of the present Treaty, the manufacture and importation of aircraft, parts of aircraft, engines of aircraft, and parts of engines for aircraft, shall be forbidden in all German territory." See *The Avalon Project at the Yale Law School: The Versailles Treaty June 28, 1919,* part 5, http://www.yale.edu/lawweb/avalon/imt/partv.htm.

6. S.H.A.A., série 2B, carton 109, ministère de la guerre, "Instruction sur l'emploi tactique des Grandes Unités" (Paris: Imprimerie nationale, 1936), 17.

7. One source left no room for doubt about this responsibility: "[I]t is the duty of the commander of the ground forces to prescribe the location of new landing fields." The source concludes, "this problem of landing field should be placed in the front rank among the thoughts of the commander relative to his air service, *even ahead of the missions given to it"* (emphasis added). The Albert F. Simpson United States Air Force Historical Research Agency (hereafter HRA), File 248.262-13, "Selection of Landing Fields," 3.

8. HRA, File 248.262-13, "Employment of Air Observation," 1. This is a military attaché report that includes translations of letters and instruction manuals from the École militaire et d'application du génie. Most of the documents in this file date from the mid-1920s, but they reflect the army's institutional opinion about how to use aviation in the later years of the world war. It is not clear whether it was the military attaché or the officers of the Air Corps Tactical School who translated the report.

9. For a brief discussion of the doctrine of the continuous front, see Capitaine J.–M. Marill, "La doctrine militaire française entre les deux guerres," *Revue historique des armées* 3 (1991): 24–34. Robert A. Doughty describes the command philosophy of the methodical battle as an intensification of the methods of the First World War in *The Breaking Point: Sedan and the Fall of France, 1940* (Hamden, Conn.: Archon Books, 1990), 7–32.

10. HRA, File 248.262-13, "Missions of Pursuit Aviation," 23.

11. HRA File 248.262-13, "Bombardment Aviation: Roles and Missions," 29.

12. Ibid.

13. HRA, File 248.262-13, "Aerostation," 33–41.

14. HRA, File 248.262-13, "Anti-Aircraft Defense," 41–48.

15. S.H.A.A., série 2B, carton 109, École supérieure de guerre, "Notes sur l'emploi de l'aéronautique par le commandement, 1928–1929," *Cours aéronautique* (Rambouillet: Imprimerie Pierre Le Roy, n.d.), iii.

16. Ibid.

17. Capitaine de réserve Waldemar Pfeiffer, "Formation de marche et action de l'aviation: D'après les expériences de la guerre," *Revue de l'aéronautique militaire* 23 (September–October 1924): 108.

18. Chef de Bataillon breveté Keller, "L'aviation dans la bataille," *Revue de l'aéronautique militaire* 27 (May–June 1925): 49. Keller later served in the personnel and operations directorates of the air staff. He chaired the committee assigned responsibility for producing the 1937 defensive aviation doctrine manual *(aviation légère de défense)* under Pierre Cot's first air ministry.

19. Colonel Félix Marie, "Du bombardment par avion," *Revue de l'aéronautique militaire* 30 (November–December 1925): 139.

20. In the late 1920s, several articles focused on studies of the operations in 1914. See for example Lieutenant Colonel breveté M. Blaise, "L'expérience de la guerre: L'exploration aérienne à la 3ème armée en août et septembre 1914," *Revue de l'aéronautique militaire* 43 (January–February 1928): 21–31; 45 (May–June 1928): 71–75; 47 (September–October 1928): 125–30; and 48 (November–December 1928): 147–54. See *Revue des Forces aériennes* 1 (August 1929): 1–41; Général Paul Armengaud, "L'Aviation et la conduite de la manoeuvre et de la bataille: Morhange," *Revue des Forces aériennes* 8 (March 1930): 261–300; Colonel breveté Guillemeney, "L'aviation et les services de renseignements dans une guerre moderne," *Revue des Forces aériennes* 11 (June 1930): 645–83. See also Colonel Voisin, "L'exploration aérienne à la 5ème Armée jusqu'à la veille de Charleroi, 21 août 1914," *Revue des Forces aériennes* 12 (July 1930): 760–84; 13 (August 1930): 891–926. And for Armengaud's views, see Général Paul Armengaud, "Aviation et manoeuvre d'aile et de dislocation: La manoeuvre et la bataille de la Marne et de l'Oureq," *Revue des Forces aériennes* 14 (September 1930): 1000–1046.

21. Commandant H. Langerin, "Action de masse aérienne dans une bataille défensive," *Revue des Forces aériennes* 6 (January 1930): 21.

22. Ibid., 61.

23. See Krauskopf, "French Air Power Policy, 1919–1939," 30–37. See also Charles Christienne and Pierre Lissarague, *A History of French Military Aviation,* translated by Francis Kianka (Washington, D.C.: Smithsonian Institution Press, 1986), 241–50.

24. Colonel breveté Guillemeney, "Le bombardement aérien des installations industrielles: Le blocus du bassin de Briey," *Revue des Forces aériennes* 15 (October 1930): 1163. This was by no means the only example of a strategic air campaign plan from the First World War. The British devised a plan to launch deep attacks against German industry. American planners also hoped to create havoc in German industries to hasten the end of the war. See HRA, File 248.222-78, Edgar S. Gorrell, "The Future of American Bombardment Aviation," 1917.

25. Guillemeney, "Le bombardement aérien des installations industrielles: Le blocus du bassin de Briey," 1166.

26. Ibid., 1182.
27. Ibid., 1188–99.
28. Army commanders feared the loss of control that independent air operations implied. Airmen too understood this danger. General Voisin wrote that "independent aviation, as an intangible block, not placing all or part of its forces at the disposition of the Armées, but above them, is an idea which produces a divergence of efforts and duality of command, both difficult to reconcile with the principle of the liaison of arms." See Général Voisin, "La doctrine de l'aviation française de combat en 1918: L'aviation de combat indépendante," *Revue des Forces aériennes* 28 (November 1931): 1300.
29. See André Le Révérend, *Lyautey* (Paris: Fayard, 1983).
30. Wing Commander RHMS Saundby, "Small Wars: Summing Up," RAF Staff College, 14th Course: Andover, 26 June 1936, 5.
31. Commandant de La Fargue, "L'aviation militaire en Tunisie: Historique, rôle, 1916–1920," *Revue de l'aéronautique militaire* 3 (May–June 1921): 57.
32. For a thorough analysis of Lyautey's methods of colonization, see William A. Hoisington Jr., *Lyautey and the French Conquest of Morocco* (New York: St. Martin's Press, 1995).
33. Henri Busson, Joseph Fèvre, and Henri Hauser, *La France d'aujourd'hui et ses colonies* (Paris: Librairie Félix Alcan, 1920). On page 530, the authors quote Eugène Aubin as an expert on Moroccan society: "In reality, the Moroccan Empire was a *fédération vague,* encompassing a great number of tribes and divisions, some of them tiny; each of these organisms possessed its own constitution, each of them guarded, above all, jealously of its independence, and desired to conserve it, keeping the country at the edge of anarchy."
34. See Dwight L. Ling, *Morocco and Tunisia: A Comparative History* (Washington, D.C.: University Press of America, 1979), chap. 3. See also Paul S. Reinsch, *Colonial Government: An Introduction to the Study of Colonial Institutions* (New York: The MacMillan Company, 1916) especially chap. 8, for an introduction to the distinctions between protectorates and other forms of colonial government.
35. See Barnett Singer, "Lyautey: An Interpretation of the Man and French Imperialism," *Journal of Contemporary History* 26 (1991): 131–57. Marshal Philippe Pétain temporarily assumed control of military operations in the protectorate after the Rif rebellion cooled.
36. S.H.A.A., série C2A, carton 34, item 21, letter from Lyautey to the *ministre de la guerre,* 12 June 1914, 3.
37. Commandant Barthélemy, "L'aviation dans l'Afrique du Nord," *Revue de l'aéronautique militaire* 1 (January–February 1921): 9.
38. Commandant Cheutin, "Rôle colonial de l'aviation militaire au Maroc," *Revue de l'aéronautique militaire* 4 (1921): 89 (emphasis added).
39. Ibid.
40. Ibid.
41. Barthélemy, "L'aviation dans l'Afrique du Nord," 102–3.

42. Médecin-Major Gravellat, "L'aviation sanitaire aux colonies," *Revue de l'aéronautique militaire* 18 (November–December, 1923): 122–24. See also Capitaine W. Breyton, "L'aviation sanitaire au Maroc en 1933," *Revue de l'Armée de l'air* 56 (March 1934): 243–64.

43. Lieutenant Colonel Cheutin, "L'aviation française au Maroc: Emploi de l'aviation." *Revue de l'aéronautique militaire* 19 (January–February 1924): 6 (emphasis added).

44. Ibid.

45. Ibid., 1–6.

46. Ibid.

47. For an analysis of Abd el-Krim's political goals, see Shannon Earl Fleming, *Primo de Rivera and Abd el-Krim: The Struggle in Spanish Morocco, 1923–1927* (New York: Garland Publishing, 1991).

48. C. R. Pennell, "Ideology and Practical Politics: A Case Study of the Rif War in Morocco, 1921–1926," *International Journal of Middle East Studies* 14 (1982): 21.

49. Simone Pesquies, "L'aéronautique militaire française dans la guerre du Rif," *Revue du nord* 72 (1990): 317–67.

50. "Emploi de l'aviation au Maroc en 1925: Aperçu général de la campagne—Ses trois grandes phases," *Revue de l'aéronautique militaire* 33 (May–June 1926): 58.

51. Ibid., 38. See also "Emploi de l'aviation au Maroc en 1925: Aperçu général de la campagne—Ses trois grandes phases," *Revue de l'aéronautique militaire* 32 (March–April 1926): 37.

52. "Emploi de l'aviation au Maroc en 1925: Aperçu général de la campagne—Ses trois grandes phases," *Revue de l'aéronautique militaire* 32 (March–April 1926): 38.

53 Ibid., 39.

54. "Emploi de l'aviation au Maroc en 1925: Aperçu général de la campagne—Ses trois grandes phases," *Revue de l'aéronautique militaire* 33 (May–June 1926): 61.

55. Cheutin, "L'aviation française au Maroc: Emploi de l'aviation," *Revue de l'aéronautique militaire* 21 (May–June 1924): 56.

56. Pesquies, "L'Aéronautique militaire française dans la guerre du Rif," 356–357.

57. Paul Armengaud, *Quelques enseignements des campagnes du Riff en matière d'aviation, 1925–1926* (Paris: Berger-Levrault, 1928), 1.

58. Ibid., 26.

59. Ibid., 7 (emphasis in original).

60. Ibid., 18.

61. Ibid., 60–61.

62. Ibid., 29.

63. For an analysis of the procurement policies of this period, see Vivier, *La politique aéronautique militaire de la France*, 83–97.

64. The French were not alone in choosing to limit aircraft purchases to a few prototype models. United States senator James Wadsworth commented that "the designers are registering tremendous improvements in every way, and therefore we

should hesitate before we purchase a large number of planes in any one year, lest we find that we have committed ourselves to the extent of our financial abilities to a type doomed to be outclassed." See Frank A. Tichenor, "Air—Hot and Otherwise: Propaganda vs. Patriotism," *Aero Digest* (July 1926): 239.

65. On the development of French foreign policy, see Néré, *The Foreign Policy of France from 1914 to 1945.* For the role of airpower in the alliance with Czechoslovakia, see Vivier, "La coopération aéronautique franco-tchécoslovaque," 70–79.

66. For a thorough study of the various attempts by the Armée de l'air to support French national policy in Eastern Europe, see Vivier, *La politique aéronautique militaire de la France,* 505–64.

67. For a concise development of the delayed economic effects of the Great Depression and its consequences for the rearmament effort, see Philippe Bernard and Henri Dubief, *The Decline of the Third Republic, 1914–1938,* translated by Anthony Forster (Cambridge: Cambridge University Press, 1985).

68. Stavinsky was a corrupt financier with alleged connections with the government and law enforcement officials. When accused of swindling millions of francs from the Municipal Credit Bank of Bayonne, he fled and ultimately committed suicide. The extreme Right, including Charles Maurras's Action française, accused the government of instituting a coverup to protect key officials. On 6 February 1934, an estimated 100,000 demonstrators gathered in the Place de la Concorde to demand justice. The resulting riot left 14 dead and 2,500 wounded. Politically, the riot caused the dissolution of the Daladier government in favor of one more acceptable to the Right.

69. Patrick Facon, "Le plan I, 1933–1937: Aux origines du réarmament aérien," *Aviation Magazine* 747 (February 1979): 86–91. Part 2, *Aviation Magazine* 748 (February 1979): 66–71.

70. Vivier, *La politique aéronautique militaire de la France.*

71. See Emmaneul Chadeau, *L'industrie aéronautique en France, 1900–1950: De Bleriot à Dassault* (Paris: Fayard, 1987).

72. Ibid., 352–64.

73. On the Popular Front, see Nicole Jordan, *The Popular Front and Central Europe: The Dilemmas of French Impotence, 1918–1940* (Cambridge: Cambridge University Press, 1992).

74. *La marcha sobre Madrid,* Monografias de la Guerra de España, no. 1 (Madrid: Libreria editorial San Martin, 1968), 25–31, especially 30 n. 11.

75. "[T]he barely qualified commanders, having earned their positions as a result of their participation in the battles of 1914–1918, most often in the *Armée de Terre,* dominated and blocked the advancement of more educated and specialized captains." D'Abzac-Epezy, *L'Armée de l'air de Vichy,* 61.

76. Vivier, *La politique aéronautique militaire de la France,* 381–87.

77. For an analysis of La Chambre's appointment to the air ministry, see Patrick Facon, *L'Armée de l'air dans la tourmente: La bataille de France, 1939–1940* (Paris: Economica, 1997), 23–26.

78. The consequences of this decision may be detected in Gamelin's appraisal that "the role of aviation is apt to be exaggerated, and after the early days of a war the wastage will be such that it will be more and more confined to acting as an accessory to the army." Anthony Admathwaite, *France and the Coming of the Second World War, 1936–1939* (London: Frank Cass, 1977), 162.

79. "Full of brilliant designers and skilled craftsmen, the aeronautical industry was a shambles, a congeries of small firms incapable of facing the world of modern productivity and unwilling to test its waters." Eugen Weber, *The Hollow Years: France in the 1930s* (New York: W. W. Norton, 1994), 254.

80. "Toward the end of September [1938] when an armed conflict in Europe seemed imminent, the American government informed France in writing that if war came the Neutrality Law would prevent it from delivering the planes which the French had ordered in May." William L. Shirer, *The Collapse of the Third Republic: An Inquiry into the Fall of France in 1940* (New York: Simon and Schuster, 1969), 356. Patrick Facon catalogs the numbers of airplanes available to the French at the beginning of the war. There were 172 Curtiss Hawk pursuit planes in the French fighter force on 3 September. This number represented 14 percent of the total pursuit strength—hardly enough to shore up the lack of air superiority capability against the Germans. See Patrick Facon, "Le plan V, 1938–1939," *Revue historique des armées* 4 (1979): 102–23.

81. See Facon, *L'Armée de l'air dans la tourmente,* 156–64. For a detailed analysis of the French efforts to purchase American airframes see Vivier, *La politique aéronautique militaire de la France,* 457–84.

82. Orville H. Bullitt, ed., *For the President, Personal and Secret: Correspondence between Franklin Delano Roosevelt and William C. Bullitt* (Boston: Houghton Mifflin, 1972), 423.

83. Pierre Cot, *L'Armée de l'air, 1936–1938* (Paris: Grasset, 1939), 69.

84. Despite the assertion in the British official history that "the size and composition of air forces to be employed in France had been decided, the necessary measures for their operation had been agreed, and plans had been made for their prompt dispatch and accommodation," this was hardly the case. See L. F. Ellis, *The War in France and Flanders, 1939–1940* (London: Her Majesty's Stationery Office, 1953), 12. Thierry Vivier argues that the airmen of the two nations differed with regard to the most important objectives for the air forces. French officers argued for targeting German aerodromes to reduce the effectiveness of the Luftwaffe. British airmen advocated attacks on German factories, production centers, petroleum refineries, and other industrial targets. See Vivier, *La politique aéronautique militaire de la France,* 557–58.

85. For an account of the destruction of British light and medium bomber forces during the Battle of France, see Denis Richards, *The Hardest Victory: RAF Bomber Command in the Second World War* (New York: W. W. Norton, 1994).

3. Writing and Publishing Reactive Air Doctrine

1. S.H.A.A., série 2B, carton 109, ministère de l'air, "Principes généraux d'emploi et d'organisation de l'Armée de l'air: Rapport au président de la république," Paris, 1 April 1933, 1.

2. Sir Michael Howard wrote: "I am tempted indeed to declare dogmatically that whatever doctrine the Armed Forces are working on now, they have got it wrong. I am also tempted to declare that it does not matter that they have got it wrong. What does matter is their capacity to get it right quickly when the moment arrives." "Military Science in an Age of Peace," *RUSI: Journal of the Royal United Services Institute for Defence Studies* 119 (March 1974): 7.

3. For details on the debate within the government and the press on the creation of the Armée de l'air, see Marcellin Hodeir, "La création du ministère de l'air vue par la presse parisienne, septembre, octobre, novembre, 1928," *Revue historique des armées* 4 (1988): 92–101. See also Thierry Vivier, "L'Armée de l'air et la Révolution technique des années trente, 1933–1939," *Revue historique des armées* 1 (1990): 32–39; and Pascal Vennesson, *Les chevaliers de l'air: Aviation et conflits au XXe siècle* (Paris: Presses de sciences po, 1997), 127–43.

4. S.H.A.A., série 2B, carton 109, ministère de l'air, "Principes généraux d'emploi et d'organisation de l'Armée de l'air: Rapport au président de la république," Paris, 1 April 1933, 3.

5. For a description of the types of doctrine and how services use it, see Dennis Drew and Donald M. Snow, *Making Strategy: An Introduction to National Security Processes and Problems* (Maxwell Air Force Base, Ala.: Air University Press, 1988), 163–74. On the relevance of doctrine and its development process, see Gary Waters, ed., *RAAF Air Power Doctrine: A Collection of Contemporary Essays* (Canberra: Strategic and Defence Studies Centre, 1990), 7–12.

6. David MacIssac wrote, "there has been no lack of theorists, but they have had only limited influence in a field where the effects of technology and the deeds of practitioners have from the beginning played greater roles than have ideas." See "Voices from the Central Blue: The Air Power Theorists," in Peter Paret, ed., *Makers of Modern Strategy: From Machiavelli to the Nuclear Age* (Princeton: Princeton University Press, 1986), 624. More recently, Phillip Meilinger observed: "Airmen from any country have seldom been accused of being thinkers, and precious few have taken up the pen to write down their thoughts on how airpower should be employed in war. Added to this is the relatively short time airpower has existed: all in the past century. As a result, there have been a limited number of books, articles, and manuals written to date that have dealt with the theory and doctrine of airpower." "The Historiography of Airpower: Theory and Doctrine," *Journal of Military History* 64 (April 2000): 467.

7. Giulio Douhet, *The Command of the Air,* translated by Dino Ferrari, 1942 (reprint, Washington, D.C.: Office of Air Force History, 1983).

8. Thierry Vivier argues that the Armée de l'air adopted Douhet's ideas about airpower. He based that assessment in part on the decision to procure the all-purpose bombardment-combat-reconnaissance (BCR) airplane. Vivier makes a convincing argument that the BCR represented an attempt to field Douhet's "battleplane." See Vivier, *La politique aéronautique militaire de la France*, 59–64. Pascal Vennesson argues that the French air force thoroughly rejected Douhet's philosophy of aerial bombardment: "No doctrine, and in any case no doctrine of long-range strategic bombardment, was imposed as an underlying ideology in the institutionalization of the Air Force." See Vennesson, *Les chevaliers de l'air*, 167–72. For a contemporary critique of Douhet's ideas and their applicability to French strategic concerns, see Colonel P. Vauthier, *La doctrine de guerre du Général Douhet* (Paris: Berger-Levrault, 1935).

9. Carl H. Builder argues that this is exactly what happened in the United States Air Force after World War II, and especially after Vietnam. See *The Icarus Syndrome* (New Brunswick, N.J.: Transaction Publishers, 1996).

10. The obvious case of a doctrine that evolved without direct combat experience is nuclear deterrence theory in the United States. See Lawrence Freedman, *The Evolution of Nuclear Strategy*, 2d ed. (New York: St. Martin's Press, 1989).

11. For a discussion of how the European powers adapted theory and doctrine to the new weapon in the interwar years, see James S. Corum, "Airpower Thought in Continental Europe between the Wars," in Meilinger, ed., *Paths of Heaven*, 151–81.

12. S.H.A.A., série 2B, carton 109, ministère de l'air, cabinet du ministre et état-major, général de l'Armée de l'air, "Circulaire confidentielle pour les cadres de l'Armée de l'air," 22 October 1933, 1.

13. Cot, *L'Armée de l'air*, 37.

14. Ibid., 131.

15. S.H.A.A., série 2B, carton 109, ministère de l'air, "Principes généraux d'emploi et d'organisation de l'Armée de l'air: Rapport au président de la république," Paris, 1 April 1933, 1.

16. Cot, *L'Armée de l'air*, 123.

17. S.H.A.A., série 2B, carton 109, ministère de l'air, cabinet du ministre et état-major, général de l'Armée de l'air, "Circulaire confidentielle pour les cadres de l'Armée de l'air," 22 October 1933, 2.

18. S.H.A.A., série 2B, carton 109, "La doctrine d'emploi de l'Armée de l'air," October 1933, 6. Although this document does not bear Cot's signature, it conforms to his style and his philosophies about airpower. Moreover, the policy issues that the author discusses reflect those of a highly placed individual in French politics.

19. S.H.A.A., série 2B, carton 109, ministère de l'air, cabinet du ministre et état-major, général de l'Armée de l'air, "Circulaire confidentielle pour les cadres de l'Armée de l'air," 22 October 1933, 2.

20. In the early days of air force independence, Cot's expressed desire for innovation and intellectual stimulation contrasts with the picture painted by Williamson Mur-

ray. For his views on intellectual stagnation in the French military during the interwar years, see "Armored Warfare: The British, French, and German Experiences," in Murray and Millett, eds., *Military Innovation in the Interwar Period,* 29–34.

21. See François Pernot, "L'Armée de l'air face aux crises des années trente: Une étude moral," *Revue historique des armées* 4 (1990): 116–27. See also Weber, *The Hollow Years.*

22. S.H.A.A., série 2B, carton 109, "La doctrine d'emploi de l'Armée de l'air," October 1933, 1–2.

23. S.H.A.A., série 2B, carton 109, ministère de l'air, cabinet du ministre et état-major, général de l'Armée de l'air, "Circulaire confidentielle pour les cadres de l'Armée de l'air," 22 October 1933, 9–10.

24. S.H.A.A., 2B, carton 109, Général de division Vuillemin, membre du Conseil supérieur de l'air, commandant du 1er Corps aérien, à M le Minstère de l'air, "Instruction sur l'emploi tactique des Grandes Unités aériennes," 29 July 1937, 3.

25. Aside from the fundamental obligation that all military forces have to support one another as they seek to fulfill their roles in national defense policy, the Armée de l'air's case was unique. The 1933 law that established the independent air service specified the supporting roles to placate army and navy leaders who feared a potential loss of control.

26. S.H.A.A., série 2B, carton 109, ministère de l'air, cabinet du ministre et état-major, général de l'Armée de l'air, "Circulaire confidentielle pour les cadres de l'Armée de l'air," 22 October 1933, 3.

27. S.H.A.A., série 2B, carton 109, "Note au sujet de la lutte aérienne," October 1933, 3.

28. Ibid., 6–7.

29. S.H.A.A., série 2B, carton 109, "La doctrine d'emploi de l'Armée de l'air," October 1933, 8.

30. Ibid., 16.

31. Ibid., 17.

32 Ibid., 13.

33. For a thorough development of the problems with French aeronautical industries, see Chadeau, *L'industrie aéronautique en France;* and Vivier, *La politique aéronautique militaire de la France,* 199–215. See also Herrick Chapman, *State Capitalism and Working-Class Radicalism in the French Aircraft Industry* (Berkeley and Los Angeles: University of California Press, 1991).

34. S.H.A.A., série 2B, carton 109, état-major de l'Armée de l'air, *Règlement de manoeuvre de l'aviation,* part 4 (Paris: Imprimerie nationale, 1937), 29.

35. The organizational law of 2 July 1934 included the stipulations: "In time of war the division of the air units mobilized between the reserve air forces and the air forces placed at the disposal of the Army and the Navy is determined by the government on the basis of operations. . . . The air forces placed at the disposal of the Army are commanded by a general officer of the Air Force placed under the au-

thority of the general officer of the Army commanding the theater of land operations in question. The air forces placed at the disposal of the Navy are commanded by a general officer of the Air Force placed under the authority of the vice-admiral commanding the theater of naval operations in question." Quoted in Christienne and Lissarague, *A History of French Military Aviation,* 253–55.

36. S.H.A.A., série 2B, carton 109, ministère de l'air, cabinet du ministre et état-major, général de l'Armée de l'air, "Circulaire confidentielle pour les cadres de l'Armée de l'air," 22 October 1933, 4.

37. The airplanes that Cot relegated to the reserves for the army's use included the early 1920s-vintage LeO 20, and the Farman biplane designs that were outclassed when the new generation of all-metal monoplanes emerged in the mid–1930s.

38. S.H.A.A., série 2B, carton 109, état-major de l'Armée de l'air, *Règlement de manoeuvre de l'aviation,* part 4 (Paris: Imprimerie nationale, 1937), 21.

39. Ibid., 24.

40. S.H.A.A., série 2B, carton 109, minstère de l'air, section 3, "Instruction générale sur l'emploi des Forces aériennes mises à la disposition de l'Armée de terre, et la D.C.A. des armées au début des hostilités," 7 July 1936, 3–4.

41. Ibid., 6.

42. Ibid., 7.

43. Ibid.

44. S.H.A.A., série 2B, carton 109, état-major de l'Armée de l'air, *Règlement de manoeuvre de l'aviation,* part 4 (Paris: Imprimerie nationale, 1937), 17.

45. Ibid., 14.

46. S.H.A.A., série 2B, carton 109, ministère de la marine, état-major général, section d'études générales, 3ème Bureau, "Observations au sujet de l'instruction du 31 mars 1937 sur l'emploi tactique des Grandes Unités aériennes," 7 August 1937, 3.

47. Ibid.

48. Ibid.

49. Ibid., 4.

50. S.H.A.A., série 2B, carton 109, état-major de l'Armée de l'air, *Règlement de manoeuvre de l'aviation,* part 4 (Paris: Imprimerie nationale, 1937), 14.

51. Ibid., parts 1, 2, 3, p. 19.

52. Ibid., p. 40.

53. Ibid., part 4, pps. 14, 20.

54. Ibid., 33.

55. The concept of mass remained ill-defined throughout the 1930s. Maintenance and logistics problems limited the number of mission-capable airplanes the Armée de l'air could field at any given time. Therefore formations could consist of as few as two planes or an entire group of thirty or more.

56. S.H.A.A., série 2B, carton 109, état-major de l'Armée de l'air, *Règlement de manoeuvre de l'aviation,* part 4 (Paris: Imprimerie nationale, 1937), 69.

57. S.H.A.A., série 2B, carton 109, état-major de l'Armée de l'air, *Règlement de manoeuvre de l'aviation,* parts 1, 2, 3, p. 113.

58. John Keegan argues that heroic forms of leadership that rely on the commander to risk all in demonstrations of personal valor do not apply to modern forms of warfare. Although Keegan specifically addresses issues of command in the nuclear context, his observations also apply to the forms of modern warfare that the French encountered in 1940. See *The Mask of Command* (New York: Viking Penguin, 1987), 311–51.

59. S.H.A.A., série 2B, carton 109, état-major de l'Armée de l'air, *Règlement de manoeuvre de l'aviation,* parts 1, 2, 3 (Paris: Imprimerie nationale, 1937), 96–119.

60. Ibid., 168.

61. One staff study even explored the possibilities of combining the effects of aviation and cavalry. The author observed: "Aviation acting to the benefit of Cavalry is called to receive general missions of the same nature as those ordered by the Commander of a Grande Unité (Corps d'Armée and Division d'Infanterie)." S.H.A.A., série 2B, carton 109, "Emploi de l'aviation en liaison avec la cavalerie," n.d., 1.

62. S.H.A.A., série 2B, carton 109, état-major de l'Armée de l'air, *Règlement de manoeuvre de l'aviation,* part 4 (Paris: Imprimerie nationale, 1937), 33.

63. S.H.A.A., série 2B, carton 109, "Règlement de manoeuvre de l'Armée de l'air, livre II: Aviation de bombardement," n.d., 10.

64. The commission appointed to study and report on the Armée de l'air's performance in the Battle of France noted the lack of night-qualified bomber crews. The inability of French pilots to fly in low-visibility conditions *(pilotage sans visibilité)* also hampered French night bombing operations in the spring of 1940. See S.H.A.A., série 3D, carton 477, état français, secrétariat d'état à l'aviation, "Enseignements aériens de la guerre, 1939–1942, Commission 'G,': Deuxième partie, les armes et les moyens d'exploitation," March 1942, 78–79.

65. S.H.A.A., série 2B, carton 109, "Règlement de manoeuvre de l'Armée de l'air, livre II: Aviation de bombardement," n.d., 26–38.

66. S.H.A.A., série 2B, carton 109, état-major de l'Armée de l'air, Règlement de manoeuvre de l'aviation, part 4 (Paris: Imprimerie nationale, 1937), 82.

67. S.H.A.A., série 2B, carton 67, état-major de l'Armée de l'air, 2ème Bureau, "Renseignements préliminaries d'ordre général sur l'importance et la vulnerabilité des objectifs militaires et de représailles," 11 January 1939, 5–6.

68. S.H.A.A., série 2B, carton 110, Capitaine Secrétant, Centre d'expériences aériennes militaires, assaut, "Rapport d'ensemble, questions nos. A3 et A5: Procédés de destruction des voies ferrées par l'aviation d'assaut," 15 April 1939. The air staff produced a detailed analysis of the German rail network. See S.H.A.A., série 2B, carton 65: "Renseignements concernant les chemins de fer allemands: 1930–1940."

69. See série 2B, carton 69, "Dossiers d'objectifs: 58 dossiers d'installations électriques allemands, 1926–1940."

70. S.H.A.A., série 2B, carton 65, "Sources d'énergie électrique allemandes: Répertoire des sources d'énergie électrique allemandes, note préliminaire," dossier 1, 21 June 1939, 14–16.

71. S.H.A.A., série 2B, carton 109, "Plan de l'instruction pratique," n.d., 3.

72. Ibid., 74.

73. Ibid., 77–83.

74. S.H.A.A., série 2B, carton 109, état-major de l'Armée de l'air, "Règlement de manoeuvre, livre I: Aviation de chasse, titre I, règlement," Tirage provisoire 1938, 18.

75. S.H.A.A., série 2B, carton 109, "Plan de l'instruction pratique," n.d., 4, 92–115.

76. S.H.A.A., série 2B, carton 109, état-major de l'Armée de l'air, *Règlement de manoeuvre de l'aviation,* part 4 (Paris: Imprimerie nationale, 1937), 140–41.

77. Ibid., 140.

78. Ibid., 146–47.

79. S.H.A.A., série 3D, carton 477, état français, secrétariat d'état à l'aviation, "Enseignements aériens de la guerre, 1939–1942, Commission 'G,': Deuxième partie, les armes et les moyens d'exploitation," March 1942, 99.

4. A Training System for a Reactive Doctrine

1. Cot, *L'Armée de l'air,* 48.

2. Ibid., 68.

3. On the political and economic challenges encountered by the leaders of the Third Republic, see Bernard and Dubief, *The Decline of the Third Republic.* Patrick Facon explains that the French dreamed of an aerial alliance with the Soviet Union as one solution to the rise of German power: *L'Armée de l'air dans la tourmente,* 20–23. Thierry Vivier shows how the Franco-Czech alliance also drew French attention during the 1930s: see "La coopération aéronautique franco-tchécoslovaque," 70–79.

4. Airpower scholars comment on the technical sophistication required of airmen and its effects on the way doctrines and institutional structures develop. Carl Builder's analysis of the United States Air Force shows how too much emphasis on technical matters can lead to stagnant doctrines and intellectual atrophy. See *The Icarus Syndrome.* See also MacIssac, "Voices from the Central Blue," 624–47.

5. S.H.A.A., série 2B, carton 10, ministère de l'air, état-major général de l'Armée de l'air, 1ère section, "Jurys d'examen: Candidats à l'École de l'air, Cours des sous-officiers élèves officiers en 1936," 27 January 1936, 2–7.

6. The Armée de l'air experienced effects similar to those of the army after the government decided to shorten the duration of mandatory service. The key difference was that because of its reliance on highly skilled personnel to fill most specialties, the air force experienced more chronic shortages than did the army throughout the 1930s, especially in the numbers of combat-ready instructors. Eugenia Kiesling writes: "The fundamental weakness of French military training came from the army's structure. For organizational reasons, the army could not simultaneously provide basic training for recruits and advanced work for the trained portion of the conscript contingent." For a thorough analysis of the effects of the personnel policies on army training efforts, see Kiesling, *Arming against Hitler,* 62–84.

7. Patrick Facon describes the ways that French strategy affected the air service's requirements for operational specialties. The aviation missions changed depending upon the preferences of the government in power. At times the politicians emphasized aerial bombardment as the solution to French strategic problems; at others, air superiority and pursuit appeared to be the preferred operating method. See Facon, *L'Armée de l'air dans la tourmente,* 35–65.

8. S.H.A.A., série 2B, carton 109, état-major de l'Armée de l'air, *Règlement de manoeuvre de l'aviation,* parts 1, 2, 3 (Paris: Imprimerie nationale, 1937), 19.

9. Ibid., 20.

10. Ibid.

11. See S.H.A.A., série 2B, cartons 10, 20 for examples of issues that required coordination between the two inspectorates.

12. S.H.A.A., série 2B, carton 109, état-major de l'Armée de l'air, *Règlement de manoeuvre de l'aviation,* parts 1, 2, 3 (Paris: Imprimerie nationale, 1937), 41.

13. Ibid.

14. S.H.A.A., série 2B, carton 10, "Schéma d'organisation des Écoles de pilotage," n.d.

15. S.H.A.A., série 2B, carton 10, état-major de l'Armée de l'air, 3ème Bureau, "Fonctionnement des Écoles élémentaires de pilotage," message 10,060-3/I.S/EMAA, 4.

16. S.H.A.A., série 2B, carton 10, "Comment obtenir le brevet supérieur de mécanicien d'aéronautique," n.d., 3.

17. Ibid.

18. S.H.A.A., série 2B, carton 10, "Comment devenir radiotélégraphiste en avion," "Comment devenir mitrailleur," "Comment devenir pilote d'avion," n.d.

19. S.H.A.A., série 2B, carton 109, état-major de l'Armée de l'air, *Règlement de manoeuvre de l'aviation,* parts 1, 2, 3 (Paris: Imprimerie nationale, 1937), 42.

20. Ibid., 50.

21. Ibid., 51.

22. See Eugen Weber, *Peasants into Frenchmen: The Modernization of Rural France, 1870–1914* (Stanford, Calif.: Stanford University Press, 1976). See also Eugen Weber, *My France: Politics, Culture, Myth* (Harvard University Press, 1992), and Weber, *The Hollow Years.* Laurence Wylie also reinforces this theme in a twentieth-century context in *Village in the Vaucluse,* 3d ed. (Cambridge: Harvard University Press, 1977).

23. S.H.A.A., série 2B, carton 109, état-major de l'Armée de l'air, *Règlement de manoeuvre de l'aviation,* parts 1, 2, 3 (Paris: Imprimerie nationale, 1937), 54.

24. Cot, *L'Armée de l'air,* 159.

25. S.H.A.A., série 2B, carton 109, état-major de l'Armée de l'air, *Règlement de manoeuvre de l'aviation,* parts 1, 2, 3 (Paris: Imprimerie nationale, 1937), 57.

26. S.H.A.A., série 2B, carton 11, état-major de l'Armée de l'air, 1er Bureau, "Groupe d'École de Chambéry," message 1773-3-I/O/E.M.A.A., 2–6.

27. S.H.A.A., série 2B, carton 109, état-major de l'Armée de l'air, *Règlement de manoeuvre de l'aviation,* parts 1, 2, 3 (Paris: Imprimerie nationale, 1937), 64.

28. Ibid., 67–69.

29. Ibid., 74.

30. S.H.A.A., série 2B, carton 12, "L'état-major de l'Armée de l'air à Monsieur le Général commandant l'École de l'air: Effectifs approximatifs des éléments de l'École de l'air stationés dans la région de Salon," February 1937.

31. S.H.A.A., série 2B, carton 12, ministère de l'air, état-major de l'Armée de l'air, 1er Bureau, "Constitution du Centre- École de Salon-de-Provence," message 569-1.0/RS/E.M.A.A., 29 June 1937.

32. S.H.A.A., série 2B, carton 12, ministère de l'air, état-major de l'Armée de l'air, 1er Bureau, le ministre de l'air à Monsieur le Général commandant la 1ère Région aérienne (Dijon), "Création du Centre-École provisoire No. 357 à Strasbourg," message 1602-1.0-RC/E.M.A.A., 30 November 1937.

33. S.H.A.A., série 2B, carton 12, ministère de l'air, état-major de l'Armée de l'air, le ministre de l'air à Monsieur le Ministre de la Défense nationale et de la guerre, état-major de l'Armée, 1er Bureau, Paris, "Occupation de la base aérienne de Strasbourg," 28 December 1937.

34. Ibid.

35. S.H.A.A., série 2B. See memoranda on various bases in cartons 11, 12.

36. S.H.A.A., série 2B, carton 10, état-major de l'Armée de l'air, 3ème Bureau, "Note pour le général commandant en chef des Forces aériennes," message 238-3.1/E.M.A.A., 8 September 1939.

37. S.H.A.A., série 2B, carton 10, ministère de l'air, état-major de l'Armée de l'air, 3ème Bureau, "École de moniteurs de pilotage," message 10,039-3/1/S/E.M.A.A., 21 September 1939.

38. S.H.A.A., série 2B, carton 11, état-major de l'Armée de l'air, 1er Bureau, note pour l'inspection générale technique, "Parc d'Istres," message 799-3/0/E.M.A.A., 15 May 1937.

39. S.H.A.A., série 2B, carton 11, état-major de l'Armée de l'air, 1er Bureau, note pour le chef d'état-major de l'Armée de l'air, "Parc d'Istres," message 1170-3-1/0/E.M.A.A., 25 August 1937, 2.

40. Ibid.

41. Ibid.

42. Ibid.

43. Ibid., 4.

44. Ibid.

45. Ibid., 7.

46. S.H.A.A., série 2B, carton 11, Le 1er Bureau de l'état-major de l'Armée de l'air à Monsieur le Général chef d'état-major de l'Armée de l'air, "Parc d'Istres" (message number illegible), 7 October 1938, 1.

47. S.H.A.A., série 2B, carton 11, le 1er Bureau de l'état-major de l'Armée de l'air à Monsieur le Général chef d'état-major de l'Armée de l'air, "Parc d'Istres" (message number illegible), 15 October 1938, 2.

48. Ibid.

49. Ibid.
50. Ibid., 3.
51. Ibid., 4.
52. S.H.A.A., série 2B, carton 10, minstère de l'air, note pour l'inspection générale des écoles, l'état-major de l'Armée de l'air, la direction du contrôle, la direction du matériel aérien militaire, la direction du personnel militaire, la direction des travaux et installations, "Réorganisation des Écoles et Centres d'instruction," message 885-S.1/1, 19 October 1939, 1.
53. Ibid., 1.
54. S.H.A.A., série 2B, carton 11, ministère de l'air, état-major de l'Armée de l'air, 1er Bureau, le ministre de l'air à Monsieur le Général commandant la 4ème Région aérienne (Aix-en-Provence), "Organisation de la base-groupe d'Écoles de pilotage d'Istres," message 919-1/1.S/E.M.A.A., 20 November 1939, 1.
55. S.H.A.A., série 2B, carton 10, ministère de l'air, direction du personnel militaire, 1er Bureau, echelon lourd, le ministre de l'air à M le Général commandant en chef les Forces aériennes, "Demande de moniteurs officiers chefs de patrouille," message 486-PM 1–2, 24 November 1939, 1.
56. S.H.A.A., série 2B, carton 10, commandement en chef des Forces aériennes, inspection et commandement supérieur de l'aviation de chasse, le général de Corps aérien d'Harcourt, inspecteur et commandant supérieur de l'aviation de chasse à Monsieur le Général commandant en chef des Forces aériennes (E.M.G.-1er Bureau), "Demande de moniteurs et chefs de patrouille pour les écoles," message 318 S/I.C., 3 December 1939, 1–2.
57. S.H.A.A., série 2B, carton 10, commandement en chef des Forces aériennes, état-major général, 1er Bureau, le Général commandant en chef Vuillemin, commandant en chef les Forces aériennes, à Monsieur le Ministre de l'air (direction du personnel militaire), message 1573-1/0.R.S./E.M.G., 14 December 1939, 1–2.
58. S.H.A.A., série 2B, carton 10, commandement en chef des Forces aériennes, état-major général, 3ème Bureau, le Général commandant en chef Vuillemin, commandant en chef des Forces aériennes, à Monsieur le Ministre de l'air (E.M.A.A., 6ème Bureau), "C.I.C. de Montpellier," message 1435-3/1.S./E.M.G, 26 November 1939, 1–2.
59. Patrick Facon relates Anatole de Monzie's description of Vuillemin as a man ill suited for the position of chief of staff of the air force. He writes that Vuillemin acquired the position because of his tendency to avoid conflict *(conformisme)* and for the weakness of his character. See Facon, *L'Armée de l'air dans la tourmente,* 14. Arnaud Teyssier offers a more balanced assessment of Vuillemin's qualifications as the Armée de l'air's senior airman in "Le Général Vuillemin, chef d'état-major général de l'Armée de l'air, 1938–1939: Un haut responsable militaire face au danger allemand," *Revue historique des armées* 2 (1987): 104–13.
60. Ironically, the German air force encountered a similar dilemma late in the war, when forced to decide between fighting current battles and preserving future combat capabilities. The Germans fared no better than had the French. Faced with in-

creasing Allied air superiority, Generalleutnant Josef Schmid, commander of the Luftwaffe's I Fighter Corps, failed to devise a solution to wrest air superiority from the increasingly aggressive enemy fighter forces. "Schmid's biggest problem was one over which he had no control. During January, despite a heavy loss of pilots, he received no pilot replacements or reinforcements. German industry was sending him all the aircraft he could use, but the number of men he had to fly them continued to decline." See Stephen L. McFarland and Wesley Phillips Newton, *To Command the Sky: The Battle for Air Superiority over Germany, 1942–1944* (Washington, D.C.: Smithsonian Institution Press, 1991), 160.

61. S.H.A.A., série 2B, carton 12, état-major de l'Armée de l'air, 1er Bureau, le ministre de l'air à Monsieur le Général commandant la 4ème Région aérienne (Aix-en-Provence), message 069-1/1.S./E.M.A.A., 8 January 1940, 1–2.

62. S.H.A.A., série 2B, carton 10, ministère de l'air, état-major de l'Armée de l'air, 1er Bureau, le ministre de l'air à MM le Général commandant la 1ère Région aérienne (Dijon), le Général commandant la 2ème Région aérienne (Paris), le Général commandant la 3ème Région Aérienne (Tours), le Général commandant la 4ème Région aérienne (Aix-en-Provence), le Général commandant la 5ème Région aérienne (Alger), "Réorganisation des bases/Centres d'instruction de renseignement et de bombardement," message 1025-1/1-S/E.M.A.A., 1 April 1940, 1–2.

63. Ibid., 2–7.

64. See S.H.A.A., série 2B, carton 10, ministère de l'air, état-major de l'Armée de l'air, 1er Bureau, le ministre de l'air à MM le Général commandant la 1ère Région aérienne (Dijon), le Général commandant la 2ème Région aérienne (Paris), le Général commandant la 3ème Région aérienne (Tours), le Général commandant la 4ème Région aérienne (Aix-en-Provence), le Général commandant la 5ème Région aérienne (Alger), "Effectifs des formations de l'intérieur," message 1078-1/1-S./E.M.A.A., 4 April, 1940. See also S.H.A.A., série 2B, carton 11, ministère de l'air, état-major de l'Armée de l'air, 1er Bureau, le ministre de l'air à Monsieur le Général commandant la 3ème Région aérienne (Tours), "Création de la base/Centre d'instruction de Cognac," message 1154-1/1-S/E.M.A.A., 12 April 1940. S.H.A.A., série 2B, carton 12, note pour l'état-major de l'Armée de l'air, 4ème Bureau, "Groupement École de l'armée polonaise" (message number illegible), 22 April 1940. S.H.A.A., série 2B, carton 12, ministère de l'air, état-major de l'Armée de l'air, 1er Bureau, "Tableaux d'effectifs de la base/École auxiliare de pilotage de l'aviation polonaise à Saint-Étienne," message 1743-1/1-S/E.M.A.A., 11 May 1940.

65. S.H.A.A., série 2B, carton 10, commandement en chef des Forces aériennes, 3ème Bureau, note de service, "Désignations d'instructeurs pour les Centres d'instruction de chasse," message 2704-3/1.S./E.M.G., 19 April 1940, 1–2.

66. Ibid.

67. S.H.A.A., série 2B, carton 11, commandement en chef des Forces aériennes, état-major général, 3ème Bureau, le Général commandant en chef Vuillemin, commandant en chef des Forces aériennes, à Monsieur le Ministre de l'air, état-major

de l'Armée de l'air, 3ème Bureau, "Zone d'instruction du C.I. de Clermont-Ferrand," message 2974-3.O.2/S/E.M.G., 28 April 1940, 1–2.

68. S.H.A.A., série 2B, carton 11, état-major de l'Armée de l'air, 1er Bureau, le ministre de l'air à Monsieur le Général inspecteur général des écoles et effectifs, "Tenue du personnel pendant les attaques aériennes," message 1570-1/1/S/E.M.A.A., 14 May 1940.

69. S.H.A.A., série 2B, carton 10, ministère de l'air, état-major de l'Armée de l'air, 6ème Bureau, "Fonctionnement des Centres d'instruction de chasse," message 1080, 23 May 1940.

70. S.H.A.A., série 2B, carton 10, ministère de l'air, état-major de l'Armée de l'air, 6ème Bureau, "Fonctionnement des Centres d'instruction de bombardement," message 1082-6/2.S./E.M.A.A., 23 May 1940.

71. S.H.A.A., série 2B, carton 11, commandement en chef des Forces aériennes, état-major général, 3ème Bureau, le Général commandant en chef Vuillemin, commandant en chef des Forces aériennes, à Monsieur le Ministre de l'air—E.M.A.A.—3ème Bureau, "Zone d'instruction de Châteauroux," message 3746-3/O.2.S./E.M.G., 31 May 1940.

72. See Weber, *The Hollow Years*, 257–72; Young, *France and the Origins of the Second World War*, 130–48; Shirer, *The Collapse of the Third Republic*, 519–60; and Pierre Boillot, "La 'drôle de guerre' et la Bataille de France vues par un sergent pilote," *Revue historique des armées* 2 (1986): 76–90.

73. S.H.A.A., série 2B, carton 10, ministère de l'air, état-major de l'Armée de l'air, 1er Bureau, le ministre de l'air à Monsieur le Général commandant en chef des Forces aériennes (état-major général, 1er Bureau), Grand quartier général aérien, "Écoles en Afrique du Nord," message 454-1/1.S./E.M.A.A., 13 October 1939, 2.

74. Ibid.

75. Ibid.

76. Ibid.

77. Ibid., 3.

78. Ibid.

79. S.H.A.A., série 2B, carton 10, commandement en chef des Forces aériennes, état-major général, 3ème Bureau, le Général commandant en chef Vuillemin, commandant en chef des Forces aériennes, à Monsieur le Ministre de l'air, état-major de l'Armée de l'air (1er Bureau), "Écoles en Afrique du Nord," message 582-3/1./S./E.M.A.A., 16 October 1939.

80. S.H.A.A., série 2B, carton 10, ministère de l'air, état-major de l'Armée de l'air, 3ème Bureau, le ministre de l'air à Monsieur le Général commandant en chef des Forces aériennes (état-major général, 3ème Bureau), "Écoles en Afrique du Nord," message 89-3/1.S./E.M.A.A., 7 November 1939, 2.

81. Ibid., 4.

82. S.H.A.A., série 2B, carton 10, ministère de l'air, état-major de l'Armée de l'air, cabinet, le ministre de l'air à M le Général commandant en chef des Forces aériennes, message 112/E.M.A.A./Cab., 25 April 1940.

83. S.H.A.A., série 2B, carton 12, ministère de l'air, état-major de l'Armée de l'air, 1er Bureau, le ministre de l'air à Monsieur le Général commandant la 5ème Région aérienne (Alger), "Création de la base-Centre d'instruction de chasse d'Oran," message 1707-1/1-S./E.M.A.A., 17 May 1940.

84. S.H.A.A., série 2B, carton 11, ministère de l'air, état-major de l'Armée de l'air, 1er Bureau, le ministre de l'air à MM le Général commandant la 4ème Région aérienne (Aix-en-Provence), le Général commandant la 5ème Région aérienne (Alger), "Repli base/groupe d'écoles d'Istres," message 1779-1/1-S/E.M.A.A., 21 May 1940.

85. S.H.A.A., série 2B, carton 12, état-major de l'Armée de l'air, 6ème Bureau, le ministre de l'air à M le Général commandant la 3ème Région aérienne (Tours), "Repli du Centre d'instruction de renseignement de Tours en Afrique du Nord," message 1149-6/2.S/E.M.A.A., 1 June 1940.

86. S.H.A.A., série 2B, carton 12, état-major de l'Armée de l'air, 1er Bureau, le ministre de l'air à Monsieur le Ministre de la Défense nationale et de la guerre, état-major de l'Armée, 1er Bureau, "Envoi à Rabat des instructeurs militaires du Département de la guerre détachés à la base/groupe d'écoles de l'air de Versailles," message 2036-1/1S/E.M.A.A., 1 June 1940.

5. Maneuvers, Exercises, and Reactive Doctrine

1. S.H.A.A., série 2B, carton 116, ministère de l'air, le ministre de l'air à M le Général commandant la 1ère Région aérienne (Dijon), M le Général commandant la 2ème Région aérienne (Paris), M le Général commandant la 3ème Région aérienne (Tours), M le Général commandant la 4ème Région aérienne (Aix-en-Provence), M le Général commandant la 5ème Région aérienne (Alger), "Ordre du jour," message 8843-C.M., 27 August 1937, 1.

2. Another institutional vehicle the Armée de l'air used to develop new operational and tactical concepts was the Centre d'expériences aériennes militaires, where service personnel studied specific problems for the air ministry and air staff. Examples of topics that occupied the Centre's attention included railway attack, dive bombing procedures, bombardment attacks against hardened bunkers, and aerial attacks against armored forces. See S.H.A.A., série 2B, cartons 110, 111.

3. Pascal Vennesson argues that institutional factors contributed significantly to the erosion of air force autonomy. He writes: "In France . . . airpower was regarded as a continuation of existing weapon systems, particularly of the cavalry's reconnaissance missions and long rang artillery. The attack on the economic potential of the enemy never fully convinced either army officers, or *airmen*" (emphasis added). See Pascal Vennesson, "Institution and Airpower: The Making of the French Air Force," *Journal of Strategic Studies* 18 (1995): 37. See also Vennesson, *Les chevaliers de l'air.*

4. See Cot, *L'Armée de l'air.* See also Néré, *The Foreign Policy of France from 1914 to 1945;* and Doughty, *The Seeds of Disaster.*

5. S.H.A.A., série 2B, carton 109, état-major de l'Armée de l'air, *Règlement de manoeuvre de l'aviation,* parts 1, 2, 3 (Paris: Imprimerie nationale, 1937), 34–44.

6. See various documents in S.H.A.A., série 2B, cartons 113, 114, 115, 116.

7. S.H.A.A., série 2B, carton 110, inspection de l'aviation légère de défense, "1ère manoeuvre combinée (3ème Régiment et 22ème Escadre)," 3 July 1933.

8. Ibid. The British developed radar as a technological solution to the problem of locating enemy formations. For a recent analysis of radar developments in the interwar period, see Alan Beyerchen, "From Radio to Radar: Interwar Military Adaptation to Technological Change in Germany, the United Kingdom, and the United States," in Murray and Millett, eds. *Military Innovation in the Interwar Period,* 265–99.

9. S.H.A.A., série 2B, carton 110, inspection de l'aviation légère de défense, "1ère manoeuvre combinée (3ème Régiment et 22ème Escadre)," 3 July 1933, 1.

10. S.H.A.A., série 2B, carton 113, "Exercises de 1934," 10 July 1934, 3.

11. "The result is that their orders use too much airpower in secondary searches to the detriment of the essential searches, and the observers do not receive the intellectual stimulation that allows them to accomplish their missions and to take the initiative." S.H.A.A., série 2B, carton 113, "Exercises de 1934," 10 July 1934, 5.

12. Christienne and Lissarrague, *A History of French Military Aviation,* 310.

13. S.H.A.A., série 2B, carton 113, ministère de l'air, état-major général de l'Armée de l'air, 3ème section, le ministre de l'air à MM le Général commandant la 1ère Région aérienne (Metz), le Général commandant la 2ème Région aérienne (Paris), le Général commandant la 3ème Région aérienne (Tours), le Général commandant la 4ème Région aérienne (Lyon), "Manoeuvres AIR-D.A.T., 1935," message 653-3.R/E.M.G., 27 June 1935, 1–2.

14. S.H.A.A., série 2B, carton 113, exercises d'application de l'aviation de défense, 1935, parti de l'attaque, pièce no. 1, "thème général," n.d., 1.

15. S.H.A.A., série 2B, carton 113, manoeuvres air-D.A.T. 1935, direction, 28 septembre, 8 heures, parti bleu, pièce no. 2, "Décision du gouvernement bleu," 1.

16. Ibid. (emphasis in original).

17. S.H.A.A., série 2B, carton 113, ministère de l'air, état-major général de l'Armée de l'air, 3ème section, le ministre de l'air à MM le Général commandant la 1ère Région aérienne (Metz), le Général commandant la 2ème Région aérienne (Paris), le Général commandant la 3ème Région aérienne (Tours), le Général commandant la 4ème Région aérienne (Lyon), "Manoeuvres AIR-D.A.T., 1935," message 653-3.R/E.M.G., 27 June 1935, 3–4.

18. Ibid., 1.

19. In the United States, the U.S. Army Air Corps reached the opposite conclusion concerning comparisons of fighter and bomber performance. Air Corps leaders believed that the multiengine bomber would outclass single-engine pursuit planes. General Oscar Westover commented: "Since new bombardment aircraft possesses [sic] speed above two hundred miles per hour, any intercepting or supporting aircraft must possess greater speed characteristics if they are to perform their mis-

sions. In the case of pursuit aviation, this increase of speed must be so great as to make it doubtful whether pursuit aircraft can be efficiently or safely operated either individually or in mass." See Wesley Frank Craven and James Lea Cate, eds., *The Army Air Forces in World War II*, vol. 1., *Plans and Early Operations, January 1939 to August 1942* (Chicago: University of Chicago Press, 1948; reprint, Washington, D.C.: Office of Air Force History, 1983), 65. For performance characteristics, see S.H.A.A., série 2B, carton 113, ministère de l'air, état-major général de l'Armée de l'air, 3ème section, le ministre de l'air à MM le Général commandant la 1ère Région aérienne (Metz), le Général commandant la 2ème Région aérienne (Paris), le Général commandant la 3ème Région aérienne (Tours), le Général commandant la 4ème Région aérienne (Lyon), "Manoeuvres AIR-D.A.T., 1935," message 653-3.R/E.M.G., 27 June 1935: Annexe III. See also H.R.A. file 248.211-26A, "Comparison of World Powers Aircraft/Engines," 15 January 1938.

20. The Bloch 200 and Amiot 143 were both products of the BCR procurement program. The Amiot was France's most modern bomber in 1935. It continued in the inventory until the disastrous campaign of 1940, when the French used it in a ground attack role against German infantry and tank formations. Its poor performance characteristics made it an easy target for fighters and antiaircraft artillery. See Christienne and Lissarrague, *A History of French Military Aviation*, 259–65, 345–63.

21. S.H.A.A., série 2B, carton 114, exercise principal de D.A.T. 1936, "Dossier du parti rouge," n.d.

22. S.H.A.A., série 2B, carton 114, exercise principal de D.A.T. 1936, "Dossier général: Pièce no. 1," n.d., 3.

23. S.H.A.A., série 2B, carton 114, exercise principal de D.A.T. 1936, "Dossier du parti rouge: Pièce no. 4," n.d. S.H.A.A., série 2B, carton 114, exercise principal de D.A.T. 1936, "Dossier du parti bleu: Pièce no. 4," n.d.

24. S.H.A.A., série 2B, carton 115, ministère de l'air, état-major de l'Armée de l'air, 3ème section, le ministre de l'air à MM le Général commandant la 1ère Région aérienne (Metz), le Général commandant la 2ème Région aérienne (Paris), le Général commandant la 3ème Région aérienne (Tours), "Organisation de l'exercise technique de l'Armée de l'air," message 471-3.R/E.M.A.A., 13 May 1936, 1–8.

25. S.H.A.A., série 2B, carton 115, le Général de division Armengaud, membre du Conseil supérieure de l'air, inspecteur de l'aviation de défense métropolitaine et des écoles, à MM le Général commandant la 1ère Région aérienne (Metz), le Général commandant la 2ème Région aérienne (Paris), le Général commandant la 3ème Région aérienne (Tours), "Exercise technique 1936: Préparation de l'aviation lourde de défense," message 61/2-S./I.A.D.M.E., 7 August 1936, 1.

26. Ibid., 3.

27. Ibid.

28. Ibid., 4.

29. S.H.A.A., série 2B, carton 115, "Compte-rendu sur l'exercise de déplacement technique de l'Armée de l'air," 15 September 1936, 6.

30. S.H.A.A., série 2B, carton 116, ministère de l'air, état-major de l'Armée de l'air, 3ème Bureau, "Instruction fixant les conditions générales d'organisation des 'grandes manoeuvres aériennes' de 1937," message 988-3-1.S./E.M.A.A., 10 May 1937, 2.

31. Ibid., 4.

32. S.H.A.A., série 2B, carton 116, ministère de l'air, état-major de l'Armée de l'air, 3ème Bureau, "Instruction fixant les conditions d'organisation des 'grandes manoeuvres aériennes' particulières aux éléments de l'Armée de l'air, annexe no. 1," message 1418-3-1.S./E.M.A.A., 28 June 1937.

33. S.H.A.A., série 2B, carton 116, ministère de l'air, état-major de l'Armée de l'air, 3ème Bureau, "Instruction fixant les conditions générales d'organisation des 'grandes manoeuvres aériennes' de 1937," message 988-3-1.S./E.M.A.A., 10 May 1937, 5.

34. S.H.A.A., série 2B, carton 109, ministère de l'air, état-major de l'Armée de l'air, *Règlement de manoeuvre,* part 5: *L'Infanterie de l'air* (Paris: Imprimerie nationale, 1938), 7.

35. S.H.A.A., série 2B, carton 116, manoeuvres de D.A.T. en 1938, "Dossier général, pièce no. 3: thème général," n.d., 1–2.

36. S.H.A.A., série 2B, carton 116, manoeuvres de D.A.T. en 1938, "Dossier du parti bleu, pièce no. 3," n.d., 1. The Armée de l'air focused on operational centers of gravity—primarily enemy air forces and land components—while the British and American versions of airpower targeted strategic centers of gravity, the vital centers of the enemy nation. For an analysis of American perspectives, see Peter R. Faber, "Interwar U.S. Army Aviation and the Air Corps Tactical School: Incubators of American Airpower," in Meilinger, ed., *Paths of Heaven,* 183–238. For the evolution of British and American bombing doctrine, see Tami Davis Biddle, "Rhetoric and Reality in Air Warfare: The Evolution of British and American Ideas about Strategic Bombing," (Ph.D. diss., New Haven: Yale University, 1995).

37. S.H.A.A., série 2B, carton 116, manoeuvres de D.A.T. en 1938, "Instruction particulière sur la concentration du parti bleu," n.d., 1–8.

38. S.H.A.A., série 2B, carton 116, manoeuvres de D.A.T. en 1938, dossier du parti bleu, pièce no. 7, "Instruction particulière sur la mise en oeuvre d'un dispositif pour le ravitaillement rapide des formations de l'Armée de l'air," n.d., 1.

39. Ibid., "Tableau 1," n.d.

40. S.H.A.A., série 2B, carton 116, manoeuvres de D.A.T. en 1938, dossier du parti bleu, pièce no. 11, "Instruction particulière pour les éléments de détection éléctromagnétique et pour les P. C. de batteries qui travaillent en liaison," n.d., 1–10, annexe I–II.

41. S.H.A.A., série 2B, carton 116, ministère de l'air, état-major de l'Armée de l'air, 3ème Bureau, le ministre de l'air à M le Général inspecteur général de la défense aérienne et inspecteur de la défense antiaérienne du territoire, membre du Conseil

supérieur de l'air; M le Général commandant la 1ère Région aérienne (Dijon); M le Général commandant la 2ème Région aérienne (Paris); M le Général commandant la 3ème Région aérienne (Tours); M le Général commandant la 4ème Région aérienne (Aix-en-Provence); M le Général commandant le 1er Corps aérien, Paris; M le Général commandant le 2ème Corps aérien, Reims; M le Général commandant l'École de l'air, membre du Conseil supérieur de l'air, Paris, "Manoeuvres de D.A.T. en 1938," message 1596-3-1-S/E.M.A.A., 29 July 1938, 2.

42. Ibid., 2–4.

43. S.H.A.A., série 2B, carton 113, "Exercises de 1934: Remarques concernant l'aviation," 10 July 1934, 12.

44. S.H.A.A., série 2B, carton 117, "Exercises d'application d'aviation de défense, 1935," 2 November 1935, 7.

45. S.H.A.A., série 2B, carton 115, "Compte-rendu sur l'exercise de déplacement technique du l'Armée de l'air," 15 September 1936, 5.

46. S.H.A.A., série 2B, carton 114, inspecteur de l'aviation de défense métropolitaine et des écoles, état-major, le Général de division Armengaud, membre du Conseil supérieur de l'air, inspecteur de l'aviation de défense métropolitaine et des écoles à Monsieur le Ministre de l'air, état-major général de l'Armée de l'air, 3ème section, "Manoeuvres air-D.A.T. en 1936," message 23/1/I.A.D.M.E. 14 January 1936, 3.

47. S.H.A.A., série 2B, carton 115, exercise technique de l'Armée de l'air, parti bleu, secteur d'opérations aériennes no. 2, le Colonel LeBlanc, commandant le secteur d'opérations aériennes no. 2 à Monsieur le Général de division, directeur de l'exercise, "Au sujet de fautes commises au cours de l'exercise à Luxeuil," message 667/S.B.C., 17 September 1936, 2.

48. S.H.A.A., série 2B, carton 113, "Exercises de 1934: Remarques concernant l'aviation," 10 July 1934, 13.

49. S.H.A.A., série 2B, carton 113, Général d'Harcourt, "Rapport sur le contrôle et l'observation de l'exécution des exercises," 2 November 1935, 4.

50. S.H.A.A., série 2B, carton 114, inspecteur de l'aviation de défense métropolitaine et des écoles, état-major, le Général de division Armengaud, membre du Conseil supérieur de l'air, inspecteur de l'aviation de défense métropolitaine et des écoles à Monsieur le Ministre de l'air, état-major général de l'Armée de l'air, 3ème section, "Manoeuvres air-D.A.T. en 1936," message 23/1/I.A.D.M.E. 14 January 1936, 2.

51. S.H.A.A., série 2B, carton 113, exercise d'application de l'aviation de défense, "Rapport sur le contrôle et l'observation de l'exécution des exercises," 2 November 1935, 21.

52. S.H.A.A., série 2B, carton 113, "Exercises de 1934: Remarques concernant l'aviation," 10 July 1934, 6.

53. S.H.A.A., série 2B, carton 117, "Exercises d'application d'aviation de défense, 1935," 2 November 1935, 58–60.

54. S.H.A.A., série 2B, carton 115, "Rapport relatif à la manoeuvre 'Air-D.A.T.' de la 2ème Région aérienne, 18 juin–1er juillet 1937," n.d., 10.

55. S.H.A.A., série 2B, carton 113, "Exercises de 1934: remarques concernant l'aviation," 10 July 1934, 5–8.
56. Christienne and Lissarague, *A History of French Military Aviation*, 253–59.
57. S.H.A.A., série 2B, carton 114, inspecteur de l'aviation de défense métropolitaine et des écoles, état-major, le Général de division Armengaud, membre du Conseil supérieur de l'air, à Monsieur le Ministre de l'air, état-major général de l'Armée de l'air, 3ème section, "Manoeuvres Air-D.A.T. en 1936," message 23/1/I.A.D.M.E. 14 January 1936, 3–4.
58. Armengaud was not the only officer to comment on the flawed command structure. The bombardment commander for the 1936 maneuvers observed: "The employment of units in their habitual peacetime configurations and commanded at every level by their normal Chiefs would seem to offer the best guarantee of satisfactory results and security." S.H.A.A., série 2B, carton 114, "Exercise principal de D.A.T.: Compte-rendu général du colonel commandant les Forces aériennes du parti bleu," 4 September 1936, 6.
59. S.H.A.A. série 2B, carton 116, after-action report for 1937 maneuvers, n.d., 16.
60. S.H.A.A., série 2B, carton 113, "Exercises de 1934: Remarques concernant l'aviation," 10 July 1934, 1.
61. S.H.A.A., série 2B, carton 117, "Exercises d'application d'aviation de défense, 1935," 2 November 1935, 5–6.

6. The Dénouement of French Airpower Doctrine: Mobilization, Offensive Plans, and War

1. S.H.A.A., série 3D, carton 477, état français, secrétariat d'état à l'aviation, "Enseignements aériens de la guerre, 1939–1942, Commission 'G,': Première partie, les conditions de la guerre moderne," March 1942, 7.
2. See Vivier, *La politique aéronautique militaire de la France*, 438–54.
3. See Kiesling, Arming against Hitler, 12–40.
4. S.H.A.A., série 2B, carton 20, "Mobilisation," n.d., 7.
5. S.H.A.A., série 2B, carton 20, "Analyse: Mobilisation de l'Armée de l'air," n.d., 4. Although there is no date stamp on this document, the references to the Armée de l'air and to the regional organization of the air service indicate that it was probably written between 1934 and 1936.
6. S.H.A.A., série 2B, carton 24, ministère de l'air, état-major de l'Armée de l'air, 1er Bureau, "Tableaux d'emploi de l'Armée de l'air dans la Métropole: Plan 'E-1,'" message 1540/I/M/RS, E.M.A.A., 17 November 1938.
7. Refer to S.H.A.A., série 2B, cartons 25–30.
8. S.H.A.A., série 2B, carton 20, le Général Garnier-Duplessix au ministre de la guerre, état-major de l'Armée, 1er Bureau, "Compte-rendu," message 525/I/I-42, 10 March 1920.
9. S.H.A.A., série 2B, carton 20, 20ème Région militaire, état-major, 1ère section, 1er Bureau, "Rapport sur l'inspection de la mobilisation en 1929," message 3393/1/S, 13 September 1929, 2.

10. S.H.A.A., série 2B, carton 20, 1ère Division aérienne, 2ème Brigade d'aéronautique, "Rapport du Général de brigade Rolland, commandant la 2ème Brigade d'aéronautique, sur l'inspection de la mobilisation du 2ème Régiment d'aviation de Strasbourg," 27 June 1929, 1.

11. See Vivier, *La politique aéronautique militaire de la France*, 85–90.

12. For a thorough analysis of the French aeronautical industry see Chadeau, *L'industrie aéronautique en France*.

13. For a concise account of General Denain's role as the architect of the interwar Frence air force, see Thierry Vivier, "Le Général Victor Denain, bâtisseur de l'Armée de l'air, 1933–1936," *Revue historique des armées* 192 (1993): 21–31.

14. S.H.A.A., série 2B, carton 20, ministère de l'air, état-major général de l'Armée de l'air, 3ème section, "Instruction provisoire sur la mise en garde de l'Armée de l'air," message 655-3-R-EMG, 20 November 1934, 1 (emphasis in original).

15. Ibid.

16. Ibid., 18.

17. S.H.A.A., série 2B, carton 20, ministère de l'air, état-major de l'Armée de l'air, 1ère section, "Instruction relative aux inspections et exercises de mobilisation en 1936," message 43-I-A-2-RS/EMG, 15 January 1936, 3.

18. Ibid., 4–5, annex.

19. S.H.A.A., série 2B, carton 20, ministère de l'air, état-major de l'Armée de l'air, 1er Bureau, "L'établissement des journaux de mobilisation dans l'Armée de l'air," message 972/1/M-E.M.A.A., 22 November 1937, 2.

20. Ibid.

21. S.H.A.A., série 2B, carton 20, ministère de l'air, état-major de l'Armée de l'air, 1ère section, "Instruction générale provisoire relative aux inspections et exercises de mobilisation dans l'Armée de l'air," message 42-IA2/R/S E.M.G., 15 January 1936, *passim*.

22. During his tenure as air minister in the Popular Front government, Pierre Cot pushed—unsuccessfully—to make the flying clubs a significant source of pilots for the air service. See Vivier, *La politique aéronautique militaire de la France*, 391–99. See also Patrick Facon, "L'aviation populaire: Entre les mythes et la réalitié," *Revue historique des armées* 2 (1982): 55–59.

23. S.H.A.A., série 2B, carton 37, minstère de l'air, état-major de l'Armée de l'air, 1er Bureau, "Modificatif no. 3 à l'instruction relative aux nivellements et déclassements des réservistes de l'Armée de l'air no. 357 I/M-RS/E.M.A.A. du 20 avril 1937," message 813 I/M-RS/E.M.A.A., 22 July 1938, annexe 1.

24. S.H.A.A., série 2B, carton 20, état-major de l'Armée de l'air, 1ère section, note pour le général, chef d'état-major général, Vice président du Conseil supérieur de l'air, "Mobilisation de l'Armée de l'air," message 639/1/M/RS, E.M.A.A., 8 July 1936, 2.

25. See Patrick Facon, "Le haut commandement aérien français et le problème du réarmement, 1938–1939," *Revue historique des armées* 3 (1989): 91–101.

26. S.H.A.A., série 2B, carton 20, ministère de l'air, état-major de l'Armée de l'air,

1er Bureau, mobilisation, "Données sommaires sur la mobilisation de l'Armée de l'air," message 20/1/M/RS, E.M.A.A., 11 January 1937, 12–13.

27. S.H.A.A., série 2B, carton 20, ministère de l'air, état- major de l'Armée de l'air, 1ère section, "Instruction générale provisoire relative aux directions aux inspections et exercices de mobilisation dans l'Armée de l'air," message 42-IA2/R/S E.M.G., 15 January 1936, 8 (emphasis in original).

28. S.H.A.A., série 2B, carton 20, état-major de l'Armée de l'air, 1er Bureau, 3ème section, "Feuille de renseignements relative à l'objet, à la forme, à l'établissement et à la remise des ordres de mobilisation et des ordres de convocation spéciale," message 877/1/M/RS, E.M.A.A., 28 October 1937, 2 (emphasis in original).

29. Kiesling, *Arming against Hitler,* 110–11.

30. S.H.A.A., série 2B, carton 20, ministère de l'air, état-major de l'Armée de l'air, 1er Bureau, le ministre de l'air à MM les généraux commandant les Régions aériennes, "Documents de mobilisation," message 1091/1/M/RS, E.M.A.A., 17 December 1937, 1.

31. S.H.A.A., série 2B, carton 24, ministère de l'air, état-major de l'Armée de l'air, 1er Bureau, "Tableaux d'emploi de l'Armée de l'air dans la Métropole: Plan 'E-1,'" message 1540/I/M/RS, E.M.A.A., 17 November 1938.

32. S.H.A.A., série 2B, carton 23, ministère de l'air, état-major de l'Armée de l'air, 1er Bureau, "Plan E (1er modificatif), fiches des renseignements concernant les éléments de l'Armée de l'air mobilisée (Métropole)," message 796/1/M/RS, E.M.A.A., 19 July 1938, *passim.*

33. S.H.A.A., série 2B, carton 20, ministère de l'air, état major de l'Armée de l'air, 3ème Bureau, "Memento de mesures pouvant être prescrites en cas de tension politique extérieure, première partie," message 959-3-0.-S., E.M.A.A., 21 April 1937. See also S.H.A.A., série 2B, carton 20, ministère de l'air, état-major de l'Armée de l'air, 3ème Bureau, "Memento de mesures pouvant être prescrites en cas de tension politique extérieure, première partie," message 95-3-0.-S., E.M.A.A., 15 January 1937.

34. S.H.A.A., série 2B, carton 20, ministère de l'air, état-major de l'Armée de l'air, 3ème Bureau, "Instruction sur la mise en garde de l'Armée de l'air dans la Métropole," message 83-3.O.S, E.M.A.A., 16 January 1939, 6.

35. S.H.A.A., série 2B, carton 20, ministère de l'air, état-major de l'Armée de l'air, 3ème Bureau, "Instruction sur la mise en garde de l'Armée de l'air en Afrique du Nord: Annexe II, mesures d'alerte" message 274-3.O.S., E.M.A.A., 8 February 1939, 3–4. Although this message references procedures for North African units, the instructions and procedures mirrored those used in the *métropole*.

36. See Christienne and Lissarague, *A History of French Military Aviation,* 241–59.

37. One exception to this general statement is Patrice Buffotot's analysis of the futile planning effort to attack Soviet oil fields in the Caucasus. See Buffotot, "Le projet de bombardement des pétroles soviétiques du Caucase en 1940: Un example des projets alliés pendant la drôle de guerre," *Revue historique des armées* 4 (1979): 78–101. Ernest R. May's recent analysis of the events that led to the Battle of

France traces the Deuxième Bureau's role in shaping French policies, but May does not describe the role that air staff planners played in formulating plans for strategic and operational bombing campaigns against targets in Germany. See Ernest R. May, *Strange Victory: Hitler's Conquest of France* (New York: Hill and Wang, 2000).

38. For the German systems, see S.H.A.A., série 2B, cartons 61–76. See S.H.A.A., série 2B, cartons 78–80 for information on target systems in Spain. For Italian targets, see S.H.A.A., série 2B, cartons 83–95.

39. For the best recent analysis of the U.S. Army Air Corps Tactical School's doctrine and influence, see Faber, "Interwar U.S. Army Aviation and the Air Corps Tactical School," in Meilinger, ed., *Paths of Heaven,* 183–238. I found no evidence in French sources to suggest that the French exchanged ideas in a systematic way with the theorists at the Tactical School during the 1930s.

40. See Phillip S. Meilinger, "Trenchard, Slessor, and Royal Air Force Doctrine before World War II," in Meilinger, ed., *Paths of Heaven,* 41–78.

41. Douhet, *Command of the Air,* 197.

42. Vivier, *La politique aéronautique militaire de la France,* 145–54.

43. S.H.A.A., série 2B, carton 64, état-major de l'Armée de l'air, 2ème Bureau, "Note annexe au répertoire des industries aéronautiques allemandes: Production de l'aluminium et les alliages d'aluminium en Allemagne," 15 March 1938, 5.

44. S.H.A.A., série 2B, carton 64, état-major de l'Armée de l'air, 2ème Bureau, "Répertoire des industries aéronautiques allemandes," 15 March 1938, 7.

45. Ibid.

46. Ibid., 8.

47. S.H.A.A., série 2B, carton 66, état-major de l'Armée de l'air, 2ème Bureau, "Répertoire des terrains allemands, note préliminaire," 31 July 1939, 8–9.

48. S.H.A.A., série 2B, carton 66, Amtliches Gemeindeverzeichnis für das Deutsche Reiche auf Grand der Volkszählung 1933 (Berlin: Verlag für Sozialpolitik, 1936).

49. S.H.A.A., série 2B, carton 66, état-major de l'Armée de l'air, 2ème Bureau, "Répertoire des terrains allemands, note préliminaire," 31 July 1939, 12–13.

50. Ibid.

51. S.H.A.A., série 2B, carton 64, état-major de l'Armée de l'air, 2ème Bureau, "Répertoire des industries allemandes des carburants," 18 November 1939, 12–13.

52. Ibid., 16.

53. Ibid.

54. Ibid.

55. Ibid., 17.

56. S.H.A.A., série 2B, carton 64, état-major de l'Armée de l'air, 2ème Bureau, message 2814-2-C/S, 20 December 1938.

57. For a thorough analysis of French fears in this area, see Weber, *The Hollow Years,* 237–56. Weber includes a photograph of a dramatic propaganda poster depicting French civil defense workers tending to civilians in the aftermath of a chemical

attack. See also Ladislas Myzyrowiecz, *Autopsie d'une défaite: Origines de l'effrondement militaire français de 1940* (Lausanne: L'âge d'homme, 1973); and Robert J. Young, "The Use and Abuse of Fear: France and the Air Menace in the 1930s," *Intelligence and National Security* 2 (1987): 88–109.

58. S.H.A.A., série 2B, carton 64, état-major de l'Armée de l'air, 2ème Bureau, message 2814-2-C/S, 20 December 1938, 12.

59. Ibid.

60. S.H.A.A., série 2B, carton 65, état-major de l'Armée de l'air, "Répertoire des sources d'énergie électrique allemandes, note préliminare," 21 June 1939, 14–16.

61. Allied air attacks against the German transportation system achieved great success in the latter days of the war. The nexus between transportation and coal production proved to be a critical connection that paralyzed the German war economy. See Alfred C. Mierzejewski, *The Collapse of the German War Economy, 1944–1945* (Chapel Hill, N.C.: University of North Carolina Press, 1988).

62. S.H.A.A., série 2B, carton 65, état-major de l'Armée de l'air, 2ème Bureau, "Les voies de communication du Reich," March–April 1937.

63. S.H.A.A., série 2B, carton 75, état-major de l'Armée de l'air, 2ème Bureau, "Dossier d'objectif, Avf-11, objectifs de pleine voie, hypothèse mixte Centre Nord," n.d.

64. S.H.A.A., série 2B, carton 67, état-major de l'Armée de l'air, 2ème Bureau, "Renseignements préliminaires d'ordre général sur l'importance et la vulnerabilité des objectifs militaires et de représailles," 11 January 1939, 5–6.

65. Ibid.

66. Ibid.

67. Ibid.

68. S.H.A.A., série 3D, carton 516, "Renseignements à tirer de la guerre: Titre 26, personnel et effectifs," n.d.

69. Ibid.

70. S.H.A.A., série 3D, carton 477, "Rapport du Colonel Boucher au Général Prételat," 1 December 1939, 2.

71. Kiesling, *Arming against Hitler,* 38–40.

72. S.H.A.A., série 2B, carton, 12, note pour le ministre, "Enquête sur non obtention de permission agricoles du Bn de l'air 136 à Agen," message 1763, 10 April 1940.

73. S.H.A.A., série 3D, carton 516, "Renseignements à tirer de la guerre: Titre 26, personnel et effectifs," n.d.

74. Ibid., 10.

75. S.H.A.A., série 3D, carton 477, "Ordre no. 21," n.d., 1. Although the document does not carry a date stamp, the heading indicates an official order and the text specifies 26 February 1940 as the effective date of the order. Additionally, the document contains a map that describes the boundaries—essentially from Paris to the north and northeastern frontiers—of the new command structure.

76. Facon, *L'Armée de l'air dans la tourmente,* 95–114.

77. Thierry Vivier offers a comprehensive study of French attempts to build an alliance system in the east: see "La coopération aéronautique franco-tchécoslovaque," 70–79; Vivier, "L'aviation française en Pologne, 60–70; Vivier, *La politique aéronautique militaire de la France,* 505–64. Patrick Facon also analyzes the diplomatic efforts to use airpower as the cornerstone of the eastern alliance, in *L'Armée de l'air dans la tourmente,* 20–23. For a riveting account of the campaign in Norway, see François Kersaudy, *Norway 1940* (1987; reprint, New York: St. Martin's Press, 1990).

78. S.H.A.A., série 3D, carton 516, "Renseignements à tirer de la guerre: Titre 26, personnel et effectifs," n.d.

79. The most recent effort is Allan R. Millett and Williamson Murray's exceptional operational history of World War II, *A War To Be Won: Fighting the Second World War* (Cambridge, Mass.: Belknap, Harvard University Press, 2000), 63–83. See also Gerhard L. Weinberg, *A World at Arms: A Global History of World War II* (Cambridge: Cambridge University Press, 1994), 122–61.

80. Robert A. Doughty, *The Breaking Point.*

81. See Martin S. Alexander, *The Republic in Danger: General Maurice Gamelin and the Politics of French Defence, 1933–1940* (Cambridge: Cambridge University Press, 1992). See also Jeffrey A. Gunsburg, *Divided and Conquered: The French High Command and the Defeat of the West, 1940* (Westport, Conn.: Greenwood Press, 1979).

82. Charles de Gaulle, *The Complete War Memoirs of Charles de Gaulle,* translated by Jonathan Griffin (New York: Simon and Schuster, 1967).

83. Boillot, Pierre, "La 'drôle de guerre' et la Bataille de France vues par un sergeant-pilote," 76–90.

84. Ibid., 84.

85. Ibid., 85–86.

86. Christienne and Lissarague, *A History of French Military Aviation,* 348.

87. Olivier Ledermann and Jean-François Merolle, *Le sacrifice: Les Breguet 693 de l'aviation d'assaut dans la Bataille de France* (Paris: IPMS France, 1994), 162–81.

88. S.H.A.A., série 3D, carton 516, "Renseignements à tirer de la guerre: Titre 26, personnel et effectifs," n.d.

89. Pierre Cot, *Triumph of Treason: Contre nous de la tyrannie,* translated by Sybille and Milton Crane (Chicago: Ziff-Davis Publishing Company, 1944), 278.

90. S.H.A.A., série 3D, carton 508, "Le Capitaine Leroy à Monsieur le Général de Corps d'Armée commandant la 2ème Région aérienne (Toulouse)," 30 August 1940, 7.

91. Ibid., 7.

7. Assessing Combat Performance and Air Doctrine

1. "Les accords italo-allemandes de Wiesbaden sur l'armée française, 29 juin 1940 (traduction du compte-rendu allemand)." See d'Abzac-Epezy, *L'Armée de l'air de Vichy*, 596.

2. De Gaulle, *The Complete War Memoirs*, 84.

3. S.H.A.A., série 3D, carton 519, secrétariat d'état à l'aviation, état-major de l'Armée de l'air, 3ème Bureau, le secrétaire d'état à l'aviation à MM le Général commandant la 29ème Région aérienne (Châteauroux), le Général commandant la 32ème Région aérienne (Limoges), le Général commandant la 33ème Région aérienne (Clermont-Ferrand), le Général commandant la 34ème Région aérienne (Lyon), le Général commandant la 35ème Région aérienne (Aix-en-Provence), le Général commandant la 36ème Région aérienne (Montpellier), le Général commandant la 37ème Région aérienne (Toulouse), le Général commandant la 38ème Région aérienne (Pau), le Général commandant supérieur de l'air en Afrique du Nord, le Général commandant de l'air au Levant, le Général commandant de l'air à la Côte Française des Somalis, "Enseignements à tirer de la guerre (Forces aériennes)," message 11087-3/1-S/E.M.A.A., 23 July 1940, 3.

4. The army also launched an investigation into the conduct of the war. The two commissions exchanged information during the course of their inquiries. See S.H.A.A., série 3D, carton 519, Secrétariat d'état à l'aviation, état-major de l'Armée de l'air, 3ème Bureau, le secrétaire d'état à l'aviation à Monsieur le Général d'Armée commandant en chef des Forces terrestres, ministre, secrétaire d'état à la guerre, "Enseignements à tirer de la guerre," message 101-3/1/E.M.A.A., 26 July 1941.

5. Robert O. Paxton's groundbreaking study of the Vichy period remains the starting point for understanding the personalities and issues that drove French society during the occupation. See *Vichy France: Old Guard and New Order, 1940–1944* (New York: Columbia University Press, 1972). Philippe Burrin offers a broader perspective of the choices available to French citizens during the occupation. See *France under the Germans: Collaboration and Compromise*, translated by Janet Lloyd (New York: New Press, 1996).

6. See Thierry Vivier, "La Commission G: Entre la défaite et l'Armée de l'air future," 113–21. See d'Abzac-Epezy, *L'Armée de l'air de Vichy*, 428–86. See also S.H.A.A., série 3D, carton 519, secrétariat d'état à l'aviation, état-major de l'Armée de l'air, 3ème Bureau, le secrétaire d'état à l'aviation à MM le Général commandant la 1ère Région aérienne, état-major, 3ème Bureau (Aix-en-Provence); le Général commandant le secteur de défense aérienne sud, état-major, 3ème Bureau (Aix-en-Provence); le Général commandant la 2ème Région aérienne, état-major, 3ème Bureau (Toulouse); le Général commandant supérieur de l'air en Afrique du Nord, état-major, 3ème Bureau (Alger); le Général commandant de l'air en Afrique Occidentale Française (Dakar), "Commission d'étude des enseignements de la guerre," message 126-3/1/E.M.A.A., 6 September 1941. S.H.A.A., série 3D, carton 519, 2ème Région aérienne, état-major, 3ème Bureau, "Note de service,"

message 2649/3, 20 September 1941. S.H.A.A., série 3D, carton 519, état-major de l'Armée de l'air, 3ème Bureau, le secrétaire d'état à l'aviation à Monsieur le Général commandant la 2ème Région aérienne (état-major, 3ème Bureau), Toulouse, "Commission 'G,'" message 205-3/1/E.M.A.A., 24 November 1941.

7. See S.H.A.A., série 3D, carton 508–519, "Rapports des Grandes Unités."

8. Marc Bloch wrote: "What drove our armies to disaster was the cumulative effect of a great number of different mistakes. One glaring characteristic is, however, common to all of them. Our leaders, or those who acted for them, were incapable of thinking in terms of a *new* war. In other words, the German triumph was essentially a triumph of intellect—and it is that which makes it so peculiarly serious." Marc Bloch, *Strange Defeat: A Statement of Evidence Written in 1940,* translated by Gerard Hopkins (London: Oxford University Press, 1949), 36 (emphasis in original).

9. See Facon, *L'Armée de l'air dans la tourmente,* 109–14.

10. See the various original reports in S.H.A.A., série 3D, cartons 508–13.

11. S.H.A.A., série 3D, carton 512, 2ème Région aérienne, Groupement d'aviation no. 18, état-major, "Compte-rendu au sujet des enseignements de la guerre par le Lt. Colonel Demery, commandant du Groupement d'aviation d'assaut no. 18," message 4477, August 1940, 8.

12. S.H.A.A., série 3D, carton 511, "Enseignements pouvant être tirés des conditions dans lesquelles furent engagées les unités de Groupement de bombardement no. 2, 22 mai au 14 juin 1940," n.d., 4.

13. For an analysis of Gamelin's role in the exercise of command and his relations with the air service, see Alexander, *The Republic in Danger.* For Weygand's assumption of command and his subsequent failed attempt to salvage French fortunes, see Shirer, *The Collapse of the Third Republic,* 698–756. General de Gaulle recorded his impression of Gamelin in his *Memoirs.* He wrote: "Listening to him, I was convinced that, by dint of carrying about with him a certain military system and applying his labour to it, he had made of it a faith. I felt too that referring himself to the example of Joffre, whom he had assisted at close quarters and to some extent inspired in the early days of the First World War, he had persuaded himself that, at his level, the essential thing was to fix one's purpose, once for all, upon a well-defined plan and then not to let oneself be deflected from it by an avatar." De Gaulle judged Weygand more sympathetically: "At one go there had fallen on his shoulders a crushing burden he was not built to bear. When, on May 20, he had taken over the supreme command, it was too late, without any doubt, to win the Battle of France. It seems likely that the realization was a surprise to him. As he had never considered the real possibilities of mechanized force, the immense and sudden effects produced by the enemy's resources stupefied him." De Gaulle, *The Complete War Memoirs,* 34–35, 50–51.

14. S.H.A.A., série 3D, carton 477, état français, secrétariat d'état à l'aviation, "Enseignements aériens de la guerre, 1939–1942, Commission 'G,': Première partie, les conditions de la guerre moderne," March 1942, 8–9.

15. Ibid., 9.

16. S.H.A.A., série 3D, carton 512, 2ème Région aérienne, 19ème Groupement d'assaut, état-major, "Rapport sur l'organisation, le fonctionnement, et l'emploi du 19ème Groupement d'assaut au cours de la guerre, 1939–1940," 13 August 1940, 6–7.

17. S.H.A.A., série 3D, carton 513, "L'aviation dans la Bataille de Flandres," 20 August 1940, 2.

18. S.H.A.A., série 3D, carton 477, état français, secrétariat d'état à l'aviation, "Enseignements aériens de la guerre, 1939–1942, Commission 'G,': Première partie, les conditions de la guerre moderne," March 1942, 10.

19. Ibid., 11.

20. Ibid., 18.

21. See, for example, S.H.A.A., série 3D, carton 513, 1ère Région aérienne, base aérienne centre de démobilisation de Nîmes, "Travail du Lieutenant Colonel Bourdier: La mission de protection en chasse d'armée," message 1321/E.M., 17 August 1940.

22. S.H.A.A., série 3D, carton 477, état français, secrétariat d'état à l'aviation, "Enseignements aériens de la guerre, 1939–1942, Commission 'G,': Première partie, les conditions de la guerre moderne," March 1942, 20.

23. Ibid., 21 (emphasis in original).

24. Ibid., 24.

25. S.H.A.A., série 3D, carton 508, Armée de l'air, 2ème Région aérienne, commandant des bases aériennes de Tarn et Garonne, et du Lot, base aérienne de Moissac, "Rapport du Commandant Levesque, ex-commandant des Forces aériennes du 8ème Corps d'armée au sujet de l'organisation et de l'emploi des Forces aériennes de renseignement," message 100/C/1, 24 August 1940, 2.

26. S.H.A.A., série 3D, carton 508, 4ème Région aérienne, base aérienne de Lyon et du Groupement nord, Lieutenant Colonel Seive de la base aérienne de Bron à Monsieur le Général commandant la 4ème Région aérienne, "Rapport sur l'organisation et l'emploi des Forces aériennes de renseignements," message 276/B.G.N, 20 August 1940, 5.

27. S.H.A.A., série 3D, carton 477, état français, secrétariat d'état à l'aviation, "Enseignements aériens de la guerre, 1939–1942, Commission 'G,': Première partie, les conditions de la guerre moderne," March 1942, 29 (emphasis in original).

28. Ibid., deuxième partie, "Les armes et les moyens d'exploitation," March 1942, 139.

29. For a discussion of the role of airborne troops in the German assault on Holland and Belgium, see Shirer, *The Collapse of the Third Republic,* 604–11. For the assault on Crete, see Weinberg, *A World at Arms,* 227–30.

30. S.H.A.A., série 3D, carton 477, état français, secrétariat d'état à l'aviation, "Enseignements aériens de la guerre, 1939–1942, Commission 'G,': Deuxième partie, les armes et les moyens d'exploitation," March 1942, 139.

31. The French military realized this vision of airborne assaults in the ill-fated attempt to defeat Vietnamese Communist forces in the First Indochina War. See Bernard B. Fall, *Street without Joy* (Mechanicsburg, Pa.: Stackpole Books, 1989).

32. The French concentrated on producing combat aircraft during the 1930s. Economic and political conditions precluded a wider research and development program that included the full range of transport aircraft. Late in the decade, the Armée de l'air considered designs for aircraft capable of transporting the Renault tank. See S.H.A.A., série 2B, cartons 165–69. Patrick Facon studied the various airplane production plans of the late 1930s: see "Le plan V," 102–23.

33. For an analysis of how French aviation industry developed, see Chadeau, *L'industrie aéronautique en France*.

34. S.H.A.A., série 3D, carton 477, état français, secrétariat d'état à l'aviation, "Enseignements aériens de la guerre, 1939–1942, Commission 'G,': Deuxième partie, les armes et les moyens d'exploitation," March 1942, 139.

35. Ibid., 148.

36. S.H.A.A., série 3D, carton 511, commandement en chef des Forces aériennes, inspection de l'aviation de bombardement, le Général de Corps aérien G. Pastier, inspecteur de l'aviation de bombardement à Monsieur le Général commandant en chef des Forces aériennes, "Enseignements de la guerre," message 108/I. B./S. C., 6 June 1940, 1.

37. Ibid., 9–10.

38. S.H.A.A., série 3D, carton 511, "Enseignements pouvant être tirés des conditions dans lesquelles Furent engagées les unités de Groupement de bombardement no. 2, 22 mai au 14 juin 1940," n.d., 11.

39. S.H.A.A., série 3D, carton 511, Capitaine Meiffren, Groupe aérien 1/23, "Enseignements à tirer de la guerre," n.d., 7.

40. S.H.A.A., série 3D, carton 477, état français, secrétariat d'état à l'aviation, "Enseignements aériens de la guerre, 1939–1942, Commission 'G,': Deuxième partie, les armes et les moyens d'exploitation," March 1942, 53.

41. See S.H.A.A., série 2B, carton 110, Capitaine Secrétant, Centre d'expériences aériennes militaires—assaut, rapport d'ensemble: Procédés de destruction des voies ferrées par l'aviation d'assaut," message 361/S, 15 April 1939. S.H.A.A., série 2B, carton 111, Centre d'expériences aériennes militaires, "Note sur l'attaque de chars par l'aviation," message 069/S, 26 January 1940.

42. Cot, *L'Armée de l'air*.

43. See Chapter 5 for the discussion of the Armée de l'air's maneuver and exercise program.

44. S.H.A.A., série 3D, carton 511, Capitaine Plique, "Rapport sur les enseignements à tirer de la guerre, 1939–1940," n.d., 7.

45. S.H.A.A., série 3D, carton 477, état français, secrétariat d'état à l'aviation, "Enseignements aériens de la guerre, 1939–1942, Commission 'G,': Deuxième partie, les armes et les moyens d'exploitation," March 1942, 60–63.

46. Ibid.

47. Ibid., 59.

48. S.H.A.A., série 3D, carton 477, "Rapport du Colonel Boucher au Général Pretelat," 1 December 1939, 8.

49. Ibid., 20–21.

50. S.H.A.A., série 3D, carton 516, "Enseignements à tirer de la guerre, titre 25, matériel: chapitre 1, avions," n.d.

51. S.H.A.A., série 3D, carton 477, état français, secrétariat d'état à l'aviation, "Enseignements aériens de la guerre, 1939–1942, Commission 'G,': Deuxième partie, les armes et les moyens d'exploitation," March 1942, 107.

52. Patrick Facon recently examined the persistence of the "myth of the 1,000 victories." He notes that partisan emotions dominate the issue, which makes resolution extremely difficult. Several sources provide conflicting data on the exact number of French aerial victories, ranging from 594 to 1,060. The statistics on French aerial losses to German fighters has a narrower range of 757–892. See Facon, *L'Armée de l'air dans la tourmente*, 247–63.

53. S.H.A.A., série 3D, carton 511, commandement en chef des Forces aériennes, inspection de l'aviation de bombardement, le Général de Corps aérien G. Pastier, inspecteur de l'aviation de bombardement à Monsieur le Général commandant en chef les Forces aériennes, "Enseignements de la guerre," message 108/I. B./S. C., 6 June 1940, 4.

54. S.H.A.A., série 3D, carton 510, "Travail du Colonel Dumemes, commandant le Groupement de chasse no. 22," 30 December 1940, 24.

55. S.H.A.A., série 3D, carton 477, état français, secrétariat d'état à l'aviation, "Enseignements aériens de la guerre, 1939–1942, Commission 'G,': Première partie, les conditions de la guerre moderne," March 1942, 11.

56. Ibid., 11.

57. S.H.A.A., série 3D, carton 477, état français, secrétariat d'état à l'aviation, "Enseignements aériens de la guerre, 1939–1942, Commission 'G,': Deuxième partie, les armes et les moyens d'exploitation," March 1942, 111.

58. Ibid., 116.

59. Ibid., 86.

60. S.H.A.A., série 3D, carton 508, commandant des Forces aériennes, 32ème Région aérienne, "Remarques sur l'organisation et la mise en oeuvre d'un groupe d'aviation d'observation de division légère mécanique," message 659/3, 29 July 1940, 3.

61. S.H.A.A., série 3D, carton 508, 1ère Région aérienne, base aérienne de Montpellier, "Rapport du Commandant Lanson, ex-commandant des Forces aériennes no. 24, sur les enseignements à tirer de la guerre," 3 June 1941, 1.

62. For a detailed daily report of the frustrations encountered by a reconnaissance unit commander as he tried to relay information to higher commanders, see S.H.A.A., série 3D, carton 508, "Emploi des Forces aériennes de renseignement: Réponse au questionnaire, annexe II," message 2644/C.I., 20 August 1940.

63. S.H.A.A., série 3D, carton 477, état français, secretariat d'état à l'aviation, "Enseignements aériens de la guerre, 1939–1942, Commission 'G,': Deuxième partie, les armes et les moyens d'exploitation," March 1942, 87–88.

64. Ibid., 92–98.

Bibliography

I. Works Primarily Cited

French Archives

Service historique de l'Armée de l'air (S.H.A.A.), Château de Vincennes, France

Série 2B: État-major de l'Armée de l'air et 3ème Bureau
Carton 10: Les Écoles et Centres d'instruction de l'Armée de l'air.
Carton 11: Documents concernants l'organisation et le fonctionnement des bases, écoles et centres d'instruction.
Carton 12: Documents concernants l'organisation et le fonctionnement des bases, écoles et centres d'instruction.
Carton 64: Notice sur la région industrielle de la Ruhr—liste d'objectifs à bombarder.
Carton 65: Renseignements concernant les chemins de fer allemands.
Carton 68: Dossiers d'objectifs—25 dossiers d'industries aéronautiques à bombarder en Allemagne.
Carton 69: Dossiers d'objectifs—58 dossiers d'installations électriques allemandes.
Carton 70: Dossiers d'objectifs—40 dossiers de dépôts et d'industries pétrolifières allemands.
Carton 71: Dossiers d'objectifs—51 villes allemandes à bombarder comme objectifs militaires et de représailles.
Carton 72: Dossiers d'objectifs—74 dossiers de terrains d'aviation allemands.
Carton 73: Dossiers d'objectifs—85 dossiers de terrains d'aviation allemands.
Carton 74: Dossiers d'objectifs—68 dossiers de terrains d'aviation allemands.
Carton 75: Dossiers d'objectifs—15 dossiers de voies ferrées allemandes.

Carton 76: Dossiers d'objectifs—44 dossiers concernant les voies navigables, les ports, les ponts, les écluses.

Carton 104: Conduite des opérations—instructions aux généraux commandants des armées aériennes (1937–38).

Carton 109: Utilisation en emploi des Forces aériennes, tactiques, règlements des manoeuvres.

Carton 110: Utilisation en emploi des Forces aériennes.

Carton 111: Utilisation en emploi des Forces aériennes—aviation de bombardement et reconnaissance.

Carton 112: Utilisation en emploi des Forces aériennes—observation, transport, autogyres.

Carton 113: Exercises et manoeuvres divers.

Carton 114: Exercises air-D.A.T.

Carton 115: Exercises et manoeuvres (1935–37).

Carton 116: Exercises et manoeuvres (1938).

Carton 117: Exercises et manoeuvres divers (1933–39).

Série C: Forces aériennes françaises et Outre-Mer
Carton 2: Aéronautique du Maroc—37e Régiment d'aviation

Série 3: Secrétariat d'état à l'aviation
Carton 329: Enseignements à tirer de la guerre.

Carton 477: Rapports divers de la Commission "G."

Carton 508: Commission G—Rapports des Grandes Unités: Zones d'opérations et Forces aériennes du corps de l'armée.

Carton 509: Commission G—Rapports des Grandes Unités: Divisions aériennes et secteurs de l'air.

Carton 510: Commission G—Rapports des Grandes Unités: Groupements et groupes de chasse.

Carton 511: Commission G—Rapports des Grandes Unités: Inspections de l'aviation de bombardment, groupement d'instruction de bombardement du sud-est, groupements et groupes de bombardement.

Carton 512: Commission G—Rapports des Grandes Unités: Groupes aériens de reconnaissance, groupes d'observation, et groupements d'aviation d'assaut.

Carton 513: Commission G—Rapports des Grandes Unités: Compagnies de l'air, compagnies de munitions, bases aériennes, bataillons de l'air, parcs, service photographique, sécurité générale, unités de transmissions, écoles, études diverses.

Carton 514: Commission G—Rapports des Grandes Unités: Organisation et emploi des commandements, états-majors de la chasse, du bombardement, de l'assaut, de la reconnaissance, de l'observation et aerostation.

Carton 515: Commission G—Rapports des Grandes Unités: Organisation et fonctionnement des services de l'Armée de l'air.

Carton 516: Commission G—Rapports des Grandes Unités: Infrastructure, matériel, personnel, effectifs, et instructions.
Carton 517: Commission G—Rapports des Grandes Unités: Aérostation.
Carton 518: Commission G—Rapports des Grandes Unités: Aérostation, attaques aériennes, activité de l'entrepôt de l'Armée de l'air 304, liaisons et transmissions, divers.
Carton 519: Rapport général de la Commission G.

United States Archives

The Albert F. Simpson United States Air Force Historical Research Agency

Books
Armengaud, Paul. *La pacification de l'Afrique encore insoumise*. Paris: Berger-Levrault, 1930.
———. *Quelques enseignements des campagnes du Riff en matière d'aviation, 1925–1926*. Paris: Berger-Levrault, 1928.
Bullitt, Orville H., ed. *For the President, Personal and Secret: Correspondence between Franklin Delano Roosevelt and William C. Bullitt*. Boston: Houghton Mifflin, 1972.
Busson, Henri, Joseph Fèvre, and Henri Hauser, *La France d'aujourd'hui et ses colonies*. Paris: Librairie Félix Alcan, 1920.
Chauvineau, Narcisse. *Une invasion, est-elle encore possible?* Paris: Berger-Levrault, 1939.
Cot, Pierre. *L'Armée de l'air, 1936–1938*. Paris: Grasset, 1939.
———. *Triumph of Treason: Contre nous de la tyrannie*, translated by Sybille and Milton Crane. New York: Ziff-Davis Publising Company, 1944.
Douhet, Giulio. *The Command of the Air*. Translated by Dino Ferrari. 1942. Reprint, Washington, D.C.: Office of Air Force History, 1983.
Ellis, L. F. *The War in France and Flanders, 1939–1940*. London: Her Majesty's Stationery Office, 1953.
Mitchell, William. *Winged Defense: The Development and Possibilities of Modern Air Power—Economic and Military*. New York: G. P. Putnam's Sons, 1925. Reprint, New York: Dover Publications, 1988.
Reinsch, Paul S. *Colonial Government: An Introduction to the Study of Colonial Institutions*. New York: The MacMillan Company, 1916.
Royse, Morton W. *Aerial Bombardment and the International Regulation of Warfare*. New York: H. Vinal, 1928.
Serre, Charles. *Les événements survenus en France de 1933 à 1945: Témoignages et documents recueillis par la commission d'enquête parlementaire*, 9 vols. Paris: PUF, 1952.
Vauthier, Arsene Marie Paul. *La défense anti-aérienne des Grandes Unités*. Paris: Berger-Levrault, 1929.
Vauthier, Colonel P. *La doctrine de guerre du Général Douhet*. Paris: Berger-Levrault, 1935.

Memoirs

Allard, Paul. *Les responsables du désastre*. Paris: Les Éditions de la France, 1941.

Astier de La Vigerie, Général. *Le ciel n'était pas vide*. Paris: Julliard, 1952.

Beaufre, André. *1940: The Fall of France*. Translated by D. Flower. New York: Knopf, 1968.

Bloch, Marc. *Strange Defeat: A Statement of Evidence Written in 1940*. Translated by Gerard Hopkins. London: Oxford University Press, 1949.

Chambrun, René. *I Saw France Fall*. New York: W. Morrow and Company, 1940.

Clostermann, Pierre. *Le grand cirque: Souvenirs d'un pilote de chasse français dans la RAF*. Paris: Flammarion, 1948.

Gamelin, Maurice. *Servir*, 3 vols. Paris: Plon, 1946–47.

Goutard, Colonel. *La guerre des occasions perdues*. Paris: Hachette, 1956.

Langeron, Lieutenant-Colonel. *Misère et grandeur de notre aviation*. Paris: Éditions Baudinière, 1941.

Reibel, Charles. *Les responsables: Ma déposition devant la Cour de justice suprême de Riom*. Paris: Éditions Baudinière, 1941.

Stehlin, Paul. *Témoignage pour l'histoire*. Paris: Robert Laffont, 1964.

Articles

"L'aéronautique militaire en Indochine: Mission 'Sud-Annam.'" *Revue de l'aéronautique militaire* 31 (1926): 5–15.

"L'aviation Britannique en Iracq." *Revue de l'aéronautique militaire* 9 (1922): 66–67.

"L'aviation militaire au Maroc (au cours du deuxième trimestre 1925)." *Revue de l'aéronautique militaire* 29 (1925): 5, 98–112.

"L'aviation militaire et la pénétration saharienne." *Revue de l'aéronautique militaire* 28 (1925): 73–83.

"Comment organiser l'aviation d'observation." *Revue de l'aéronautique militaire* 13 (1923): 1–6.

"Emploi de l'aviation au Maroc en 1925: Aperçu général de la campagne—Ses trois grandes phases." *Revue de l'aéronautique militaire* 32 (1926): 36–42.

"Engagements volontaires au régiment d'aviation du Maroc." *Revue de l'aéronautique militaire* 26 (1925): 41.

"Les manoevres aériennes de 1924." *Revue de l'aéronautique militaire* 25 (1925): 1–4.

"Les opérations aériennes au Maroc, de septembre à décémbre 1922." *Revue de l'aéronautique militaire* 13 (1923): 10–12.

"Les opérations aériennes au Maroc en juillet–août 1922." *Revue de l'aéronautique militaire* 11 (1922): 111–14.

"Les opérations aériennes au Maroc en mai–juin 1922." *Revue de l'aéronautique militaire* 10 (1922): 83–86.

"Les opérations aériennes au Maroc en mars–avril 1922." *Revue de l'aéronautique militaire* 9 (1922): 53–58.

"Les opérations aériennes dans le Djebel Druse." *Revue de l'aéronautique militaire* 30 (1925): 6, 122–25.

"Organisation de l'aéronautique militaire." *Revue de l'aéronautique militaire* 31 (1926): 1–4.

"L'organisation des terrains d'aviation: Projets-types pour terrain de régiment et terrain de magasin général." *Revue de l'aéronautique militaire* 24 (1924): 131–38.

"La participation de l'aviation aux grandes manoevres anglaises de septembre 1925." *Revue de l'aéronautique militaire* 30 (1925): 126–29.

"Travail de l'aéronautique d'Indo-Chine." *Revue de l'aéronautique militaire* 27 (1925): 56–57.

Armengaud, Paul. "L'Aviation et la conduite de la manoeuvre et de la bataille: Morhange." *Revue des Forces aériennes* 8 (March 1930): 261–300.

———. "Aviation et manoeuvre d'aile et de dislocation: La manoeuvre et la bataille de la Marne et de l'Oureq." *Revue des Forces aériennes* 14 (September 1930): 1000–1046.

Barthélemy, Commandant. "L'aviation dans l'Afrique du Nord." *Revue de l'aéronautique militaire* 1 (January–February 1921): 7–13.

Bloch, D. P. "Notes sur la balistique aérienne." *Revue de l'aéronautique militaire* 20 (1924): 37–40.

Boniface, Lieutenant. "Le personnel de l'aviation." *Revue de l'aéronautique militaire* 6 (1921): 130–32.

Casse, Lieutenant-Colonel. "Faut-il des 'Divisions aériennes'?" *Revue de l'aéronautique militaire* 5 (1921): 5, 98–99.

Cheutin, Commandant. "Rôle colonial de l'aviation militaire au Maroc." *Revue de l'aéronautique militaire* 4 (1921): 85–91.

———. "L'aviation française au Maroc." *Revue de l'aéronautique militaire* 16 (1923): 77–81.

———. "L'aviation française au Maroc: Organisation, composition, répartition et emploi de l'aviation militaire au Maroc." *Revue de l'aéronautique militaire* 17 (1923): 100–104.

———. "L'aviation française au Maroc: Emploi de l'aviation." *Revue de l'aéronautique militaire* 19 (January–February 1924): 1–6.

———. "L'aviation française au Maroc: Emploi de l'aviation (suite)." *Revue de l'aéronautique militaire* 20 (1924): 2, 26–30.

———. "L'aviation française au Maroc: Emploi de l'aviation (fin)." *Revue de l'aéronautique militaire* 21 (May–June 1924): 3, 50–56.

Dagnaux, Capitaine. "L'aviation de bombardement: Son rôle, ses moyens, son état actuel." *Revue de l'aéronautique militaire* 4 (1921): 79–84.

———. "Les instruments de navigation expérimentés au cours d'un voyage en Afrique du Nord, 27 Octobre–9 Janvier 1924." *Revue de l'aéronautique militaire* 20 (1924): 31–32.

De La Fargue, Commandant. "L'aviation militaire en Tunisie: Historique, rôle, 1916–1920." *Revue de l'aéronautique militaire* 3 (May–June 1921): 3, 50–58.

Estienne, Lieutenant. "Comment réaliser un service aérien à travers le Sahara." *Revue de l'aéronautique militaire* 11 (1922): 95–100.

———. "La reconnaissance photographique d'armée: Ce qu'elle doit être." *Revue de l'aéronautique militaire* 13 (1923): 13–16.

Gravellat, Médecin-Major. "L'aviation sanitaire aux colonies." *Revue de l'aéronautique militaire* 18 (November–December 1923): 122–24.

Guillemeney, Colonel breveté. "Le bombardement des installations industrielles: Le blocus du bassin de Briey," *Revue des Forces aériennes* 15 (October 1930): 1151–90.

Hébrard, Capitaine. "De l'aviation de bombardement de nuit." *Revue de l'aéronautique militaire* 22 (1924): 87–90.

Keller, Chef de Bataillion breveté. "L'aviation dans la bataille." *Revue de l'aéronautique militaire* 27 (1925): 3, 50–55.

Picqué, R. "L'état actuel de l'aviation sanitaire." *Revue de l'aéronautique militaire* 19 (January–February 1924): 15–20.

Romatet, J. "Organisation de l'aéronautique militaire." *Revue de l'aéronautique militaire* 1 (1921): 3–6.

Tichenor, Frank A. "Air—Hot and Otherwise: Propaganda vs. Patriotism." *Aero Digest* (July 1926): 239.

Voisin, Général. "La doctrine de l'aviation française de combat en 1918: L'aviation de combat indépendante." *Revue des Forces aériennes* 28 (November 1931) 895–914.

Woelflin, Capitaine. "L'emploi de l'aviation tel qu'il est conçu par les allemands: Étude du règlement 'Führung und Gefecht der verbundenen Waffen' en ce qui concerne l'aviation." *Revue de l'aéronautique militaire* 20 (1924): 41–44.

———. "L'emploi de l'aviation tel qu'il est conçu par les allemands: Étude du règlement 'Führung und Gefecht der verbundenen Waffen' en ce qui concerne l'aviation (fin)." *Revue de l'aéronautique militaire* 21 (1924): 60–62.

II. Additional Sources

Books

d'Abzac-Epezy, Claude. *L'Armée de l'air de Vichy, 1940–1944.* Vincennes: Service historique de l'Armée de l'air, 1997.

Adamthwaite, Anthony. *France and the Coming of the Second World War, 1936–1939.* London: Frank Cass Publishers, 1977.

Alexander, Martin S. *The Republic in Danger: General Maurice Gamelin and the Politics of French Defence, 1933–1940.* Cambridge: Cambridge University Press, 1992.

Avant, Deborah D. *Political Institutions and Military Change: Lessons from Peripheral Wars.* Ithaca: Cornell University Press, 1994.

Azema, Jean-Pierre. *De Munich à la Libération, 1938–1944.* Paris: Éditions du Seuil, 1979.

Azema, Jean-Pierre, and François Bédarida. *La France des années noires.* Paris: Éditions du Seuil, 1993.

Bedarida, François. *La stratégie secrète de la drôle de guerre: Le conseil suprême interallié, septembre 1939–avril 1940*. Paris: Presses de la fondation nationale des sciences politiques/CNRS, 1979.

Bernard, Philippe, and Henri Dubief. *The Decline of the Third Republic, 1914–1938*. Translated by Anthony Forster. Cambridge: Cambridge University Press, 1985.

Berque, Jacques. *French North Africa: The Maghrib between Two World Wars*. Translated by Jean Stewart. London: Faber, 1967.

Bidwell, Rubin. *Morocco under Colonial Rule: French Administration of Tribal Areas 1912–1956*. London: Cass, 1973.

Blanchard, Anne, et al. *Histoire militaire de la France*, 3 vols. Paris: PUF, 1992.

Boog, Horst, ed. *The Conduct of the Air War in the Second World War: An International Comparison*. Proceedings of the International Conference of Historians in Freiburg im Breisgau, Federal Republic of Germany, from 29 August to 2 September 1988. New York: Berg Publishers, 1992.

Brunschwig, Henri. *French Colonialism, 1871–1914: Myths and Realities*. London: Pall Mall Press, 1966.

Builder, Carl H. *The Icarus Syndrome*. New Brunswick, N.J.: Transaction Publisher, 1996.

Burrin, Philippe. *France under the Germans: Collaboration and Compromise*. Translated by Janet Lloyd. New York: New Press, 1996.

Chadeau, Emmanuel. *L'industrie aéronautique en France, 1900–1950: De Blériot à Dassault*. Paris: Fayard, 1987.

Chapman, Herrick. *State Capitalism and Working-Class Radicalism in the French Aircraft Industry*. Berkeley and Los Angeles: University of California Press, 1991.

Christienne, Charles, and Pierre Lissarague. *A History of French Military Aviation*. Translated by Frances Kianka. Washington, D.C.: Smithsonian Institution Press, 1986.

Cohen, Eliot A., and John Gooch. *Military Misfortunes: The Anatomy of Failure in War*. New York: Vintage Books, 1991.

Corvisier, André, and André Martel. *Histoire militaire de la France*, vol. 4, *De 1940 à nos jours*. FEDN-IHCC, 1985.

Craven, Wesley Frank, and James Lea Cate, eds., *The Army Air Forces in World War II*, vol. 1., *Plans and Early Operations, January 1939 to August 1942*. Chicago: University of Chicago Press, 1948. Reprint, Washington, D.C.: Office of Air Force History, 1983.

De Gaulle, Charles. *The Complete War Memoirs of Charles de Gaulle*. Translated by Jonathan Griffin. New York: Simon and Schuster, 1967.

Doughty, Robert A. *The Breaking Point: Sedan and the Fall of France, 1940*. Hamden, Conn.: Archon Books, 1990.

——. *The Seeds of Disaster: The Development of French Army Doctrine, 1919–1939*. Hamden, Conn.: Archon Books, 1985.

Drew, Dennis, and Donald M. Snow. *Making Strategy: An Introduction to National Security Processes and Problems*. Maxwell Air Force Base, Ala.: Air University Press, 1988.

Duroselle, Jean Baptiste. *Politique étrangère de la France: La décadence, 1932–1939.* Paris: Imprimerie nationale, 1979.

Facon, Patrick. *L'Armée de l'air dans la tourmente: La bataille de France, 1939–1940.* Paris: Economica, 1997.

——. *Le bombardement stratégique.* Paris: Éditions du Rocher, 1996.

——. *Le haut commandement aérien français et la crise de Munich, 1938.* Vincennes: Service historique de l'Armée de l'air, 1987.

Fleming, Shannon Earl. *Primo de Rivera and Abd el-Krim: The Struggle in Spanish Morocco, 1923–1927.* New York: Garland Publishing, 1991.

Frankenstein, Robert. *Le prix du réarmament français, 1935–1939.* Paris: Publications de la Sorbonne, 1982.

Freedman, Lawrence. *The Evolution of Nuclear Strategy.* 2d ed. New York: St. Martin's Press, 1989.

Futrell, Robert Frank. *Ideas, Concepts, Doctrine: Basic Thinking in the United States Air Force,* vol. 1, *1907–1960.* Maxwell Air Force Base, Ala.: Air University Press, 1971. Reprint, 1989.

Gunsburg, Jeffrey A. *Divided and Conquered: The French High Command and the Defeat of the West, 1940.* Westport, Conn.: Greenwood Press, 1979.

Hoisington, William A., Jr. *Lyautey and the French Conquest of Morocco.* New York: St. Martin's Press, 1995.

Holley, I. B., Jr. *Ideas and Weapons: Exploration of the Aerial Weapon by the United States during World War I; A Study in the Relationship of Technological Advance, Military Doctrine, and the Development of Weapons.* New Haven: Yale University Press, 1953. Reprint, Washington, D.C.: U.S. Government Printing Office, 1983.

Ingram, Norman. *The Politics of Dissent: Pacifism in France, 1919–1939.* Oxford: Clarendon Press, 1991.

Jordan, Nicole. *The Popular Front and Central Europe: The Dilemmas of French Impotence, 1918–1940.* Cambridge: Cambridge University Press, 1992.

Keegan, John. *The Mask of Command.* New York: Viking Penguin, 1987.

Kersaudy, François. *Norway 1940.* Paris: Tallandier, 1987. Reprint, New York: St. Martin's Press, 1990.

Kier, Elizabeth. *Imagining War: British and French Military Doctrine before World War Two.* Princeton: Princeton University Press, 1997.

Kiesling, Eugenia. *Arming against Hitler: France and the Limits of Military Planning.* Lawrence, Kans.: University Press of Kansas, 1996.

Le Révérend, André. *Lyautey.* Paris: Fayard, 1983.

Le Goyet, Pierre. *La défaite, 10 mai–25 juin 1940.* Paris: Economica, 1990.

Ledermann, Olivier, and Jean-François Merolle. *Le sacrifice: Les Breguet 693 de l'aviation d'assaut dans la Bataille de France.* Paris: IPMS France, 1994.

Ling, Dwight L. *Morocco and Tunisia: A Comparative History.* Washington, D.C.: University Press of America, 1979.

May, Ernest R. *Strange Victory: Hitler's Conquest of France.* New York: Hill and Wang, 2000.

Meilinger, Phillip S., ed. *The Paths of Heaven: The Evolution of Airpower Theory.* Maxwell Air Force Base, Ala.: Air University Press, 1997.

Michel, Henri. *La défaite de la France, septembre 1939–juin 1940.* Paris: PUF, 1980.

Millett, Allan R., and Williamson Murray. *A War To Be Won: Fighting the Second World War.* Cambridge, Mass.: Belknap, Harvard University Press, 2000.

Murray, Williamson, and Allan R. Millett, eds. *Calculations: Net Assessment and the Coming of World War II.* New York: Free Press, 1992.

———. *Military Innovation in the Interwar Period.* Cambridge: Cambridge University Press, 1996.

Mierzejewski, Alfred C. *The Collapse of the German War Economy, 1944–1945.* Chapel Hill, N.C.: University of North Carolina Press, 1988.

Myzyrowiecz, Ladislas. *Autopsie d'une défaite: Origines de l'effondrement militaire français de 1940.* Lausanne: L'âge d'homme, 1973.

Néré, J. *The Foreign Policy of France from 1914 to 1945.* Translated by Translance. London: Routledge and Keegan Paul, 1975.

Omissi, David. *Air Power and Colonial Control: The Royal Air Force, 1919–1939.* Manchester: Manchester University Press, 1990.

Paxton, Robert O. *Vichy France: Old Guard and New Order, 1940–1944.* New York: Columbia University Press, 1972.

Paret, Peter, ed. *Makers of Modern Strategy: From Machiavelli to the Nuclear Age.* Princeton: Princeton University Press, 1986.

Posen, Barry R. *The Sources of Military Doctrine: France, Britain, and Germany between the World Wars.* Ithaca: Cornell University Press, 1984.

Prochasson, Christophe. *Les intellectuals, le socialisme, et la guerre, 1900–1938.* Paris: Éditions du Seuil, 1992.

Pujo, Bernard. *Le général Pujo et la naissance de l'aviation française.* Vincennes: Service historique de l'Armée de l'air, 1988.

Richards, Denis. *The Hardest Victory: RAF Bomber Command in the Second World War.* New York: W. W. Norton, 1994.

Roberts, Stephen H. *The History of French Colonial Policy, 1870–1925.* Hamden, Conn.: Archon Books, 1963.

Rosen, Stephen Peter. *Winning the Next War: Innovation in the Modern Military.* Ithaca: Cornell University Press, 1991.

Scham, Alan. *Lyautey in Morocco: Protectorate Administration, 1912–1925.* Berkely and Los Angeles: University of California Press, 1970.

Seive, Fleury. *L'aviation d'assaut dans la bataille de 1940.* Paris: Berger-Levrault, 1948.

Shirer, William L. *The Collapse of the Third Republic: An Inquiry into the Fall of France in 1940.* New York: Simon and Schuster, 1969.

Vaisse, Maurice, ed. *Ardennes, 1940.* Paris: Henri Veyneir-Kronos, 1991.

Vennesson, Pascal. *Les chevaliers de l'air: Aviation et conflits au XXe siècle.* Paris: Presses de sciences po, 1997.

Vivier, Thierry. *La politique aéronautique militaire de la France, janvier 1933–septembre 1939.* Paris: Éditions l'Harmattan, 1997.

Waters, Gary, ed. *RAAF Air Power Doctrine: A Collection of Contemporary Essays.* Canberra: Strategic and Defence Studies Centre, 1990.

Weber, Eugen. *The Hollow Years: France in the 1930s.* New York: W. W. Norton, 1994.

———. *My France: Politics, Culture, Myth.* Cambridge: Harvard University Press, 1992.

———. *Peasants into Frenchmen: The Modernization of Rural France, 1870–1914.* Stanford, Calif.: Stanford University Press, 1976.

Weinberg, Gerhard L. *A World at Arms: A Global History of World War II.* Cambridge: Cambridge University Press, 1994.

Wright, Gordon. *The Ordeal of Total War, 1939–1945.* New York: Harper and Row, 1968.

Wylie, Laurence. *Village in the Vaucluse.* 3d ed. Cambridge: Harvard University Press, 1977.

Young, Robert J. *France and the Origins of the Second World War.* New York: St. Martin's Press, 1996.

———. *In Command of France: French Foreign Policy and Military Planning, 1933–1940.* Cambridge: Harvard University Press, 1978.

Dissertations

Coox, A. D. "French Military Doctrine, 1919–1939: Concepts of Ground and Aerial Warfare." Ph.D. diss. Cambridge: Harvard University, 1951.

Davis Biddle, Tami. "Rhetoric and Reality in Air Warfare: The Evolution of British and American Ideas about Strategic Bombing." Ph.D. diss. New Haven: Yale University, 1995.

Dean, William T. "The Colonial Armies of the French Third Republic: Overseas Formation and Continental Deployment, 1871–1920." Ph.D. diss. Chicago: University of Chicago, 1999.

Gunsburg, Jeffrey A. "Vaincre ou mourir: The French High Command and the Defeat of France." Ph.D. diss. Durham, N.C.: Duke University, 1974.

Harvey, Donald J. "French Concepts of Military Strategy, 1919–1939." Ph.D. diss. New York: Columbia University, 1953.

Krauskopf, Robert W. "French Air Power Policy, 1919–1939." Ph.D. diss. Washington, D.C.: Georgetown University, 1965.

Articles

d'Abzac-Epezy, Claude. "Clément Ader, précurseur ou prophète?" *Revue historique des armées* 3 (1991): 65–77.

André, Eric. "Le Général Roques, inspecteur permanent de l'aéronautique." *Revue historique des armées* 3 (1988): 57–67.

Astorkia, Madeline. "Les leçons aériennes de la guerre d'Espagne." *Revue historique des armées* 2 (1977): 145–73.

Ausems, André. "The Luftwaffe's Airborne Losses in May 1940: An Interpretation." *Aerospace Historian* (September 1985): 184–88.

Ayache, Germain. "Les implications internationales de la guerre du Rif, 1921–1926." *Hesperis-Tamuda* 15 (1974): 181–224.

Beyerchen, Alan. "Clausewitz, Nonlinearity, and the Unpredictability of War." *International Security* 17 (1992): 59–90.

Bourdes, Lieutenant-Colonel. "La création de l'arme aéroportée française." *Revue historique des armées* 2 (1977): 62–86.

Breche, Yves. "Les officiers de l'Armée de l'air à travers la littérature militaire." *Revue historique des armées* 2 (1977): 113–44.

Breuguet, Emmanuel. "La place de l'aviation française de renseignement dans la guerre de 1939–1940." *Revue historique des armées* 4 (1988): 102–11.

Buffotot, Patrice. "Le projet de bombardement des pétroles soviétiques du Caucase en 1940: Un example des projets alliés pendant la drôle de guerre." *Revue historique des armées* 4 (1979): 78–101.

Chadeau, Emmanuel. "L'industrie française à la vielle de la première guerre mondiale." *Revue historique des armées* 2–3 (1981).

———. "Préhistoire des politiques industrielles françaises: L'aéronautique, 1928–1940." *L'information historique* 49 (1987): 153–60.

Christienne, Charles. "Ader et Mitchell: Deux penseurs aéronautiques." *Revue historiques des armées* 1 (1982): 24–41.

Christienne, Charles, and Patrice Buffotot. "L'aéronautique militaire française entre 1919 et 1939." *Revue historique des armées* 2 (1977): 9–40.

Cohen, Victor. "Lyautey." *Quarterly Review* 295 (1957): 180–93.

Dournel, Jean-Pierre. "L'image de l'aviateur français en 1914–1918." *Revue historique des armées* 1 (1976): 95–122.

Facon, Patrick. "Aperçus sur la doctrine d'emploi de l'aéronautique militaire française, 1914–1918." *Revue historique des armées* 3 (1988): 80–90.

———. "Arme ou armée? Aviation réservée ou aviation organique? L'aéronautique militaire à l'école de la Première guerre mondiale." *Revue historique des armées* 4 (1994): 67–75.

———. "L'aviation dans une revue interarmes de l'entre-deux-guerres, 1923–1938." *Revue historique des armées* 2 (1977): 103–11.

———. "L'aviation populaire: Entre les mythes et la réalité." *Revue historique des armées* 2 (1982): 55–59.

———. "Douhet et sa doctrine à travers la littérature militaire et aéronautique française de l'entre-deux guerres: Une étude de perception." *Revue historique des armées* 1 (1988): 94–103.

———. "Le haut commandement aérien français et la crise de Munich." *Revue historique des armées* 3 (1983): 10–17.

———. "Le haut commandement aérien français et le problème du réarmament, 1938–1939." *Revue historique des armées* 3 (1989): 91–101.

———. "Le plan V, 1938–1939." *Revue historique des armées* 4 (1979): 102–23.

——. "La visite du général Vuillemin en Allemagne, 16–21 aôut 1938." *Revue historique des armées* 2 (1982): 110–21.

Fleming Shanon E., and Ann K. Fleming. "Primo de Rivera and Spain's Moroccan Problem, 1923–27." *Journal of Contemporary History* 12, no. 1 (1977): 85–99.

Goyet, Colonel P. "Évolution de la doctrine d'emploi de l'aviation française entre 1919 et 1939." *Revue d'histoire de la Deuxième guerre mondiale* 19 (1969): 3–41.

Hodeir, Marcellin. "La création du ministère de l'air vue par la presse parisienne, septembre, octobre, novembre, 1928." *Revue historique des armées* 4 (1988): 92–101.

Howard, Michael. "Military Science in an Age of Peace." *RUSI: Journal of the Royal United Services Institute for Defence Studies* 119 (1974): 3–11.

Kirkland, Faris Russell. "The French Air Force in 1940: Was It Defeated by the Luftwaffe or by Politics?" *Air University Review* 36 (1985): 101–17.

Laine, Serge. "L'aéronautique militaire française au Maroc." *Revue histoirique des armées* 5 (1978): 107–19.

Marill, J.–M. "La doctrine militaire française entre les deux guerres." *Revue historique des armées* 3 (1991): 24–34.

Millet, Jérôme. "L'aviation militaire française dans la guerre du Rif." *Revue historique des armées* 1 (1987): 46–58.

Pernot, François. "L'Armée de l'air face aux crises des années trente: Une étude morale." *Revue historique des armées* 4 (1990): 116–27.

——. "L'image de l'aviateur dans la presse française de 1940 à 1944: La recherche d'un modèle." *Revue historique des armées* 191 (1993): 85–95.

Pesquies, Simone. "L'aéronautique militaire française dans la guerre du Rif." *Revue du nord* 72 (1990): 317–67.

Teyssier, Arnaud. "L'Armée de l'air et l'aviation d'assaut, 1933–1939: Histoire d'un malentendu." *Revue historique des armées* 1 (1989): 98–109.

——. "Le Général Vuillemin, chef d'état-major général de l'Armée de l'air, 1938–1939: Un haut responsable militaire face au danger allemand." *Revue historique des armées* 2 (1987): 104–13.

Vaisse, Maurice. "Le procès de l'aviation de bombardement." *Revue historique des armées* 2 (1977): 41–61.

Vennesson, Pascal. "Institution and Airpower: The Making of the French Air Force." *Journal of Strategic Studies* 18 (1995): 36–67.

Vivier, Thierry. "L'Armée de l'air et le problème du réarmement aérien au procès de Riom." *Revue historique des armées* 2 (1990): 92–102.

——. "L'Armée de l'air et la révolution technique des années trente, 1933–1939." *Revue historique des armées* 1 (1990): 32–39.

——. "L'aviation française en Pologne, janvier 1936–septembre 1939." *Revue historique des armées* 193 (1993): 60–70.

——. "La commission G: Entre la défaite et l'Armée de l'air future, 1941–1942." *Revue historique des armées* 3 (1989): 113–21.

——. "La coopération aéronautique franco-tchécoslovaque, janvier 1933–septembre 1938." *Revue historique des armées* (March 1993): 70–79.

———. "Le douhétisme français entre tradition et innovation, 1933–1939." *Revue historique des armées* 3 (1991): 89–99.

———. "Le Général Victor Denain, bâtisseur de l'Armée de l'air, 1933–1936." *Revue historique des armées* 192 (1993): 21–31.

———. "Pierre Cot et la naissance de l'Armée de l'air, 31 janvier–8 fevrier 1934." *Revue historique des armées* 4 (1990): 108–15.

Young, Robert J. "The Use and Abuse of Fear: France and the Air Menace in the 1930s." *Intelligence and National Security* 2 (1987): 88–109.

Index

Levant, 28
Luftwaffe, ix, 30, 62, 116, 117, 118, 121, 125, 126, 148
lutte aérienne, x, 39, 40, 41, 42, 43, 48, 51, 52, 53, 54, 56, 59, 61, 81, 82, 87, 88, 97, 103, 115, 116, 118, 123, 137, 140, 150, 153, 155, 157, 158
Lyautey, Marshal Hubert, 16, 17, 18, 19, 20, 21, 22, 23, 24, 155
Maginot Line, x
maintenance, 7, 19, 54, 62, 69, 72, 73, 75, 80, 90, 132, 145, 151
Messerschmidt 109 aircraft, 125, 147
methodical battle, 11, 84, 124
mobilization, x, 5, 7, 24–25, 31, 40, 50, 63, 85–89, 95, 105–14, 122–23, 151, 158
Morane 225 aircraft, 87
Morane 406 aircraft, 126
Musée de l'air, 4, 135

O

offensive: operations, x, 11, 15, 16, 22, 37, 39, 40, 41, 42, 43, 50, 52, 53, 54, 59, 75, 76, 82, 83, 86, 87, 88, 89, 90, 91, 95, 96, 100, 102, 134, 139, 140, 141, 143, 150; plans, 27, 115–22, 158, 159; power, 17, 35, 147, 155, 160
operational: aspects of air warfare, 5, 11, 15, 24, 34, 35, 50, 51, 62, 63, 65, 75, 83, 85, 97, 102, 109, 113, 115, 126, 143, 149, 150, 160; centers of gravity, 86, 140, 155, 160; commands, 7, 43, 73, 78, 79, 80, 83, 89, 95, 107, 111, 123, 140, 151, 152; concepts, 21, 36, 43, 59, 60, 61, 66, 81, 82, 83, 84, 91, 95, 100, 104, 114, 155; effectiveness, 2, 5, 7, 29, 60, 68, 82, 105, 110, 114, 119, 125, 144, 155, 158; exercises, 87; level of war, 1, 2, 3, 30, 33, 35, 53, 59, 114, 139, 142, 151, 152, 153; objectives, 7, 35, 38, 86, 102, 115, 118, 121, 147, 156, 159; planning, x, 6, 7, 38, 49, 111, 119, 120, 121, 124, 158

P

Pétain, Marshal Philippe, 4, 132, 134
Plan E, 111, 112
Plan I, 28, 30
Poland, 27, 122, 124
politique des prototypes, 26, 48, 107
Popular Front, 4, 28, 29, 60, 106
Protectorate, 16, 17, 19, 20, 21, 22, 24

pursuit, 11, 12, 14, 17, 30, 31, 40, 43, 49, 50, 51, 52, 54, 56, 57, 58, 64, 74, 75, 79, 83, 84, 86, 87, 88, 91, 107, 114, 125, 139, 141, 144, 145, 147, 148, 149, 150, 152, 158

R

rail: line, 55, 147; marshaling yards, 15, 120, 147; networks, 55, 120; railroad, 111, 120, 143, 146; railway, 15, 55, 56, 111; traffic, 15; yards, 15
reactive: airpower, 1, 6, 32, 41, 106; doctrine, x, 7, 26, 35, 81, 102, 154, 157, 158–59, 160
reconnaissance, 1, 11, 12, 16, 17, 20, 27, 30, 40, 41, 42, 43, 48, 52, 57, 58, 59, 64, 79, 84, 85, 91, 95, 98, 99, 103, 104, 107, 125, 126, 142, 144, 147, 149, 150, 151, 152, 160
Règlement de manoeuvre de l'aviation, 48, 49, 51, 52, 54, 58, 83
Reich, Third, 56, 116, 122
Republic, Third, xi, 4, 5, 27, 33, 39, 134, 154
resistance movement, 5, 134, 135
Rif War, 9, 16, 17, 18, 21, 22, 24, 25, 26, 154, 155
Riom trial, 4, 5
Royal Air Force, ix, 147
Rumania, 27

S

Salon-de-Provence, 69, 71, 75, 79
Stavinsky affair, 28
Strasbourg, 69, 70, 107, 117
strategic: bombardment, 2, 6, 10, 16, 26, 35, 154; environment, 1, 6, 28, 36, 38, 39, 42, 51, 61, 66, 103, 124, 137, 156, 157, 160; forces, 6; level of war, 1, 33, 34, 35, 59, 114, 115, 153, 160; objectives, 17, 34, 35, 102, 117, 120, 121, 142, 147; operations, 2, 14, 15, 51, 62, 86, 142, 143, 147, 153, 155, 159; planning, 7, 82, 115, 119, 120, 121, 138; posture, 59, 60; power, 38

T

tableaux d'effectifs de guerre, 104, 107
tableaux d'emploi de l'Armée de l'air dans la métropole, 111
Tétu, General Marcel, 123, 126
37th Aviation Regiment, 16, 19, 20, 21, 22, 24, 89, 155